English Words: History and Structure is concerned primarily with the learned vocabulary of English, the words borrowed from the classical languages and French. It initially surveys the historical events that define the layers of vocabulary in Old English (c. 450–1066) Middle English (1066–1476), Early Modern English (1476–1776), and Present-Day English. It is both an introduction to some of the basic principles of linguistic analysis and a helpful manual for vocabulary discernment and enrichment. Exercises to accompany each chapter and further readings on recent loans and the legal and medical vocabulary of English are available on-line at *http://uk.cambridge.org/linguistics/resources/englishwords*

- Introduces students to some basic linguistic terms needed for the discussion of phonological and morphological changes accompanying word formation.
- Designed to lead students to a finer appreciation of their language and greater ability to recognize relationships between words and discriminate between meanings.
- An informative appendix discusses the history and usefulness of the best known British and American dictionaries.
- On-line readings and exercises designed to deepen and strengthen the knowledge acquired in the classroom.

ROBERT STOCKWELL is Professor Emeritus at the Department of Linguistics, University of California, Los Angeles. He is co-editor of *Linguistic Change and Generative Theory* (with R. Macaulay, 1972), co-author of *Major Syntactic Structures of English* (with Paul Schachter and Barbara Partee, 1973) and author of *Foundations of Syntactic Theory* (1977).

DONKA MINKOVA is Professor of English at the University of California, Los Angeles. She has published widely in the fields of English and Germanic historical phonology and syntax, historical dialectology and English historical metrics. She is the author of *The History of Final Vowels in English* (1991).

English Words:
History and Structure

ROBERT STOCKWELL AND
DONKA MINKOVA

PUBLISHED BY THE PRESS SYNDICATE OF THE UNIVERSITY OF CAMBRIDGE
The Pitt Building, Trumpington Street, Cambridge, United Kingdom

CAMBRIDGE UNIVERSITY PRESS
The Edinburgh Building, Cambridge CB2 2RU, UK
40 West 20th Street, New York, NY 10011–4211, USA
477 Williamstown Road, Port Melbourne, VIC 3207, Australia
Ruiz de Alarcón 13, 28014 Madrid, Spain
Dock House, The Waterfront, Cape Town 8001, South Africa

http://www.cambridge.org

First published 2001
Fourth printing 2005

Printed in United Kingdom at the University Press, Cambridge

Typeface Monotype Times New Roman 10.5/13pt   *System* QuarkXPress™   [SE]

A catalogue record for this book is available from the British Library

Library of Congress cataloguing in publication data

Stockwell, Robert P.
   English words: history and structure / by Robert P. Stockwell and Donka Minkova.
      p.   cm.
   Includes bibliographical references and index.
   ISBN 0 521 79012 3 (hardback)   ISBN 0 521 79362 9 (paperback)
      1. English language – Etymology.   2. English language – Morphology.   3. English
   language – Word formation.   4. Vocabulary – Problems, exercises, etc.   I. Minkova,
   Donka, 1944–   II. Title.
   PE1571.S76 2001
   422 – dc21   00–052896

ISBN 0 521 79012 3 hardback
ISBN 0 521 79362 9 paperback

Wittgenstein:

"The limits of my language are the limits of my world."

Contents

An introduction to the textbook

This book is about the origins of English words, about their etymology. It is important to realize, however, that it is not about **all** possible origins, it is not about **all** the ways in which English has introduced new words into the language, but rather it is primarily about a particular subset, that portion of the vocabulary which is borrowed from the classical languages (Latin and Greek) either directly, or indirectly through French.

This (very large) portion of our vocabulary is a familiar subject. Greek and Latin roots in the English language have been studied and described for many centuries. Departments of Classical Languages traditionally offer courses under titles like "Classical Roots in English," and in the past a decent education necessarily included a full program in the classics. At the beginning of the twenty-first century, however, it is extremely rare for students entering college to have a clear idea what Latin is, or whether English is derived from it or not, and even what it means for a language to be "derived," in any sense, from another. The word *cognate* is not only generally unknown to undergraduate students, it often remains conceptually obscure, because it is simply not one of the topics we grow up with these days.

We take the view that people cannot call themselves "educated" who do not have a minimal acquaintance with the history and structure of the words in their own language. It doesn't take much: if you use a dictionary a lot, you probably don't need this book. But people don't usually use a dictionary to do more than settle an argument about spelling, pronunciation, or hyphenation. It should be used for **much** more. Learning to appreciate those additional uses is one of the benefits we hope to provide to our readers.

Another benefit is learning to appreciate relationships between words that even the best dictionaries don't always make clear. These relationships are part of what linguists call **morphology**. Morphology, the form of words, is the least regular part of language. The shapes that words take is part of the legacy of history, very specifically the legacy of history, whereas both the phonetic aspects of language and the syntactic aspects are probably largely innate.

1

A question which everyone wonders about, and often asks of instructors, is "How many words does English have?" And even more commonly, "How many words does the typical educated person know, approximately?" There are no verifiable answers to these questions. We can tell you how many headwords a given dictionary has (or claims to have), or how many words Shakespeare used in his plays (because it is a closed corpus of texts, and we can count the number of different words – about 21,000 if you count *play*, *plays*, *playing*, *played* as a single word, and all similar cases, almost 30,000 if you don't). A very generous estimate of the vocabulary of a really well-educated adult is that it may reach up to 100,000 words, but this is a wildly unverifiable estimate. We can quote the *Oxford English Dictionary*'s claim to have 500,000 headwords in its recent second edition, but that figure is not particularly meaningful because it includes ancient as well as modern words, and most of the ancient words are unknown to us. They are obsolete and of antiquarian interest only.

One thing is certain: well over 80 percent of the total vocabulary of English is borrowed. The more we know about the sources and processes of linguistic borrowing, the better our chances of coping with technical vocabulary and educated usage in general.

To use this book, one must have a good dictionary. We have attached a discussion of dictionaries, both British and American, in Appendix I. We recommend that it be read before you purchase a new dictionary so that you will understand better what sort of book to shop for. All the major dictionaries are available also in electronic form: they must be purchased separately and installed in your computer. The electronic spell-checker and the thesaurus included in word-processing programs are **not** good enough. Such applications are primarily for spelling, hyphenation, and for finding synonyms. They will not help you discover the history and multiple meanings of words.

The book is accompanied by a workbook arranged to correspond to the chapters of this book. In addition, it includes a special chapter on recently borrowed words from both ancient and modern languages, and one on technical vocabulary in law and medicine. The Workbook is available on the Cambridge University Press website (http://www.cambridge.org).

1   Word origins

The two general themes of this book are the historical origins and the structure of English words. Our word stock is huge. It is useful to divide it up between words that belong to the common language that everybody knows from an early age and words that are learned in the course of our education. The former, the core vocabulary, is nearly the same for everyone. The latter, the learned vocabulary, is peripheral and certainly not shared by everyone. The core vocabulary is not an area where we need special instruction – the core vocabulary is acquired at a pre-educational stage. Our learned vocabulary is a different matter. It varies greatly in size and composition from one individual to another, depending on education and fields of specialization. No single individual ever controls more than a fraction of the learned vocabulary. Often the extent of one's vocabulary becomes a measure of intellect. Knowledge about the history and structure of our words – both the core and the learned vocabulary – is a valuable asset.

The vocabulary of English is not an unchanging list of words. New words enter the language every day, and words cease to be used. The two sources of new words are borrowing and word-creation. In fields of higher learning, like the life sciences, physical sciences, medicine, law, and the social sciences, English has usually borrowed words from other languages to get new words to cover new concepts or new material or abstract phenomena. Words referring to notions and objects specific to other cultures are often borrowed wholesale. We may borrow a word as a whole, or just its central parts (the roots). We have borrowed mainly from Latin, Greek, and French. We will leave the discussion of borrowing for later chapters. In this chapter, we will focus on the patterns of vocabulary innovation – the creation of new words – that occur within English.

We now address this topic: where do our new words originate – how do they get created – when we don't borrow them? Other than borrowing, we can count ten main sources of words in English. All but the first involve the creation of new words. These are by inheritance, by creative imagination, by blending, by joining initial letters of a phrase, by shortening, derivation, conversion, compounding, by using names as ordinary words, and by some rare echoic processes.

1   Inheritance

For the most part, the core vocabulary has been part of English for many centuries, passed down with minor changes. Much of it is shared with closely related languages like Dutch, the Scandinavian languages, and the classical languages Latin and Greek. The notion of what it means to be a closely related language is the topic of Chapter 2. For the moment the notion of relationship can be understood in a pre-scientific sense, as in "family relationship."

The core vocabulary includes all of the common prepositions (*by, for, to, on, in, of, with, among, etc.*). They are learned well before the age of five. Similarly conjunctions like *and, but, or.* They are an essential part of the glue that holds sentences together. Other core words are the auxiliary and linking verbs (*be, is, was, were, are, am, have, can, could, may, might, will, would, shall, should, must, ought to*), and many common verbs having to do with perception and the senses (*feel, think, touch, hear, see*), and common names of body parts and kinship (*face, mouth, eyes, hand, foot, leg, mother, father, brother, sister*). If we look just at the 1,000 most common words of English, over 800 of them are of this type. Many of them can be traced back as far as language history allows us to go – about 8,000 years before the present time. Some of the others have popped up in the language during more recent times – the last two or three millennia – and in many instances their origins remain mysterious. For instance, *brunt* as in "to take the brunt of the attack," has been in the language since 1325, but it remains of unknown origin; *blear(y)*, from the fourteenth century, origin also unknown; *duds*, as in "to wear fancy duds," from the middle of the fifteenth century, also unknown. Closer to our times, *copacetic, posh* are from the beginning of the twentieth century; their etymology is unknown.[1] *Snazzy* is from the first Roosevelt administration starting in 1933, but no one knows its ancestry.

In addition to its core vocabulary, English has a rich supply of learned words (*learned*, in this meaning, is pronounced as two syllables). The learned vocabulary is different from the core vocabulary in that most of it is acquired through literacy and education. It tends to be associated with technical knowledge and professional skills, though there is also a large part of it which is associated with humanistic education and the literary tradition. Vocabulary enrichment in all of those areas has drawn heavily on borrowed words and roots. Most of this

---

[1] *Posh*, it should be pointed out, has been claimed to be a blend of "Port Out, Starboard Home," the wealthy way to travel on a Mediterranean cruise, to avoid having the sun in your porthole. The *Oxford English Dictionary* considers this etymology to be without foundation.

book is devoted to finding out when and how such vocabulary came into English. But first we need to examine the sources of other words, words that are not part of the inherited core vocabulary and that are not borrowed from the classical languages. These are words which are created by inventive minds, and they follow a small number of patterns.

2   Neologisms (Creation *de novo*)

Though one might think it an easy matter to create a new word (without basing it on some pre-existing word or part of a word) for some new idea or new artifact, such creations are extremely rare. *Blurb* is such a word, created in 1907 to refer to the embellished descriptions on the jackets of books. *Kodak* was created by George Eastman, founder of the camera company that bears his name. Of the word itself, Eastman is reported to have said that it was "a purely arbitrary combination of letters, not derived in whole or in part from any existing word."[2] *Nylon, Orlon, Dacron, Kevlar*, and *Teflon* are others, invented by wordsmiths within the companies that manufacture these products. Probably except for *nylon* these are not part of the core vocabulary. Even the *-on* ending of these words is obviously by analogy with words like *electron* and therefore, unlike *Kodak*, these words are not completely made up from scratch. Another word like *Kodak* is *quark*, which first appears in Joyce's *Finnegans Wake* in the phrase "Three Quarks for Muster Mark," taken over by physicists to mean "Any of a group of sub-atomic particles (originally three in number) conceived of as having a fractional electric charge and making up in different combinations the hadrons, but not detected in the free state" (*OED*). In the world of marketing, such creations generally are the result of massive commercial research efforts to find a combination of sounds that does not suggest something they do not want to suggest, words that have a pleasant ring to them and that are easy to pronounce. But most of the new words that even advertising experts come up with are derived from old words. For instance, the headache remedy named *Aleve* clearly is intended to suggest *alleviate*. The skin cream called *Lubriderm* is intended to suggest lubricating the *derm*, which suggests skin because of its occurrence in familiar forms like *dermatology, epidermis, dermatitis.* On the other hand another famous headache remedy, *Tylenol*, is

---

[2] The original source of this quotation appears to have been in a letter quoted in a biography of Eastman by Carl W. Ackerman (*George Eastman*, New York 1930). It was picked up by H. L. Mencken, the great Baltimore journalist whose major contributions to scholarship were his monumental studies of the distinctive words and phrases of American English (*The American Language* and two *Supplements*, New York, 1936 [4th edn., the supplements in 1945 and 1948]).

like *Kodak*, created *de novo*. *Frigidaire* is a clever coinage for a particular brand of refrigerating device. *Kleenex* is a similarly catching proprietary commercial name based on clean and the pseudo-scientific suffix -*ex*

3   Blending

Creations by blending are also called *portmanteau words*, following Lewis Carroll (Charles L. Dodgson), the author of *Through the Looking Glass*. He wrote:

> Well, "slithy" means "lithe and slimy" . . . You see it's like a portmanteau – there are two meanings packed up into one word. . . . "Mimsy" is "flimsy and miserable" (there's another portmanteau).

Of course, to appreciate what Carroll was saying, you have to realize that portmanteau itself is a rather old-fashioned word for "suitcase," originally designed for carrying on horseback. Other examples of blends created by him are *chortle*, from *chuckle* and *snort*; and *galumph*, from *gallop* and *triumph*. In blending, parts of two familiar words are yoked together (usually the first part of one word and the second part of the other) to produce a word which combines the meanings and sound of the old ones. Successful examples, in addition to Lewis Carroll's whimsical literary examples above, are *smog*, a blend of *smoke* and *fog*, *motel* from *motor* and *hotel*, *heliport* from *helicopter* and *airport*, *brunch* from *breakfast* and *lunch*, *flurry* from *flutter* and *hurry*, *flush* from *flash* and *gush*. Sometimes we lose track of the components of the new blend. The origin of the word is then no longer transparent. *Vaseline* is such a word. It was based on German *wasser* "water" and Greek *elaion* "oil." It was made up in 1872 by the man who owned the company that produced it. It is still a "proprietary term" (as *Kodak* and *Tylenol* and the other commercial terms above are), that is, it is trademarked and owned by the company that manufactures it. It is not uncommon for new technical terms to be created by blending. *Medicare*, the Social Security term covering medical care for the elderly in the United States, is now totally established, though it dates from as recently as 1965. *Medicaid* is the same sort of blend. In medical practice, a term like *urinalysis*, obviously from *urine* plus *analysis*, is so transparent in its derivation that one hardly notices that it is a separate blended word. In the field of chemistry, developing rapidly in the nineteenth century, new compounds and chemical substances required new names, which were chiefly blends: *acetal* (*acetic* and *alcohol*), *alkargen* (*alkarsin* and *oxygen*), *carborundum* (*carbon* and *corundum*), *chloral* (*chlorine* and *alcohol*), *phospham* (*phosphorus* and *ammonia*), and many more. Blending is an area of word formation where cleverness can be rewarded by instant popularity: *sexploitation* from the seventies, the *Chunnel* from the eighties are common words now. On a lighter note, the reward can even be amusement: unpleasant as the phenomena they describe are, the words *guesstimate*, *testilying*, *pagejacking*, *spamouflage*, *compfusion*, and *explornography* will probably elicit a smile.[3]

4   Acronyms

Acronyms (*acr-o* "tip, point" + *onym* "name") are a special type of blend. A typical acronym takes the first sound from each of several words and makes a new word from those initial sounds. If the resulting word is pronounced like any other word it is a true acronym. True acronyms are, for example, ASCII (pronounced [ass-key]) (American Standard Code for Information Interchange), NASA (National Aeronautics and Space Administration), WAC (Women's Army Corps pronounced to rhyme with lack, sack, Mac), SHAPE (Supreme Headquarters Allied Powers Europe), and NATO (pronounced to rhyme with Cato) is for North Atlantic Treaty Organization. *Laser* stands for Light Amplification by Stimulated Emission of Radiation. Some of the most famous acronyms of World War II included FU-, as in FUBAR (F***ed Up Beyond All Recognition) and the GI favorite SNAFU (Situation Normal All F***ed Up). Often, however, to make an acronym pronounceable, we take not just the initial sounds but, for example, the first consonant and the first vowel together. Thus *radar* comes from *radio detecting and ranging*. *Sonar* is from *sound navigation and ranging*, where the first two letters of each of the first two words form the basis of the acronym. Few of us realize that the now very common noun *modem* was similarly formed from *modulator–demodulator*. Sometimes acronyms are based on even larger chunks of the words they abbreviate: COMECON stands for the Council for Mutual Economic Assistance – the organization of the pre-1990 East European counterpart to the Common Market. A similar formation is the name of the computer language FORTRAN (Formula Translation). These are half-way between blends and acronyms. When an acronym becomes fully accepted as a word, it often comes to be spelled with lower-case letters, like other words:

---

[3] *Pagejacking* is an Internet scam by which web porn operators clone legitimate web pages. The last three words are from the list of new words available on the web page of the *American Dialect Society*: http://www.americandialect.org/adsl.shtml. They are defined as follows: *spamouflage* as "the non-spam-like header on a spam email message," *compfusion* as "confusion over computers," and *explornography* as "tourism in exotic and dangerous places."

modem, radar came to be treated that way, as well as *okay*; and indeed in the case of *snafu* some young people may not even realize that it disguises an obscene word.

4.1   Initialisms

If the letters which make up the acronym are individually pronounced, like COD, such acronyms are called *initialisms*. America seems to have been the great breeding ground of initialisms. They are rare in English before the twentieth century (GOP and OK are early examples, both dating from the middle of the nineteenth century). TNT (trinitrotoluene) dates from just before World War I. That war produced only a smallish number of acronyms – for example WAAC (Women's Army Auxiliary Corps) and WREN (Women's Royal Naval [Service]). It was during the first administration of Franklin Delano Roosevelt, starting in 1933, and then during World War II, that the fashion for acronyms and initialisms really got moving. The name for American soldiers was GI's (for General Issue), and the vehicle they drove, the Jeep, was a pronunciation of GP – General Purpose (vehicle). UFO (Unidentified Flying Object) is from the early 1950s. Roosevelt created many new government agencies, nearly all of which were referred to by initialisms (WPA Works Progress Administration, NRA National Recovery Administration, CCC Civilian Conservation Corps, FCC Federal Communications Commission, FTC Federal Trade Commission), to the point where the practice became respectable and started a trend that is now enormously productive in all areas of life. In the US, we pay taxes to the IRS (Internal Revenue Service), our driver's licenses are issued by the DMV (Division of Motor Vehicles), we watch NBC (National Broadcasting Company), ABC (American Broadcasting Company), and CBS (Columbia Broadcasting System). It would be unfair any longer to think of the trend as American: the BBC (British Broadcasting Corporation) can be heard all over the world, the ICA (Institute of Contemporary Art) Café in London is known to locals and visitors alike, and Dubliners ride their DART, while the people in Berkeley and San Francisco ride their BART (Bay Area Rapid Transit).

In more recent times, the proliferation of initialisms and acronyms has been much aggravated by the ubiquity of computer abbreviations: e.g., HTTP Hypertext Transfer Protocol, DRAM dynamic random-access memory, CPU central processing unit, as well as further government agency naming (DOD Department of Defense, DOE Department of Energy, HEW Health, Education and Welfare). The word acronym itself came into being in 1943, near the end of FDR's life. Al Smith, the New York City mayor who ran for president in 1928 with FDR as his vice-presidential candidate, referred to the trend to create more and more initialisms as "making alphabet soup." Al Smith could not have known it, but in the Gale *Dictionary of Acronyms, Initialisms & Abbreviations*, the initialism AAAAAA is recorded as the name of an organization the Mayor would have joined: The Association for the Alleviation of Asinine Abbreviations and Absurd Acronyms. (This is also an example of a reverse acronym: see below.)

4.2   Reverse acronyms

An interesting phenomenon in recent years, a sort of political offshoot of normal acronymic coinage, has been the rise of reverse acronyms – the creators start with a word they want as their name, say, for example, CORE, and then they work from those four letters to find four words which represent something like the idea they want to be associated with. CORE is the acronym for Congress of Racial Equality, NOW is the acronym of the National Organization of Women, MADD is the acronym of Mothers Against Drunk Drivers, CARE is the acronym for Cooperative for American Remittances to Europe. Organization names such as AID (Agency for International Development), AIM (American Indian Movement), HOPE (Health Opportunity for People Everywhere), PUSH (People United to Serve Humanity) have instant appeal and are easy to remember. Recently the Microsoft Corporation announced a new program which it calls DNA, for Windows Distributed interNet Architecture. It is obviously a reverse acronym in two ways: it picks up and capitalizes on a familiar acronym, namely DNA (deoxyribonucleic acid) and it has to fudge a bit to get the three letters DNA out of the actual phrase – it ignores the W of Windows, and the I of Internet. No doubt the benefits of appearing to be familiar, famous, and scientifically distinguished are worth the fudge. A rather nice case of the opposite motivation, namely to poke fun at oneself, appears in the acronym of an investment group which is called the University Park Investment Group – UPIG, naturally. A similar jest, which at the same time pokes fun at a super-secret agency of the Federal government, is to be heard in the phrase "A CYA operation." A small hint: the first two words are "Cover Your . . ."

Another widespread recent phenomenon is acronyms based simply on some popular phrase. People can produce acronyms or initialisms from any common phrase and from just about any string of words, most of them used only within a business or a shop. A popular restaurant chain on the West Coast of the US calls itself TGIF (Thank God it's Friday), memos start with FYI (for your information), individuals are referred to as DEWMs pronounced [DOOMs] (dead European white males).

The frequency of alphabet soup is such as to justify the production of numerous editions of the Gale dictionary, with over 400,000 entries in its eleventh edition (1987). On the other hand, alphabet soup easily and quickly disappears from the language: among the many examples above, it is a fairly good bet that not every reader knew NRA, WPA, or CCC, and those who are not into computers would have been unfamiliar with several more of the above examples. Of the 400,000 in Gale's dictionary, an ordinary person would be unlikely to know more than two or three hundred. Very large numbers of them are abbreviations for technical terms. For instance, no one but a medical expert would be likely to recognize TMJ as an initialism for temporomandibular joint.

5   Creation by shortening

Shortening may take any part of a word, usually a single syllable, and throw away the rest, like *quiz* from *inquisitive*, *phone* from *telephone*, *plane* from *airplane*, *flu* from *influenza*. Shortening is sometimes called "clipping." The process often applies not just to an existing word, but to a whole phrase. Thus *mob* is shortened from *mobile vulgus* "fickle rabble." *Zoo* is from *zoological gardens*. *Ad* and British *advert* are transparently based on *advertisement*. In many cases it is apparent that they are deliberate shortenings to save time and space in lists. Many shortenings have entered the language and speakers have lost track of where they came from. How many people would recognize *gin* as in *gin and tonic* as coming from *Genève*? Look up *whiskey* to discover what it is shortened from: the form will be completely unfamiliar to you.

Much less commonly we find what are called back formations like *edit* from *editor*, where the final *-or* is wrongly analyzed as a suffix (like the *-er* of *worker*, *employer*, *builder*) and is therefore treated as removable. To *burgle*, from *burglar*, is formed in the same way. Most examples of back formations are no longer transparent. One does not ordinarily realize, for instance, that *cherry* is a back formation from *ciris*, with the final -s having been wrongly analyzed as a plural suffix. The verb *grovel* is a misanalysis of *groveling*, which was originally *grufe* "face down" plus *-ling* "one who." There are not many of these, and except for very recent ones like *burgle* they are always opaque. They came into the language, after all, because the form they came from was itself opaque and open to the wrong analysis.

6   Derivation

6.1   Derivation by affixation

Up to this point, this chapter has described ways of creating new words which are not immediately transparent to the native speaker. The processes of what is called **derivational morphology** are, in many instances, so obvious that significant numbers of derivations are not even treated by dictionaries as separate entries. Since most of this book is about the complexities of derivational morphology, we do not want to anticipate details here. Roughly, derivation consists in making up new words by adding endings to more basic forms of the word. Mostly these derivations require no special definition or explanation because they follow regular rules. For example, from the *Chambers Dictionary*, under the headword *active*, we find these derived words: *activate, activation, actively, activeness, activity, activism, activist.* Four of them are given no further explanation at all, two of them are given only the very briefest explanation because the meaning has become slightly specialized, and one – *activate* – is treated at more length because it has a technical sense that requires explanation. The question is, when is a derived form merely that, predictable and comprehensible by general rules of the language, and when does the derived form require treatment as a separate word? The line is not really clear, and different decisions are found in different dictionaries. But the basic principle is this: if the new word can be fully comprehended given a knowledge of the meaning of the base and also of the endings, then it is not a new word and should not receive independent dictionary treatment, because just by knowing the parts you also know the whole. But if the new word is not transparent in that way, then it requires full definition. Examine each of these pairs of words. The members of each pair obviously have a historically based derivational relationship:

graceful	disgraceful	spectacle	spectacles
hard	hardly	late	latter
new	news	custom	customs
civic	civics	sweat	sweater

The word on the right comes from the one on the left, but the relationship is obscured because some sort of change has occurred in the meaning of the derived form (on the right) which cannot be understood by general rules of the language. Under these conditions we must then say that the derived form is a new word (in the new meaning).

6.2   Derivation without affixation

Consider the following pairs of sentences in which the same words appear in different functions (e.g., as a noun and as a verb):

This is a **major** oversight.
She graduated with a **major** in geography.
She **majored** in geography.

My **account** is overdrawn.
I can't **account** for where the money went.

They weighed **anchor** at 6:00 a.m.
Tom Brokaw **anchored** the news at 6:00 p.m.

They gave aid and **comfort** to the enemy.
They **comforted** the enemy.

We don't have any **doubt** it's correct.
We don't **doubt** that it's correct.

It's no **trouble** at all.
Don't **trouble** yourself.

In all these cases the verb or adjective and noun look alike and sound alike. There is reason to believe that the verbs are derived from the nouns. They are called "denominal verbs" for that reason, and they are said to be derived by a process of **conversion** – the noun is converted into a verb. In one sense such converted words are not new items in the lexicon. They are already there in another function (they are nouns, in these cases; but there are also adjective/adverb–verb pairs like *near, idle, clear, smooth, obscure,* and many more). The process of conversion is, furthermore, extremely productive today: we can *chair a meeting, air our opinions, panel the walls, weather the storm, storm the gates, e-mail the students, floor our enemies, polish the car, try to fish in troubled waters,* and so on. Conversions that have been around long enough are normally shown with a single entry in the dictionary, with the identification n., a., v., meaning that the form occurs as noun, adjective, and verb all three. Recent, or surprising, conversions often get separate entries in the dictionaries.

7   Compounding

This is the largest, and therefore the most important, source of new words. To produce new words by compounding, what we do is put together two words in a perfectly transparent way, and then various changes take place which cause the compound to lose its transparency.

A clear example from very early English is the word *Lord*, which is an opaque form of *loaf* "bread" (you can see the "l" and the "o" still) and *warden* "guardian" (you can see the "rd" still). A less extreme example, without the phonetic complication, is a word like *hoe-down* "noisy dance associated with harvests and weddings in the old South and West." The *Oxford English Dictionary* gives it as the equivalent of an earlier sense of *breakdown*, now obsolete in the relevant meaning. In neither case can one infer the meaning from knowing the meaning of the constituent parts. It is therefore an opaque compound. Other examples of the "Lord" type which were once compounds and are now recognizable only as fully assimilated single words include *woman* from *wife + mon* ("female" + "person"), *good-bye* from *God be with you*, *holiday* from *holy day*, *bonfire* from *bone fire*, *hussy* from *house wife*, *nothing* from *no thing*.

A full description of compounds is far beyond our scope, but because it is the largest and most important source of new words in the English vocabulary, outside of borrowing, we shall try to convey some sense of the variety of words that have come into English through the process of compounding. We will not include those compounds that are now totally opaque, like *Lord* – which of course is no longer felt to be a compound at all – but will include examples of those that are transparently composed of two familiar elements that have taken on a unique new meaning that cannot be inferred totally from the meaning of the elements, like *airship* or *frogman* or *icebox* or *hovercraft*. By unique new meaning we mean that *airships* are not ships, *frogmen* are not frogs, an *icebox* is not a box made of ice, and *hovercraft* do not hover.

We begin by distinguishing between syntactic compounds and lexical compounds.[4] One can always figure out what a syntactic compound means. Such compounds are formed by regular rules of grammar, like sentences, and they are not, therefore, listed in a dictionary. So if someone were to say,

"Playing quartets is fun."

We know, just from the rules of grammar, that they could also say,

"Quartet playing is fun."

Quartet playing is therefore a syntactic compound. Other transparent syntactic compounds are *shoemaker* (someone who makes shoes), *bookkeeper* (someone who keeps the books in order), *washing machine* (we wash things with the machine), *candlelight* (light provided by

[4] We have drawn examples freely from a truly great piece of scholarship, *The Categories and Types of Present-Day English Word-Formation*, by Hans Marchand, 2nd edn. 1969, C. H. Bech'she: Munich.

candles), *birdcage* (a cage for birds), *playgoer* (someone who goes to plays regularly). In fact the majority of compounds we use on a daily basis are the transparent syntactic ones.

On the other hand, we cannot figure out what *ice cream* or *iced cream* means just from the rules of grammar. We cannot compute the sense of *ice cream* from something like,

They iced the cream.

Therefore *ice cream* is a lexical compound which (if we don't know the meaning already) has to be looked up in a dictionary like a totally novel word. *Crybaby* must also be treated as a lexical compound, because it refers not to babies that cry but to people who act like babies that cry, i.e., who complain when anything makes them unhappy. Similarly, *girl friend* is not just a girl who is a friend, nor is *boy friend* just a boy who is a friend. Both of these compounds actually can mean what they appear to mean on the surface, but usually they mean more than that. *Sweetheart* is not a "sweet heart," whatever that would be, but it is an opaque compound that has been in the language since the thirteenth century. *Highlight*, as in "the highlight of my day," is opaque from the seventeenth century. One can see how such a compound becomes opaque: it starts its life as a transparent description of lighting which causes some object to stand out, and then it is generalized or extended to refer to anything which stands out in one's memory or experience. As soon as this extension of the meaning is taken, then – at least in this meaning – the compound is opaque. *Bull's-eye*, which most speakers of modern English would associate with the center of a target as the primary sense, originally referred to the central protuberance formed in making a sheet of blown glass. Its earliest occurrence is a slang name for a British coin, the crown, from the beginning of the eighteenth century. The transfer of meaning to "center of a target" is simply an extension of the notion "center" which is a function of the way glass is blown, starting as a hot glob and gradually expanded outward in all directions from the center.

All of the compounds exemplified above have two parts, and their meaning is a function of the interaction of these parts plus the context of use that may gradually change them from transparent to opaque. Are there also phrasal compounds made up of more than two words? Is *maid of honor* or *good-for-nothing* or *man of the world* or *jack-of-all-trades* a phrase or a compound, and do we care? There is, unfortunately, no easy answer. Where the meaning is not obviously computable, some dictionaries list them as lexical compounds: e.g., the *Oxford English Dictionary* does not list *jack-of-all-trades*, but the much smaller *Webster's Collegiate* does. *Maid of honor* is listed by both, whereas *good-for-nothing* is not listed by any, nor is *man of the world*, though in both these instances there would seem to be good reason to single them out as having special properties: one can know about men and about the world without knowing what man of the world really means, and good-for-nothing refers to a special kind of worthlessness, usually laziness.

8   Eponyms

These are new words based on names (*epi-* "upon" *onym* "name"). All eponyms necessarily involve some degree of change in the meaning of the word: *watt*, for example, refers to a unit of electrical power, not to the individual who invented the steam engine. The number of new words of this type in fields like biology, physics, and medicine is very large, since new discoveries are very often named for their discoverers. Quite often we take the name of an individual, a character familiar from mythology, history, or folklore, a place name, a brand name, and so on and extend its scope beyond the original individual reference, thereby turning what is called a proper noun, i.e. somebody's name, into a common noun, i.e. a word like boy, girl, doctor, house, town that does not refer to a particular individual but to a class of individuals sharing relevant defining properties. Even proper nouns, of course, can be of several types: those which are associated with real people, those that are associated with imaginary creatures or mythological figures, those that are associated with places. All three types have provided words in English based on their names. Some examples:

8.1   Based on personal names

boycott (Charles Boycott, an English land agent in Ireland)
dahlia (developed by Anders Dahl, a Swedish botanist)
cardigan (Earl of Cardigan, nineteenth century; a style of waistcoat that he favored)
derrick (the name of a hangman at a London prison in the time of Shakespeare and Queen Elizabeth I)
guy (In Britain, Guy Fawkes Day, November 5; for the Catholic conspirator, member of the Gunpowder Plot in Great Britain, 1606. Since he was held up to ridicule, and in Britain the word still means "a person of odd or grotesque appearance," it is apparent that American English has generalized and neutralized the word.)
lynch (Capt. William Lynch, a planter in colonial Virginia, originated lynch law in 1780)
nicotine (Jacques Nicot introduced tobacco into France in 1560)

ohm (unit of electrical resistance, named for nineteenth-century German physicist, Georg Simon Ohm)

sadistic (eighteenth-century Marquis de Sade, infamous for crimes of sexual perversion)

sandwich (eighteenth-century British nobleman, the Earl of Sandwich, who brought bread and meat together to the gambling table to provide sustenance for himself, and started the fast food industry)

8.2   Based on geographical names

bikini (the islands where the atom bomb was tested; presumably gets its meaning from the style of female native costumes encountered there)

cheddar (a village in Somerset whence the cheese first came)

china (short for chinaware, from china-clay, employed in the manufacture of porcelain, originally made in China)

denim (cotton cloth now, originally serge, made in the town of Nîmes, southern France, hence serge de Nim)

hamburger (the word is an Americanism; from Hamburg steak, some form of pounded beef, found in Hamburg in the nineteenth century and brought to the US by German immigrants, though the word and specific concept of the hamburger originated in the US)

jean (from the Italian city of Genoa, where the cloth was first made, as in blue jeans)

port (shortened from Oporto, the chief port for exporting wines from Portugal)

sardonic (should be sardinic, coming from the island of Sardinia; the vowel change is based on the Greek form; refers to a type of sarcastic laughter supposed to resemble the grotesque effects of eating a certain Sardinian plant)

sherry (a white wine from, originally, Xeres, now Jerez de la Frontera, in Spain; the final <s> was deleted on the mistaken view that it was the plural suffix, an instance of what is known as morphological reanalysis)

spartan (from the ancient Doric state of Laconia, in the south of Greece; the meaning comes from their chosen lifestyle, which eschewed luxuries)

turkey (an American bird, confused in America at first with an African Guinea-bird, brought into Europe through Turkey, whence the name: but certainly a confusing sequence of borrowing and renaming!!!)

8.3   Based on names from literature, folklore, and mythology

atlas (he was condemned by Zeus, the leader of the Greek gods [called Jupiter by the Romans], to support the earth on his shoulders; the

name was assigned by an imaginative early anatomist to the top vertebra of the neck, the one which supports the head; it came to refer to a
collection of maps because many early publications of world geography showed drawings of Atlas holding the world up on his shoulders)

casanova (Giovanni Jacopo Casanova de Seingalt. He wrote vividly
about his sexual adventures throughout most of Europe)

chimera (a mythological Greek monster, purely a creature of the imagination)

morphine (Morpheus was the son of the Greek god of sleep)

nemesis (after the name of a Greek goddess who punished violations of
all forms of rightful order and proper behavior)

panic (noises which caused fear in the flocks by night were attributed in
ancient Greece to Pan, who was the God of misdeeds; a panic is irrational behavior in the herd)

platonic (Plato was an early Greek philosopher; the word originally
referred to the kind of interest in young men that Socrates, the first
great Greek philosopher, is supposed to have had. As originally used,
it had no reference to women, though now its main reference is to a
non-sexual relationship between men and women)

saturnine (as the *OED* says, "sluggish, cold, and gloomy in tempera-
ment"; one wonders why a car should be named after it. Presumably
the sense of saturnine is based on the fact that Saturn was the most
remote of the seven planets known to ancient astronomers)

satirical (a satyr was a creature with a mixture of human and animal
properties, and supposed to be gifted with a prodigious sexual appe-
tite; the word satire refers originally to theatrical pieces which hold
these qualities, and others, up to ridicule)

8.4   Based on commercial brand names

Band-aid® is commonly generalized to refer to any small bandage for a
cut or scratch, and it has moved out into general use in metaphors
like "The IRS needs major reforms; we've had enough of these taxa-
tion band-aids!"

Jello® a particular brand of jellied emulsion, is generalized to refer to
any edible substance of the same type.

Levis® a brand of canvas trousers, now refers to any denim-like, rough
and ready, trousers.

Tampax® is one of many brands of feminine hygiene devices, generalized to them all.

Xerox® especially as a verb ("to xerox something"), has come to mean
"to copy by any dry process."

Zipper®, based on the echoic word (see below) *zip*, which imitates the
sound of speeding objects. The verb is from 1852, the noun 1926.

9   Other sources

It is part of the common mythology about language that many words must have come from efforts to imitate the sounds that the words represent. There are in fact only a few legitimate instances of this sort, and they are called **echoic** words. Bloomfield[5] distinguished between those words that are actually imitative, like *oh!*, *ah!*, *ouch!*, those that are coined to sound like a noise made by some object or creature, such as *bang, blah, buzz, burp, splash, tinkle, ping, cock-a-doodle-doo, meow, moo, baa, cuckoo, bob-white, whip-poor-will*, and those that have the property that "to the speaker it seems as if the sounds were especially suited to the meaning." His examples are *flip, flap, flop, flitter, flimmer, flicker, flutter, flash, flush, flare, glare, glitter, flow, gloat, glimmer, bang, bump, lump, thump, thwack, whack, sniff, sniffle, snuff, sizzle, wheeze*. The total number of any of these types of words that may be called roughly echoic is very small, in English or any other language. It is not a major resource for expanding the vocabulary.

Another rather unimportant, though often amusing, resource for expanding the vocabulary is through a process called **reduplication**, in which part or all of a word is repeated.[6] Only a few of these examples are more than trivial expansions of the vocabulary: *dum-dum* (type of bullet), *bonbon, tom-tom, fifty-fifty, hula-hula, so-so, boob tube, brain drain*.

So much for the ways of introducing new words into English without borrowing them. Since well over 80 percent of the total vocabulary of English is borrowed, we turn now to the rest of the book to study many aspects of the history of borrowed words in English.

---

[5] Leonard Bloomfield, *Language*, New York: Henry Holt, 1933: 156.
[6] A recent study, from which our examples are taken, is John M. Dienhart, "Stress in Reduplicative Compounds: Mish-Mash or Hocus-Pocus," *American Speech* 74.1: 3–37 (1999).

2 The background of English

A quick scan of a couple of pages in a dictionary that records the origin of our vocabulary reveals that many entries in it are historically "un-English." This is not surprising; languages travel with the people who speak them. No language in the world today uses vocabulary which is entirely free of foreign influence, just as no country's population can remain completely indigenous. A genetically "pure" language is as hard to imagine as a genetically "pure" population. Like the society we live in, the language we speak is a product of history. Like nations and governments, languages differ in their attitude and adaptability to external pressure. History tells us how periods of hostility, isolation, self-sufficiency, follow upon periods of openness, constructive interaction, and peaceful coexistence with the outside world. The overall inventory of words used in a language is the outcome of centuries of political and cultural history. In many ways our vocabulary mirrors the events which have taken place in the history of English-speaking peoples. The purpose of this chapter is to highlight the important socio-historical events and circumstances which have shaped our vocabulary. We start with some basic notions and facts about the place of English within the enormously broad picture of languages of the world.

1   The family history of English

Language families. The "family tree" is a commonly used metaphor in the classification of languages. Like human families, some language families are larger than others, some families stick together for long periods of time, while others drift apart, some families are mobile, others stay put. The parallel between the genetic relatedness of languages and the human family, or any minimal social unit which produces offspring, is scientifically imperfect, but it is still a helpful way of thinking about language in its historical context. The analogy with the family tree allows us to talk about "parent" languages evolving into "daughter" languages, about the splitting of families into branches of languages, about the maintenance and severance of family ties and the continuity of shared characteristics.

In terms of its ancestry, English comes from a large and mobile family whose daughter languages have developed considerable independence. Without specialized knowledge, the genetic similarities between English and the languages related to it are not immediately obvious. One way of establishing the historical links between languages is by looking into their vocabularies. As will be shown in this chapter, the English vocabulary today reveals layers of words that correspond to its family history. Some of these words are shared with languages from which English has been separated for millennia; only a trained philologist can detect their common traits. Sometimes, however, genetic relatedness is recognizable, either because of the "sameness" it involves, or because genetic history has been enhanced by external history. We start by identifying the parent-family and the family branches and smaller groups from which English originates. As we describe the family and its branches, we will evaluate the strength of the genetic and social links of English to the other daughter languages.

Indo-European. The family of languages to which English belongs is called *Indo-European*, a name which derives from the geographical range over which these languages were spoken before some of them spread to the New World: roughly from India to Iceland. *Indo-* refers to the fact that many of the daughter languages from earliest recorded times were spoken on the Indian subcontinent, and *European* refers to the fact that from equally early times most of the languages of Europe are descended from that common ancestor also. The term is strictly historical; in the twenty-first century descendants of Indo-European languages are spoken across the globe, in many countries in the continents of Africa, Australia, the Americas. Not all European languages are Indo-European in origin. Hungarian, Estonian, and Finnish belong to the language family called *Finno-Ugric*; Basque (in the northwest corner of the Iberian peninsula) is not known to be related to any other language of which we have any record. In India, the southern one-third of the subcontinent is occupied by speakers of a family of languages that are not related to Indo-European. The family is called *Dravidian*. It includes languages like Telugu and Tamil. Another name for the Indo-European family, which appears in etymological references, is *Proto-Indo-European*. *Proto-* means "first, earliest form of." In the context of language study, *Proto-* means that we have no actual records of this language but that scholars have been able to reconstruct in a significant degree of detail what the earliest form of the language was like.

Indo-European is only one of perhaps as many as 600 language families that are not demonstrably related to one another. Ultimately, they must be related because there is good reason to believe that human languages are all designed in basically similar ways and that human language was invented only once in all of history. However, we have no idea, other than speculation based on modern languages, what the earliest languages were like. Our knowledge of specific languages goes back only about 7,000 years, whereas human languages have existed in forms probably not very different from modern languages for as much as a million years, quite probably a lot longer in some more primitive form. Our direct access to ancient languages begins only when systems of writing were invented and preserved on clay tablets, the earliest ones in the Indo-European family dating from the middle of the second millennium B.C., i.e. around 3,500 years ago. (In other language families of the Near East, where writing was first invented, the clay tablets date from about 6,000 years ago.) Our indirect access to the earliest forms of Indo-European, through comparison of ancient recorded languages with each other, allows us to establish fairly reliable reconstructions of Indo-European as it existed, probably in an area north of the Caspian Sea, about 5,500 years ago. This date, as the etymology editor of the Third Edition of the *American Heritage Dictionary*, Calvert Watkins, writes, is "the latest possible date for the community of Proto-Indo-European proper" (p. 2088). This is also the approximate date archaeologists have established for the spread of the wheel through Europe. Though we cannot prove there was a connection between the spread of the wheel and the spread of the Indo-European languages, speculation along these lines seems reasonable.

The chart below represents, in a very simplified form, the way in which various Indo-European languages "branched off" from the proto-language. The time line is an approximation. For obvious reasons we have included only branches which have living descendants.[1]

The Indo-European family is among the most studied of all language families, though other families such as Semitic, to which Arabic and Hebrew belong, and Finno-Ugric, to which Hungarian, Finnish, and Estonian belong, have also been deeply studied, to say nothing of the ancient linguistic traditions of China.[2] The last century has been a

---

[1] Indo-European languages of which there are no living descendants are Illyrian, Thracian, Phrygian, Anatolian, and Tocharian. The cross, †, marks "dead" languages. Sanskrit is included in the chart because of its importance for reconstructing Indo-European. Our time-depth calculations are intended to approximate the dates at which each of the older languages were still more or less cohesive units, at least linguistically. These estimates are based on opinions cited in Calvert Watkins' essay on "Indo-European and the Indo-Europeans," which precedes the Root Appendix in the *American Heritage Dictionary*, 3rd edn. 1992: 2081–89, the opinions of various contributors to *The World's Major Languages*, ed. by Bernard Comrie (Oxford University Press, 1987), and the opinion of Leonard Bloomfield as expressed in *Language*, Ch. 4 "The Languages of the World" (New York: Holt, 1933).

[2] According to recently published data (*National Geographic Magazine*, August 1999), Mandarin Chinese is by far the most broadly used language in the world, with 885 million speakers. This is significantly more than the total number of speakers of the next three largest languages taken together. The three runners-up happen to be Indo-European: English, with 322 million speakers, Spanish, with 266 million speakers, and Bengali, with 189 million speakers.

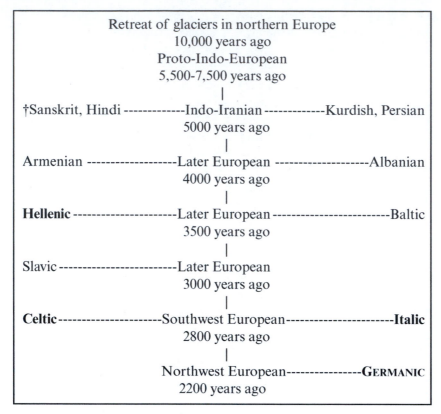

Retreat of glaciers in northern Europe
10,000 years ago
Proto-Indo-European
5,500-7,500 years ago
|
†Sanskrit, Hindi -------------Indo-Iranian -------------Kurdish, Persian
5000 years ago
|
Armenian -------------------Later European --------------------Albanian
4000 years ago
|
Hellenic ---------------------Later European ------------------------Baltic
3500 years ago
|
Slavic ------------------------Later European
3000 years ago
|
Celtic ----------------------Southwest European----------------------**Italic**
2800 years ago
|
Northwest European----------------**GERMANIC**
2200 years ago

The IE Family of Languages

time of unprecedented interest in the structure and history of previously undescribed language families, from Austronesian and Bantu, to Yupik (spoken in Alaska and Siberia) and Zaparoan (spoken in Peru).

The discovery that some geographically distant languages, such as Hindi, Greek, and English, belong to the same family, was made by a British judge, Sir William Jones. He was stationed in India, and his interest and knowledge of many tongues led him to notice that words in Sanskrit, Greek, and Latin showed similarities that could not be accidental. In 1786 he announced that these languages must have "sprung from a common source, which, perhaps, no longer exists," laying the foundations of a scientific field called Comparative-Historical Indo-European Linguistics. Intense research over the last 200 years has produced many important insights into the relationship, history, and structure of the Indo-European languages. Indeed, understanding the structure of the present-day English vocabulary would be impossible without the enlightening results of Indo-European scholarship.

The chart above includes the "productive" branches of Indo-European. Not all branches are equally important for English. The boldfaced groups (Celtic, Hellenic, Italic) have had the strongest influence on our vocabulary, either because of territorial overlap or proximity, or for historical, social, and cultural reasons. Occasional contacts with other languages in the chart, such as Hindi, Persian, and Russian, have also left some traces, but their effect on English is not due to shared origin. The contribution of these languages to our vocabulary is similar to the contribution from unrelated languages like Japanese, various American Indian languages, or Maori. We start with some information on the branches of Indo-European whose relationship to English is evident only in more recent borrowings.

1.1   Indo-European

Indo-Iranian. Indic is the source of the languages spoken by the descendants of a huge migration into the Indian subcontinent from the Indo-European homeland. Most of the languages of northern and central India, among them *Hindi, Urdu, Bengali,* and *Gujerati,* are descendants of Indic. Among the earliest texts of any surviving Indo-European language are the hymns which form the basic part of the scriptures of the Brahmin religion, the compositions known as the *Rig-Vedas,* dating from about 1200 B.C.; these are known to us through much later documents. *Sanskrit* is the classical language of the texts of the Brahmin religion as it was formalized and codified in the fourth century B.C. The other branch of this family, the Iranian branch represented earliest by *Old Persian,* is the ancestor of modern *Kurdish* and modern *Persian,* which is an Indo-European language even though, under the influence of Islam, it is written in the Arabic alphabet.

Armenian and Albanian are the ancestors of those two modern languages, respectively, and are generally viewed as independent non-branching lineages, though Armenian has two major dialects (East and West).

Balto-Slavic, includes the Baltic languages (Lithuanian and Latvian, though not Estonian, which is a Finno-Ugric language) and the Slavic languages. The ancestor of all Slavic languages is *Old Church Slavonic.* The *Cyrillic* alphabet, now the most widely used non-Roman alphabet in Europe, was devised during the ninth century in the course of translating the Scriptures into Old Church Slavonic. The Slavic languages are *Russian, Ukrainian,* and *Byelorussian* to the east, *Bulgarian, Macedonian, Serbo-Croatian,* and *Slovene* to the south, and *Polish, Czech, Slovak,* and *Sorbian* to the west.

The Indo-European branches and their daughter languages which are more directly responsible for the shape of our modern vocabulary are Celtic, Hellenic, and Italic.

The Celtic languages.[3] Celtic languages were once spread over most of western Europe, especially along the coastal areas and certainly throughout the British Isles. Celtic is the oldest language group of record in the geographical territory which later became Ireland and Great Britain. The Celts were in Britain when the Romans arrived in the time of Julius Caesar, in 55 B.C. After the Romans left, around A.D. 400, the Celts who remained in southern England were responsible for inviting mercenary warriors from across the North Sea: that was the first-known contact between Celtic-speaking and Germanic-speaking peoples. The idea did not work out well for the Celts: the Germanic mercenaries soon took over, and much of the Celtic population was either assimilated or pushed to the outlying areas of the British Isles: Scotland, Ireland, Cornwall to the south-west, Wales, the Isle of Man.

The daughter languages of the Celtic group are: Irish, Welsh, Scottish Gaelic, Cornish, Breton, and probably the now virtually extinct †Manx. Irish (also known as Irish Gaelic) is spoken natively by about a quarter of a million people in Ireland and taught in school for a number of years throughout the Republic of Ireland, even though English remains the main language. It is also used by about 60,000 people in Britain. Welsh is one of the languages used by 500,000 people in Wales. The number of people speaking Scottish Gaelic in Britain is about 70,000. The last speaker whose mother-tongue was Cornish reportedly died in 1777, and today the language is familiar to fewer than 200 people in Britain. Breton, which was transplanted into western France by Celtic speakers fleeing from the fifth-century Germanic invaders of Britain, is spoken by some 300,000 people.[4]

Hellenic. The oldest Homeric poems are thought to date back at least to 800 B.C., and records of ancient Greek dialects exist from the seventh century B.C. Athenian Greek, also called *classical Greek*, was spoken in Athens from about 450–350 B.C. *Koiné* is the variety of Greek that had come into being by the time of Jesus; it is a mixed, de-regionalized language which is the direct ancestor of Modern Greek. It is of interest also because it is the language of St. Paul, whose epistles in the New Testament were written in koiné. It rivals Latin in its importance as a source of influence on the English vocabulary. The Romans adopted and modified many Greek words and roots. In English, Greek vocabulary comes both directly from the Hellenic source, and indirectly, through Latin. As we shall see, the influence is entirely through

---

[3] The first letter of the *Celtic* language group is pronounced [k], unlike the name of the Boston professional basketball team, which begins with [s].
[4] The figures, compiled by the European Bureau of Lesser Used Languages, were published in *The Guardian* July 14, 1999.

higher education and scholarship, especially in the life sciences, which tend to use Greek as their main source of technical coinages.

Italic. This is the branch of Indo-European whose daughter languages have had the most pervasive and lasting effect on the composition of the English vocabulary. The group includes †Latin, French, Spanish, Portuguese, Catalan, Italian, Rumanian, Sardinian, and Rhaeto-Romance.

Latin is attested since the sixth century B.C. It started out simply as the language of ancient Rome, and it was just one of a number of Italic languages. The economic, military, and cultural success of the Romans secured a dominant position for Latin. That language soon swamped all others in the family, as well as non-Indo-European languages like Etruscan that were at one time spoken on the Italian peninsula. The use of Latin by the Roman Catholic Church later played a major role in the spread and continuity of the Latin language, throughout the Middle Ages and indeed to the present day. All the modern Italic languages listed above, also commonly referred to as the *Romance* languages, are simply what Latin became in different parts of the Roman Empire. Thus, modern Italian is the direct descendant of Latin in Italy; modern Spanish is one of the direct descendants of Latin on the Iberian peninsula, modern French is a development of the speech of Romans living in France during the third republic, and so on. Technically speaking, the language differentiation that produced the various branches of Italic meant that Latin "died" as a language acquired naturally and effortlessly by children at home. However, Latin had such enormous cultural prestige that during the Middle Ages and the Renaissance, it continued to be the language of scholars throughout western Europe, and it was studied by educated English speakers throughout the last century. Thus, Latin is a dead language as no one learns it natively, but it has been and is very much of a "living" dead language in the sense that it is still used in the liturgy by the Roman Catholic Church. It is still spoken in the priesthood and in certain scholarly circles.

Italian is the national language of Italy, standardized on the basis of the literary language of Tuscany (Florence) that developed during the Renaissance, with substantial influence from Rome in modern times.

Spanish is the national language of Spain and its former colonies throughout the Americas, including most of South and Central America except Brazil.

Portuguese is the national language of Portugal and Brazil.

French. The modern standard language is based on the variety spoken in Paris, the seat of French government and culture. Although this variety has had much influence on English in relatively recent times, in earlier history the French of Normandy (northern France), which was imported into England with William the Conqueror and his soldiers in 1066, was the source of thousands of words borrowed from French into English.

Other Romance languages include *Catalan*, spoken in Barcelona and surrounding areas, *Sardinian*, *Rumanian*, and *Rhaeto-Romance*, the latter spoken in Switzerland. These languages have had no contact with English, hence no influence.

1.2   The Germanic branch

The closest relatives of English are the languages belonging to the *Germanic* branch of Indo-European. "Germanic" is not to be confused with "German." German is the name of the modern language spoken in Germany. Like English, Danish, Dutch, etc., it is one of the descendants of a common Germanic ancestor spoken between 2,200 and 2,000 years ago.

Germanic is further divided into two subgroups with living descendants, *North Germanic* and *West Germanic*. A third group, *East Germanic*, has died out completely. East Germanic is historically important because much of our earliest information about the Germanic languages comes from an East Germanic language called *Gothic*, the language of the Visigoths. Gothic has been extinct since the Middle Ages; one major manuscript, a translation of the Greek New Testament, dates from the middle of the fourth century A.D. The chart shows, in outline form, the Germanic branch of Indo-European as it survives today.

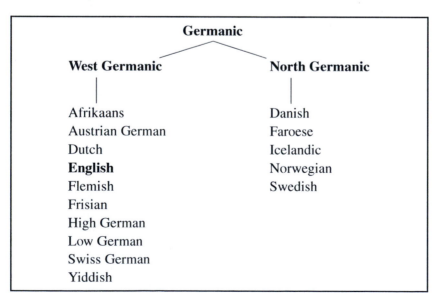

	Germanic	
West Germanic		**North Germanic**
Afrikaans		Danish
Austrian German		Faroese
Dutch		Icelandic
English		Norwegian
Flemish		Swedish
Frisian		
High German		
Low German		
Swiss German		
Yiddish		

North Germanic. Geographically, North Germanic is subdivided further into *East Nordic*, including *Swedish* and *Danish*, and *West Nordic*, including *Norwegian*, *Icelandic* and *Faroese*. Swedish is spoken mainly in Sweden, and to some considerable extent also in Finland. Danish is spoken mainly in Denmark. Both Swedish and Danish, though they are distinct languages, can be used as a "common currency" by most Scandinavians. Norwegian has two major varieties spoken in Norway. Icelandic is the language of the oldest Scandinavian documents, except for inscriptions on stones found mainly in Sweden; these documents survive in Icelandic from the twelfth century A.D. Faroese, closely similar to Icelandic, is spoken in the Faroe Islands in the North Atlantic Ocean.

The distinction between East and West Nordic is primarily of historical settlement interest, since Iceland and the Faroe Islands were settled mainly from Norway. In modern times, the relevant distinction is between *Mainland Nordic* and *Insular Nordic*. An educated Scandinavian from any of the mainland areas finds it fairly easy to get along linguistically with any other mainland speaker, but not at all with insular speakers. What has happened to the Scandinavian languages – a major re-grouping – is an interesting example of how historical linguistic boundaries may become blurred and replaced through long periods of trade, population movements, and shared government.

West Germanic. The languages in this group, listed alphabetically on the chart, can be divided according to historical geographical criteria into *Low Germanic* and *High Germanic*. Low Germanic comprises *Frisian*, *Dutch*, *Afrikaans*, *Flemish*, and *English*, while High Germanic includes *High German* (or simply *German*), *Austrian* and *Swiss German*, and *Yiddish*.

The designations "high" and "low" in the classification of the West Germanic languages should be taken quite literally, in their topographical sense, and not as value judgments. *Low* refers to all the Germanic languages of the flat lowlands of northern Germany and the Netherlands and their descendants. *High* refers to all the Germanic languages of the mountainous southern parts of the area, i.e. the Alps and the hills north of them. The standard language of modern Germany is called High German because it is historically based on the southern varieties, though it is now a standardized school language, not fully identical with any of the native varieties.

Frisian is spoken on the coast and coastal islands of the Netherlands along the north coast almost over to Denmark; of all the Germanic languages, this language is most similar to English. *Flemish* is one of the two official languages of Belgium. *Dutch* is spoken in the Netherlands, and *Afrikaans* is the offspring of Dutch spoken in South Africa after the seventeenth century. *(High) German* is used in government, and institutionalized in grammars and dictionaries of "standard" German. *Austrian* and *Swiss German* are the national varieties used in those two countries. The three languages are as mutually intelligible, or unintelligible, as are the varieties of English spoken in different geographical regions, from Scotland to Alabama, and from New Zealand to New York. Taken together, Austrian German, Swiss German, and German, represent the second most widely spoken Germanic language in the world, used natively by about 98 million speakers.

The "youngest" language within High Germanic is Yiddish. During the Middle Ages, High German expanded vigorously into Poland, the Baltic countries, and Russia, though it did not replace the local languages. At that time there were very large numbers of Jews in this area who learned High German and modified it with loanwords from the Slavic languages and Hebrew; they carried this language with them to western Europe and to America. The name "Yiddish" is from *jüdisch*, from German *Jude* "a Jew."

1.3   English

Our earliest records of how Germanic-speaking people invaded the British Isles and settled there come from brief remarks made by Continental historians. From an anonymous fifth-century chronicler we learn that in 441–42 the Germanic tribe of the Saxons conquered Britain after prolonged harassment.[5] No other contemporary documentation of these early events exists. About a century later, the Celtic preacher and chronicler Gildas, told a somewhat more elaborate story of the conquest. According to him, the Saxons were invited to Britain to help protect the island from an invasion from the north. In return for their military services, the Saxons were given land and were allowed to settle in the eastern parts of Britain. The authoritative *Ecclesiastical History of the English People*, written in 731 by the English cleric Bede, dates the first landing of the Germanic warriors in Britain to the year **449**. This is the date that histories of English usually identify as the year of birth of *The English Language*. Obviously, the useful metaphor does not tell the whole story: it took many successive waves of new settlers and at least another hundred years before the demographic and linguistic character of Britain was changed.

As noted earlier, the Celts were the first Indo-European occupants of Britain. The southern British Celts had been first subdued and thereafter ruled and sheltered by the Romans. Julius Caesar's attempt at an

---

[5] For more information on the early records of the Germanic conquest of Britain, see Jacek Fisiak, *An Outline History of English*: Volume I, 1995: 31–41, also A. C. Baugh and T. Cable, *A History of the English Language*, 4th edn., Englewood Cliffs, New Jersey: Prentice-Hall, Inc. 1993: 45–48.

early invasion in 55–54 B.C. did not result in occupation, unlike the results elsewhere in the Roman Empire, in particular Gaul (where the Latin spoken by Caesar's legions became, ultimately, modern French). It was during the rule of the emperor Claudius (from A.D. 43) that the Roman invasion was followed by a more permanent occupation and military control. For about four hundred years thereafter, Britain was a province of the Roman Empire. By the beginning of the fifth century, however, maintaining occupation forces in that outlying territory became too costly for the Romans, who were constantly subjected to the attacks of the belligerent Germanic tribes on the Continent. A highly simplified version of the events that followed is that when the Romans pulled out, with all of them gone by A.D. 400, the Celts in the south of the island were relatively defenseless. It was then that they invited Germanic mercenary soldiers to come over from northern Europe and protect them from invading Vikings, as well as from marauding Celts from the north and from Ireland (the Scots and the Picts). The mercenaries came mainly from three tribes, the *Angles*, the *Saxons*, and the *Jutes*. The language takes its name from the Angles: *Angle-ish*. The name of the country *England* comes from *Angle-land.*

The entire documentation concerning the early history of English is in Latin. Most of it is heavily "recycled" long after the time of the first invasions and settlements. The Germanic tribes, pagan and illiterate, left no records of their first exploits across the English Channel, though some of the early heroic poetry preserved in Anglo-Saxon may reflect details of their customs and traditions. The archaeological evidence, too, is scanty at best. Place names are of some help: since *-ing* is a Germanic ending, meaning "belonging to, of the kind of," it is assumed that place names such as *Harting, Hastings, Reading, Woking* testify to early Germanic presence in these locations. Similarly, place names ending in *-ham* meaning "settlement, home," as in *Birmingham, Durham, Grantham, Nottingham, Oakham* probably also indicate early settlement in the respective places, but scholars working with this kind of evidence call for extreme caution.[6] Combining the various sources of information, historians are confident, however, that the language was indeed brought to Britain from the territory of what is northwestern Germany today around the middle of the fifth century. There is also agreement that at least some of the ships of Germanic mercenaries arrived at the invitation of the Celts in southern Britain, after the Romans had withdrawn their military forces to protect Rome from barbaric invasions. The subsequent history of rapid expansion of the Germanic-speaking population and the formation of English kingdoms

---

[6] For those interested in the subject, Cecily Clark's chapter "Onomastics" in volume I of the *Cambridge History of the English Language* (1992) is an excellent survey of these issues.

on previously Celtic lands, leaves no doubt that the invasion resulted in gradual, but relentless expulsion of the Celtic speakers from the central parts of the island. Though the earliest preserved written records of the language did not appear until about the first quarter of the eighth century, we can assume that the beginnings of *Old English* go back to the middle of the fifth century.

2   Historical influences on the early vocabulary of English

Territorial proximity and a shared genetic source can account only partially for the degree of closeness between English and its sister languages. Genetic similarities are obscured or even completely disguised by time, cultural, economic, and demographic factors. Indeed, for the structure of the vocabulary, nothing is as important as the historical context in which the language evolved. *All* aspects of language are constantly changing, but vocabulary is the part that reacts most readily and rapidly to external influences. As shown below, English has changed its vocabulary so dramatically that in terms of word stock it can no longer be considered a Germanic language. This section looks into the historical and cultural factors that defined the composition of the early vocabulary of English; it also covers the events and circumstances that led to its "hybridization."

The history of the English language is traditionally divided into:

> *Old English* (c. 450–1066)
> *Middle English* (1066–1476)
> *Early Modern English* (1476–1776)
> *Modern English* (1776–present)

The historical period during which Old English was spoken is known as Anglo-Saxon. We talk of Anglo-Saxon literature, the *Anglo-Saxon Poetic Records*, Anglo-Saxon religion, law, and culture. The end of Old English/the beginning of Middle English is dated at 1066 to coincide with the *Norman Conquest*. Clearly, a single historical event cannot cause the language to change overnight; the cut-off date is a convenience. In some of its features Old English was still Old English until the end of the eleventh century, and characteristic traits of Middle English had started to develop before 1066. The same principle holds for the time-span of the other periods.

2.1   The indigenous vocabulary of Old English

The pre-Germanic words. Many words used in Old English, and surviving to this day, can be traced back to the Indo-European parent language. Such words have been in the language, essentially unchanged except for some aspects of their pronunciation, for perhaps 7,000 years. We assume that the Indo-European language family began, at least in Europe, not long after the end of the last Ice Age, when the glaciers covering all of Europe north of the Alps gradually melted and opened up huge territories where humankind had not lived before. Surviving from this earliest period are words denoting natural phenomena, plants, animals, kinship terms, verbs for basic human activities, adjectives for essential qualities, numerals, pronouns: *moon, tree, brother, mother, do, be, new, long, that, me, two, mine.*

Early Germanic words. When Germanic became an independent branch of the Indo-European family about 2,200 years ago, many new words came into existence. Again, these are words which refer to everyday life, natural phenomena, land and sea: *sand, earth, starve, make, fox, find.* Other uniquely Germanic items are *boat, broad, drink, drive, fowl, hold, house, meat, rain, sail, storm, thief, wife, winter.* There are also some suffixes which are not found outside the Germanic linguistic branch: *-dom* (as in *freedom, kingdom, stardom, bugdom*) and *-ship* (as in *friendship, lordship, kinship, stewardship*), are typical examples. Later still, when English was separated from its continental relatives in the fifth century, some words not found elsewhere in Germanic appeared in Old English: *bird, woman, lord, lady, sheriff.*

2.1.1   Earliest loanwords

The vocabulary of Old English, estimated roughly at about 25,000–30,000 words, was mostly homogeneous in origin. Yet even at this early stage in the language, contacts with other peoples brought in *some* foreign words. There are three major sources of "outside" vocabulary in Old English: Celtic, Latin, and Scandinavian.

Celtic. The demographic history of the British Isles prior to the Germanic invasions and settlements might lead us to expect traces of Celtic vocabulary in Old English. Such traces are not abundant, however. The newcomers gradually drove the indigenous Celts to the periphery of the country, or assimilated them. Lack of contact, and presumably socio-economic differences had the effect of isolating Celtic from Old English. Consequently, the Celtic languages were not a significant source of new words, except for a few everyday words such as *bin, cradle, dun, crag, curse, loch, cross, ancor* "hermit." As is common in such historical situations, however, the Anglo-Saxons adopted many geographical names: *Kent, Dover, York, London* (?), *Thames, Esk, Avon.* Of Celtic origin are also the place names ending in – *combe* "valley," *-torr* "rock, peak." We also find Celtic–English hybrids: *Yorkshire, Devonshire, Canterbury*; the first part of these place names is Celtic, while *-shire, -bury* are Old English.

Latin. About 3 percent of the Old English word stock comes from Latin, or in some cases, from Greek through Latin. Manuscript writing in Anglo-Saxon times was done primarily in the monasteries, where monks and scribes who were educated in Latin and often fluent in it, practiced their craft. Many of the surviving Anglo-Saxon records where the Latin loanwords appear, are translations of religious or scholarly material; it is therefore difficult to estimate the extent to which the "ordinary" speaker of Old English was familiar with these non-Germanic words. The passage of time has made these very early borrowings from Latin an integral part of our language and has obscured the difference between their points of entry. Still, based on various philological criteria, we can identify two main groups of Latin words recorded in extant Old English texts.

Continental borrowings. Before they invaded the British Isles in the fifth century, the Anglo-Saxon tribes had been in contact with Latin speakers on the continent. The first set of Latin loanwords in Old English is therefore shared with other branches of Germanic. Many words, reflecting the military, administrative, and commercial dealings between the Roman Empire and the pre-Old English Germanic tribes, were carried over from the continent into Old English: e.g., *camp*, *mile*, *street*, *cheese*, *wine*, *gem*, *linen*, *wall*. These words must have been part of the core vocabulary of the first bands of Germanic warriors crossing the English Channel in the middle of the fifth century.

Christianity and monastic culture. The most significant early influence of Latin on English comes through the adoption of Christianity by the Anglo-Saxons. This important cultural and political event took place in England between the end of the sixth and the middle of the seventh centuries, and its impact was felt on the language for several centuries thereafter. A large number of the Latin words borrowed in that period were words related to the Christian religion and religious practices: *abbot*, *candle*, *congregation*, *devil*, *disciple*, *eternal*, *martyr*, *mass*, *pope*, *noon*, *offer*, *testament*. The monasteries were not only centers of religion, they were centers of scholarship and writing. Through increased literacy and enhanced interest in translating the religious and philosophical treatises popular in Europe at the time, a great many learned words entered the language: *alphabet*, *describe*, *discuss*, *history*, *mental*, *paper*, *school*, and the word *translate* itself. Other Latin borrowings from that period have become common everyday words: *fever*, *giant*, *port*, *mount*, *pear*, *plant*, *polite*, *radish*. Like the continental borrowings, the Latin words adopted during Anglo-Saxon times through religion and learning have blended completely with the native vocabulary; it is only the number of syllables in the longer words that betrays their origin to a speaker of modern English. In the centuries following the adoption of Christianity and the subsequent rise in literacy, new words, especially for "elevated" usage, continued to be borrowed from classical and medieval Latin, from its Romance descendants French, Italian, and Spanish, and later, during the Renaissance, from New Latin. We return to the contribution of these languages to the English vocabulary in Chapter 3.

2.1.2   The Scandinavian element

One of the major influences on the early vocabulary and grammar of English comes from its North Germanic neighbors. From the eighth century until the eleventh century, the Anglo-Saxons were subjected to a series of attacks and invasions by Scandinavian seafarers. One can think of these invasions as the second Germanic onslaught on Britain, only this time the invaders and the invaded were close relatives, linguistically speaking. The Scandinavians (also known as *Vikings*) spoke Old Norse, the precursor of Danish and Norwegian in the North Germanic subgroup. The earliest written texts in Old Norse do not appear until the eleventh century (but inscriptions using the pre-Christian Runic alphabet exist from the third century A.D.). Judging from the written records, there was probably a considerable degree of mutual intelligibility between English and the language of the Vikings. During the Anglo-Saxon period, a very significant part of the northeast Midlands of England had to be surrendered to the Viking invaders. In 878 the English King Alfred (871–99) signed a treaty establishing the *Danelaw*, or Danish area, an independently administered Danish territory to the northeast of a boundary stretching approximately from London to Chester. Although the territory changed hands again in the next century, the Viking raids continued unabated and culminated in the complete usurpation of the English throne by Danish kings between 1014 and 1042.

Reconstructions of Viking customs and way of travel suggest that many of the seafarers arrived in England without womenfolk. Intermarriages must have been common as more and more of the invaders became settlers and inhabitants of what they came to see as their own country. These social and historical circumstances would have been very favorable for the transfer of vocabulary from Scandinavian to Old English. The first linguistic link between Vikings and Anglo-Saxons is found in the large number of Scandinavian place names in the northern and eastern parts of England, as many as 1,400. These are place names ending in -*by* "settlement" (*Carnaby, Ellerby, Rugby, Thirtleby*), -*thorpe* "hamlet" (*Barleythorpe, Grimsthorpe, Hamthorpe, Hilderthorpe, Low Claythorpe, Fridaythorpe*), -*thwaite* "clearing" (*Hampsthwaite, Hunderthwaite, Husthwaite*). Demographically, it is hard to reconstruct reliably the extent to which the Scandinavian invasions, victories, and settlements swelled the ranks of the Anglo-Saxon population. However, there are more than 750 Scandinavian name-forms in records concerning medieval Yorkshire and Lincolnshire alone, the best known of which is the ending *-son*, as in *Henryson, Jackson, Robertson.* Judging by the density of Scandinavian place names and the considerable rate of survival of *-son* names, we can assume that the newcomers represented a large and vigorous minority. There were probably as many Scandinavian speakers as English speakers living in the Danelaw. As the lexicon is the language layer most responsive to socio-political and cultural changes in the history of a nation, it is easy to see why English borrowed almost 1,000 words from Scandinavian between the eighth and the eleventh centuries.

Unlike the adoption of Latin vocabulary, which was initiated and promoted primarily by a small subsection of the population, the learned priests, monks, and scribes, the adoption of Scandinavian words did not involve special education or writing skills. It occurred naturally in the mixed households, in the fields, and in the marketplace, among people at comparable levels of cultural development. In addition to the propitious social conditions, the borrowing of words was facilitated by the linguistic closeness of Scandinavian and Old English. It is not surprising that loanwords that came into English during this period are not easily recognizable as foreign, nor are they marked as belonging to a special more literate or more elevated level of usage. Scandinavian borrowings in English from the period between the ninth and the twelfth centuries are common words such as *bag, call, cast, die, fellow, hit, knife, root, skin, sky, ill, until, wrong,* the prepositions *till* and *fro* (as in *to and fro*), and the pronouns *they, them, their.* There is probably Scandinavian influence on the pronoun *she,* the verb form *are,* and the quantifiers *both* and *same.* In some regional varieties of English today Scandinavian words exist side by side with the more familiar word from the standard language: *garth* vs. *yard, kirk* vs. *church, nay* vs. *no, trigg* vs. *true.* Since the Vikings spoke a Germanic language, sharing words with Old English, but pronouncing them differently, we find that one and the same word with two pronunciations, Scandinavian and Old English, has evolved into a pair of historically related words which are now two separate lexical items. Such pairs in present-day English are *dike* vs. *ditch, scrub* vs. *shrub, skirt* vs. *shirt.*

2.2 English becomes a hybrid

The Norman Conquest. The next important historical event which has left a lasting mark on the composition of the English lexicon is the Norman Conquest of Britain in **1066**. In that year, William, Duke of Normandy, attacked and defeated the English army at Hastings on the south coast of England. He was then crowned king of England, replacing the Saxon line which had begun with Alfred the Great's grandson Ecgberht in 802. By the end of the eleventh century the positions of influence, prestige, and learning in England were occupied by Norman nobility, churchmen, and clerics. The exact number of new settlers following the Conquest is unknown, though some scholarly estimates have been offered. Here is how one well-known source describes the social and demographic consequences of the Conquest:

> One may sum up the change in England by saying that some 20,000 foreigners replaced some 20,000 Englishmen; and that these newcomers got the throne, the earldoms, the bishoprics, the abbacies, and far the greater portion of the big estates . . . and many of the burgess holdings in the chief towns.[7]

The key to understanding the enormous effect of the Norman Conquest on the vocabulary of English is in the political and social standing of the conquerors. William of Normandy lived on as king of England for twenty years after his conquest. During that time members of the Saxon aristocracy were executed or driven away from their castles and their lands. Their property was now in the possession of Norman barons and retainers who had come with William or had followed him soon thereafter. This led to a new correlation between social standing and language: the peasants working in the fields or doing the manual jobs around the noblemen's estates were speakers of English, and the overlords spoke French. In terms of sheer numbers, the speakers of English were unquestionably the dominant group: they constituted between 90–98 percent (or even more) of a total population of approximately 1,500,000.[8]

The numerical and social discrepancies between speakers of French and speakers of English worked against the development of widespread bilingualism. Nevertheless, the linguistic barriers between the two groups were not impenetrable. Given their dependence on local labor, the conquerors had to communicate with the conquered. The French-speaking upper clergy had to talk to the lower clergy and listen to the preachers whose sermons had to be in English. Instructions had to be given and understood in every walk of life. The majority of the population spoke English natively, but many people must have learned enough French to fulfil requests and obey orders from their French overlords. A smattering of French would have been sufficient for some

---

[7] Cited in Baugh and Cable's *A History of the English Language*, p. 111 from a statement by F. York Powell in H. D. Traill (ed.) *Social England*, vol. I, p. 346.
[8] The demographic estimates are from *The Shape of English: Structure and History*, by Roger Lass, London: J. M. Dent and Sons, 1987: 56.

French words to gain access to English; that was enough of an opening to allow the initial trickle to become a flood.

The Norman French masters, on their part, gradually got out of touch with their French origins. At the beginning of the thirteenth century King John who, like William, had started out as King of England and Duke of Normandy, lost his Norman title and territory. This forced many of the French-speaking nobility in England to abandon their continental ties, either because their lands in Normandy had been confiscated, or because they themselves divided their posses-sions between their offspring, discontinuing the practice of having lands both in England and in Normandy. As new generations came along and constant travel between the two countries was made unnec-essary, the Normans in England assimilated linguistically to the (Middle) English-speaking majority. Although the interaction between the two languages following the Conquest resulted in quite dramatic vocabulary changes, the language of England remained *English*.

The linguistic influence of the Norman Conquest is marked by an interesting historical fact: though French-speaking, the Normans were just a couple of generations removed from their North Germanic Viking ancestry themselves. The word Norman is a reduced form of "North-man," the name of the Scandinavian tribes that had raided the north of France since the middle of the ninth century and had estab-lished the Dukedom of Normandy in 911. The variety of French that the Normans brought to England was different from the variety of French spoken around Paris and in southern France. During the imme-diate post-Conquest period in England, Norman French was the main donor of Romance vocabulary. Norman French (also known as Anglo-French or Anglo-Norman) was one of the provincial dialects of French. As the political scene in England changed after the end of the twelfth century, the linguistic connections between English and French shifted to central and southern France. Middle English was receptive to new Romance vocabulary from both sources. Originally driven by dem-ographic and economic necessity, the influence of French grew during the thirteenth century and after through English–French political con-tacts and through the cultural prestige of French in Europe. The massive influx of French words in post-Conquest England changed the proportion of Germanic vs. non-Germanic words in the language. Old English had a relatively *homogeneous* lexicon, while Middle English became lexically *heterogeneous*.

2.2.1   French loanwords in Middle English

The unprecedented enrichment of the lexicon through borrow-ing altered the etymological composition of English after the Conquest. Data on the exact number of words borrowed from French is difficult to obtain, but according to one estimate the number of French words adopted during the Middle English period was slightly over 10,000. Of these, about 75 percent have survived and are still used in present-day English.[9] The large volume of new words changed the etymological balance from approximately 3 percent of foreign (Latin) words in Old English, to 25 percent of borrowed words in Middle English. At no other time in the history of English had such a dramatic change in the composition of the vocabulary occurred. Moreover, this was only the beginning. The trend of borrowing from other languages that was started with the post-Conquest English–French mixture was to continue steadily throughout the history of English and it is still with us today.

Interestingly, at these early stages of massive diversification of the vocabulary of English, there seem to be no negative attitudes to borrowed words. Literacy in medieval times was very much an accomplishment related to social standing. It is likely therefore that the large majority of the people who could read and write were either members of the Norman aristocracy, or people trained to serve the Normans in some capacity: clerks, scribes, chroniclers, religious and court writers, scholars, poets. This situation might conceal both potential negative attitudes and the rate at which new words were actually adopted by speakers of English. Thus, an early record of a French word is no guarantee that that word was familiar and current throughout the linguistic community. Conversely, we can imagine that many words, especially words which would not make their way easily into religious, legal, or didactic writing, might have been used in the spoken language for decades before they actually went on record.

More manifestly, the class-based distinction between the literate and the illiterate is reflected in the type of words that Middle English borrowed from French. The two chronological layers of borrowings discussed below show how the new political and social realities shaped the English lexicon.

Early post-Conquest borrowings. For approximately the first two centuries after the Conquest the source of new words was mainly Norman French. Though the Normans were Scandinavian in origin, they had adopted the language and culture of medieval France. William and his men spoke French when they first came to England, but the linguistic assimilation that had happened to the Northmen in Normandy was replicated in England. From about the middle of the thirteenth century, English was gradually replacing French (and Latin) as the language of government, administration, and learning. By the middle of the fourteenth century French was taught as a foreign language, even in

[9] See Baugh and Cable: *A History of the English Language*, p. 174.

ethnically Norman households. For reasons which perhaps have much to do with the keeping and survival of records, the overall number of documented borrowings before 1250 is relatively modest: about 900.[10] Among the words which entered English at that early stage are such common words as *air, beast, beauty, color, dangerous, diet, feast, flower, jealous, journey, judge, liquor, oil, part, peace, soil, story, tender*. Many of the early borrowings also reflect social class relations: *baron, noble, servant, throne*.

Central French. In 1204 King Philip of France took Normandy from England, severing the immediate administrative and political ties between the dukedom and the Anglo-Norman rulers of England. England's military, economic, and cultural interests shifted to central France. From the thirteenth century on, therefore, the French spoken in and around Paris became the source of new loans in English. As in earlier times, the word stock was enriched with words reflecting the leading position of the new aristocracy in the legal, military, administrative, political, religious, and cultural spheres. Many Old English words in these areas were either duplicated or replaced by Romance borrowings: *army, assembly, council, defense, empire, mayor, navy, parliament, record, soldier, state, statute, tax*. Predictably, words from the fields of literature, art, science, medicine came into the language in large numbers, including the words *literature, art, science, medicine*, and *number* themselves: *figure, grammar, image, logic, music, pain, physician, poet, remedy, romance, study, surgeon, tragedy*. Many of these loanwords can be traced back to classical Greek and Latin.

After the fourteenth century English became once again the dominant language of administration, commerce, art, and learning. From that point onwards, the rate at which common words were adopted from *any* foreign source into the language slowed down. The rapid and far-reaching vocabulary growth of Middle English permanently changed our lexicon, making it an etymological hybrid. Already contemporaries of Chaucer (d. 1400) would not have considered originally French words like *very, river, city, mountain, anchor, close, glue, haste, ease*, and so on as "foreign"; such words had become an inseparable part of English. French borrowings could now combine with English words to produce new compounds: *breast-plate, freemason, knight errant* (English + French), *commonweal, cornerstone, gentleman* (French + English). The language was now ready to produce mixed-origin formations such as *talkative, unknowable, wizard* (English roots + Romance suffixes), and *colorless, cheerful, spousehood* (Romance roots + English suffixes). English had turned an adverse political situation to its own benefit.

---

[10] The estimate is from Baugh and Cable: *A History of the English Language*, p. 164.

3 Composition of the Early Modern and Modern English vocabulary

The linguistic period identified as *Early* Modern English began some time during the second half of the fifteenth century. There is no single historical event comparable to the Norman invasion of 1066 for Middle English which can be taken conveniently as the boundary between Middle and Early Modern English. The language changes which characterize the transition of Middle to Early Modern English coincide chronologically with several major cultural and social changes. The most notable among these is the introduction of the printing press, by Sir William Caxton, in **1476**. This year is commonly taken as the cut-off date because it marks a turning point in the production and accessibility of books. Another historical event which coincides roughly with the beginning of Early Modern English is the discovery of the New World in **1492**. While its effect on our word stock was not as immediate as the availability of printed books, the discovery of the Americas has had extraordinary consequences for the composition of the English lexicon.

The end-point of Early Middle English coincides with two important events which occurred in the second half of the eighteenth century. We have already mentioned the appearance of the first really influential dictionary of English, the *Dictionary of the English Language* in two volumes by Samuel Johnson in **1755**. That dictionary boosted enormously the prestige of English lexicographical research. It was the first dictionary to use quotations extensively, and it contributed more than any other eighteenth-century work to the establishment of spelling standards. Another demarcation point of immense cultural and social significance is the American Revolution of **1776**, when along with their political independence Americans began to develop more linguistic autonomy relative to British English. Enclosed within these four dates 1476/1492 at one end, and 1755/1776 at the other, are the three centuries that comprise Early Modern English.

The Early Modern linguistic period, roughly 1476–1776, does not overlap completely with the usual chronological boundaries of the *Renaissance*. Most histories identify the Renaissance with the time prior to the revolutionary events of the middle of the seventeenth century: the English Civil War of the 1640s, Oliver Cromwell's Protectorate, and the Restoration of Charles II in 1660. The broader time-span for Early Modern English is justified for two reasons. First, the cultural aftermath of the Renaissance continued beyond the political events in the seventeenth century. The revival of classical learning had a powerful and permanent effect on the intellectual life of the following century. Second, even at that highly literate stage in the history of the language, recorded "first" entries of new words in the language can be mistaken by one or two generations. Since the focus in this book is on "words," we will ignore the time differences and will use Renaissance and Early Modern English as loosely synonymous terms.

The main cultural difference between Middle and Early Modern English, stated in the most general terms, is in the number of people who had access to books and could read. Heightened literacy means wider exposure to new texts and new words; the more people read, the smoother the channels for the adoption of new words. Living in highly literate societies, we may find it shocking that reading was not common before the end of the fifteenth century. Medieval peasants were almost all illiterate, and most of the nobility were able to read only with considerable effort, if at all. Although literacy was highly respected and could ensure one a privileged place in society, reading and writing were skills expected only from the clergy and specially trained copyists known as scriveners. After 1476 the reading scene began to change dramatically. More than 20,000 titles, several million individual copies of books or pamphlets, were printed in the fifty-to-sixty years after Caxton set up the first printing press in London.[1] Books became part of everyday middle-class life. Easy access to printed materials brought about reforms of the educational system, and within three generations the inhabitants of England, the lower classes as well as the nobility, went from 2 percent literacy to as high as 50 percent or even 60 percent. Virtually all middle- and upper-class males learned to read. Women of the aristocracy were generally literate also, but it was a skill not taught to most females until the Industrial Revolution about 200 years later.

The rise of literacy in Early Modern English was accompanied by a rapid expansion of the lexicon. According to one estimate based on counting entries in the *OED*,[2] as many as 4,500 new words were

---

[1] These numbers are cited in Baugh and Cable, *A History of the English Language* (1993: 195).

[2] Charles Barber, *Early Modern English*, Edinburgh: Edinburgh University Press, 1997, at p. 220. Our figures are a recalculation of Barber's original counts which cover 2 percent of the entries in the first edition of the *OED*, i.e. Barber's 2 percent count amounts to about ninety-five words per decade.

recorded in English during each decade between 1500 and 1700. Two-thirds of these words were creations based on already existing roots and affixes,[3] but an impressive one-third were straight borrowings. Eliminating new words of unknown origin, and words not recorded after 1700 (one-third of the entries), English adopted for permanent use over 20,000 borrowings in two centuries. In Middle English the corresponding estimate for double that time is about 7,500 surviving borrowings; the different numbers are due to the availability of books and the popularization of literacy and education in Early Modern English. New intellectual activities, the rediscovery and reappraisal of the ancient philosophical, religious, and literary masterpieces went hand in hand with the realization that like Greek and Latin, English should be capable of expressing the full range of abstract ideas and subtle emotions conveyed in the classical writings. Vocabulary enrichment was one of the consequences of the unparalleled interest in the classical heritage; the Renaissance was not only a time of re-birth, but also a time of growth and expansion.

The word *Renaissance* itself expresses the idea of looking back and looking forward at the same time. Its first element, *re-* means "again," or "backwards from a certain point," and *nais-* "be born" is a form that developed in French from the Latin root *nasc-* still found in words like *nascent, native, nation*. What may come as a surprise is that *Renaissance* is not a word that speakers of Early Modern English would have recognized. The word was borrowed from French in the eighteenth century in the strictly religious sense of "re-birth," and it was only later, since about the 1840s, that *Renaissance* developed its present-day cultural and historical associations.

2   Vocabulary enrichment during the Renaissance

The great intellectual movement of reinvention and reinterpretation of the classical models began in Italy during the early Middle Ages, spread in Europe, and reached England during the fifteenth century. From that time on, the importance of French loans decreased, while English turned increasingly towards Latin and Greek for new learned words. Scholarly and everyday words continued to be borrowed from French in the sixteenth century: *fragrant* (1500), *elegance* (1510), *baton* (1520), *accent, adverb* (1530), *amplitude* (1540), *cassock* (1550), *chamois* (1560), *demolish* (1570), *pounce* (1580), *admire* (1590), *avenue*

---

[3] The terms will be explained fully in Chapter 4. For the moment, "affixes" can be taken as meaning roughly "word endings," in the case of those that typically occur at the ends of words, or "word beginnings," in the case of those that typically occur at the beginnings of words, as indicated by the hyphens in the examples.

(1600),[4] yet the *Chronological English Dictionary* shows that as the century advances, the share of words identified as French goes down at the expense of words from Latin and Greek.

During the Renaissance proficiency in Latin and Greek became equivalent to being educated. Much of the scholarly work and academic writing was conducted in Latin. To a well-educated Renaissance person Latin was like a second language; it was taught, read, and used for learned discourse. Much energy and enthusiasm went into translating the classics into English. The translators often found it easier to introduce a new word for an unfamiliar notion than to worry about coining an English equivalent and risk being misunderstood. An interesting example of how widespread this practice was comes from a count of the Latin innovations in a *c.* 1485 translation by John Skelton, a prominent poet and writer. In turning *The History of the World* by Diodorus Siculus into English, Skelton introduced more than 800 Latin words new for the language, many of which are recorded by the *OED* as later borrowings.[5]

Learned words make up the largest portion of the new Latin vocabulary. From the fields of classical civilization, philosophy, religion, and education, Early Modern English added words such as: *alumnus, arena, contend, curriculum, elect, exclusive, imitate, insidious, investigate, relate, sporadic, transcendental.* Among the loanwords from the fields of mathematics and geometry, botany, biology, geography, medicine are: *abdomen, antenna, calculus, cerebellum, codex, commensurable, compute, evaporate, lacuna, larva, radius, recipe, species.* Along with these, a substantial number of everyday words were also adopted; they probably started out as specialized words, but quickly became part of the common vocabulary: *frequency, parental, plus, invitation, susceptible, offensive, virus.* An important aspect of the process of borrowing during these two centuries was the naturalization of a great many affixes from Latin: *-ence, -ancy, -ency* < Latin *-entia, -antia, -y*; Latin *-ius, -ia, -ium, -ous,* and Latin *-os, -us, -ate* were borrowed unchanged. Borrowed prefixes such as *ante-, post-, sub-, super-* became part of the productive morphology of English.[6]

Classical Greek was another source of learned words during the Early Modern English period, though the path of entry of Greek words into English is often indirect. The ancient Romans knew and

---

[4] The dates are from the *Chronological English Dictionary* by Finkenstaedt, Leisi and Wolff, Heidelberg: Carl Winter Universitätsverlag, 1970.

[5] The example is cited in Baugh and Cable, *A History of the English Language*, p. 210, fn. 1.

[6] "Productive" means that they are still used to make up new words: *postwar* (1908), *subset* (1902), *superstar* (1925). Other affixes in the language are no longer productive, like the fossilized *-th* in *growth, warmth, health, wealth,* or *with-* in *withstand, withdraw, without.*

admired the Hellenic heritage; the vocabulary of Latin included many learned Greek words. Similarly, French had adopted many Greek words, either through Latin, or directly. The Greek words we use today are therefore as likely to have come into English through Latin and French, as they are through direct borrowing. Greek words which came through Latin, and possibly through French, are words such as *atheism, atmosphere, chaos, dogma, economy, ecstasy, drama, irony, pneumonia, scheme, syllable.* Direct borrowings from Greek are *asterisk, catastrophe, crypt, criterion, dialysis, lexicon, polyglot, rhythm, syllabus.* In some cases such as *epicenter, chromatic,* the Greek first elements of the words: *epi-* "on, upon," *chromat-,* combine with the Latin elements *centre* < Old French *centre,* Latin *centrum, -ic* < Old French *-ique,* Latin *-icus.*

The adoption and assimilation of the hundreds of new words from the classical languages are not easy to trace. The ultimate sources can be obscured by intermediate borrowings and changes: Latin borrowed very freely from Greek, and it is often hard to distinguish between words borrowed directly from Latin, and words borrowed from Latin through French. Nevertheless, it is beyond doubt that during Early Middle English three or four times more words were borrowed from an immediate classical source through reading and translating classical texts than words coming directly from French. We will return to the identification of the source or sources of borrowed words in Section 3.

Other European Languages. The New World. The Renaissance spirit of intellectual renewal and discovery manifested itself in adventurous travel and heightened political, economic, and cultural interest in other countries and peoples. The conditions for the adoption of words from languages other than French and the classical tongues were good. For the first time in the history of the language, very many speakers of English were exposed to the customs and achievements of other Europeans. More and more members of the rising English merchant class maintained active ties with their European partners in travel and navigation, manufacture and commerce. Compared to classical borrowings, the volume of Early Modern English borrowings from other European or non-European languages is not overwhelming, but they set a trend that has been steady and increasing to this day: the trend to welcome words not just from the highly prestigious languages of the past, but from any other contemporary language.

Along with French, Italian was the source of many borrowed words. During the first two centuries of the period the words borrowed from Italian were distributed evenly between words having to do with everyday life, military activities, architecture, and the arts. From that period we have inherited *artichoke* (1531), *gondola* (1549), *squadron* (1562), *stanza* (1588), *fresco* (1598), *bazaar* (1599), *balcony* (1619), *opera* (1644), *vermicelli* (1669), *rotunda* (1687). At the beginning of the eighteenth century, Italian music and especially Italian opera became very fashionable in England, and with that came a new wave of Italian loanwords. Indeed, there was a real explosion of new musical words in English. Here is a small selection of some of these words with their dates of entry:[7]

adagio	1746	impresario	1746
allegretto	1740	lento	1724
andante	1742	libretto	1742
aria	1742	maestro	1724
bravo	1761	mezzo-soprano	1753
cantata	1724	moderato	1724
coda	1753	operetta	1770
coloratura	1753	oratorio	1727
concerto	1730	pianissimo	1724
contralto	1730	pianoforte	1767
crescendo	1776	soprano	1730
divertimento	1759	sotto voce	1737
duet	1740	tempo	1724
falsetto	1774	trombone	1724
forte	1724	violoncello	1724

The addition of the Italian musical terms to English illustrates well the importance of innovation, leadership, and prestige to the composition of the vocabulary. During the eighteenth century it became impossible to speak about western music in English without using an Italian word. At the end of the twentieth century it is probably impossible to speak about computers in any language without using some English words.

During the Renaissance and after there were strong commercial and cultural ties between Britain and the Low Countries. Early loans from Dutch into English are words like *foist*, v. (1545), pickle, v. (1552), *yacht* (1557), *rant*, v. (1598), *knapsack* (1603), *trigger* (1621), *drill*, v. (1622), *smuggle*, v. (1687). These are not learned or specialized words; the same tendency for borrowing popular words from Dutch continued in the eighteenth century:

bully	v.	1710	ogle	v.	1700
cookie	n.	1730	roster	n.	1727
crap	n.	1721	scoop	n.	1742
gin	n.	1714	scuffle	v.	1766
kid	n.	1769	snuffle	n.	1764
kit	v.	1725	track	v.	1727

---

[7] All dates are from the *Chronological English Dictionary.* Some of the dates of the pre-1700 loans are cited in Barber, *Early Modern English*, pp. 229-231.

There is an interesting difference between Dutch and the Italian borrowings. The Italian words, in addition to being more specialized, are all nouns, while the words borrowed from a related Germanic language, Dutch, are a fair blend of verbs and nouns. Clearly, Dutch words were adopted through direct contacts between people speaking English and Dutch, while the Italian terms must have been transmitted mostly on paper. The structural closeness between Dutch and English probably allowed English speakers to produce sentences mixing the two languages, where the foreign item could either point to new objects (nouns), or also describe new types of action (verbs).

Spanish and Portuguese borrowings also reflect the cultural traditions and accomplishments and the naval and military exploits of the countries of origin. Spain and Portugal led Europe in the colonization of the New World, and some of the words borrowed from Spanish had been borrowed into Spanish from American Indian languages. Early borrowings from Spanish include *guava* (1555), *hammock* (1555), *negro* (1555), *potato* (1565), *mestizo* (1588), *buoy* (1596), *cargo* (1602), *masquerade* (1654), *siesta* (1655). Some eighteenth-century loans from these languages are:

adobe	1748	jerk	1707
albino (Portuguese)	1777	lasso	1768
banjo	1764	mantilla	1717
cocoa	1707	mesa	1775
demarcation	1727	palaver (Portuguese)	1733
fandango	1700	poncho	1748
flotilla	1711	quadroon	1707
hacienda	1760	torero	1728

Compiling statistics about the exact sources of the new words in Early Modern English is hard because of uncertainties surrounding their etymologies. Nevertheless, an approximate picture of how the vocabulary changed is useful. A count of the new loanwords between 1500 and 1700 in a sample of 1848 words of "reasonably certain etymology" in the *OED* shows that the sources break up as follows:[8]

Latin	393
French	121
French or Latin	20
Greek	35
Italian	16
Spanish/Portuguese	16

---

[8] Barber *Early Modern English*, p. 221. The chart is based on the same 2 percent sample of the *Oxford English Dictionary* used to estimate the overall number of borrowings during the period 1500–1700.

German/Dutch	9
Other languages	15
Loanwords total	**625**

Latin was by far the most important donor of new words during the first two centuries of Early Modern English. Closer to the end of the eighteenth century, the balance changed in favor of the living languages of travel and commerce. Modern English continues to coin new terms using Latin and Greek roots. The trend which started with the Renaissance, and which was so prominent during the eighteenth century, is also with us: for genuinely new words covering unfamiliar geographical areas, customs, and civilizations, English turns to the living modern languages. A special chapter dedicated to the most recent borrowed vocabulary of English is included in the on-line Workbook.

3   Transmission, etymology, source identification

The biological metaphor of language families is convenient for describing the evolution of languages from a common source, but it says nothing about the way our vocabulary reacts to outside influences. Like biological families, languages can grow and move away from their original genetic pool by borrowing and absorbing new (grammatical) features and (lexical) items. Unlike people, however, languages never grow old or become dysfunctional with time. Instead, focusing only on the vocabulary, languages constantly renew themselves by discarding unnecessary words, changing the meaning of existing words, by creating or borrowing new lexical items. The vocabulary turnover in English has been quite remarkable; etymologically, the English we speak now does not look like the offspring of Old English at all. More than 80 percent of the vocabulary used a thousand years ago has been replaced with words borrowed since the Norman Conquest.

The *transmission* of borrowed vocabulary into English has been both direct (oral transmission), and indirect, mediated by writing, education, and literacy. Face-to-face communication is the easiest and most obvious line of linguistic transmission. When the Roman troops battled or traded with the pagan Germanic tribes in the early centuries of the Christian Era, it must have been the immediate exchanges between them that led to the adoption into Germanic of words such as *chalk, cheese, street, wall, wine*. It must have been through direct conversation with the Scandinavian settlers that the words *bag, call, fellow, skin* came to be part of the vocabulary of English after the tenth century. Some words borrowed from the Anglo-Normans after 1066 must also have been heard and learned in conversation: *air*, *beast*, *mountain*, *river*, *story*, *very*. Oral transmission continues to be part of our everyday experience: words like *bagel*, *cockroach*, *gumbo*, *macho*, *moccasin*, *pajamas*, *sherbet*, *sushi* are words which were probably heard, understood, repeated in everyday conversations long before they were written down in documents and recorded in dictionaries.

The situation is quite different with learned words, which of course comprise a very large portion of our borrowed vocabulary. They do not come directly from the battlefield, the marketplace, or a bilingual family setting, and their meanings tend to be more abstract. The transmission of "bookish" words is more likely to change their meaning in some way, sometimes quite radically. Often one and the same Indo-European root with several meanings emerges with different meanings in Old English, French, Latin, Greek, and so on. Words which start out from the same root, but which merit separate dictionary entries, are called *cognates*. We will return to a more specific description of cognates in the following chapter; here we only illustrate the way cognates enter the language and the vast variation of form and meaning that occurs during the process of transmission.

Let us start with a simple example. Old English and other Germanic languages borrowed from Latin the word *discus* "a flat round plate." In Old English this word was used to refer to the flat plates on which food was served, and it also came to mean platter, or bowl, and, by extension, the food itself. The form of the word was changed from *discus* to *disc*, pronounced the same way as our word *dish*. It is most likely that the word was transmitted directly from speaker to speaker. Then, in the seventeenth century, the French word *disque*, or its source, Latin *discus*, was borrowed again, this time strictly with the meaning of "flat surface," especially the surface of the sun, the moon, etc. The word was pronounced [disk], spelled either *disc* or *disk*, first recorded in 1664. It must have come into the language through the medium of education or reading. This second borrowing quickly spread to medical, zoological, and botanical uses; later it evolved into a technical term, as *disc brake*. The musical meaning of *disc* "phonograph record" was first recorded in 1888. After the war the word *discotheque* was coined in French, borrowed into English in 1951, where it produced *disco* by shortening in 1964. The word was modified yet again and given a specialized new meaning more recently with the introduction of the *compact disc* (1979). The invention and popularization of computers gave it new life and new meanings too: *floppy disk*, *hard disk*, *disk drive*, and the diminutive *diskette*. But that's not all: during the seventeenth century the word *discus* was borrowed, directly from the Greek word *diskos*, with its specialized athletic meaning that we associate with the Olympic discipline of discus throwing. Adding to the richness of this cognate group is the Old French version of the Latin *discus* which turns up in English as *dais* "raised platform."

Another intriguing example of the vagaries of transmission is provided by the Indo-European root **bha-* "speak," whose word-family shows how repeated contacts, the reading and production of literary or administrative documents, can change meaning. The Latin forms of the same root are *fa-*, *fe-*, and the Greek forms are *pha-*, *phe-*. The word *fame*, "being spoken about" was borrowed in Middle English from Latin or French and it meant just having a reputation, good or bad. It probably came into the language orally. Its cognate *infamy*, a fifteenth-century loan, entered the language through Latin legalistic texts, in which the word *infamia* had no English counterpart; the transmission was mediated. Another cognate, the rhetorical term *euphemism* "the avoidance of offensive terms," "speaking well" (where *eu-* means "well, good"), was a purely literary seventeenth-century borrowing from Greek. The word *infant* (first recorded in 1382) may have been borrowed either orally or through literacy, but *infanta* "the daughter of a king of Spain or Portugal" (1601), was strictly a learned word borrowed through political discourse. Both words have the negative prefix *in-* "not": *infant* originally meant "one who does not speak," or simply "not speaking," while *infanta* assigns a very special and restricted meaning to the "one who does not speak." Since the word can be used only in reference to a royal female offspring in Spain and Portugal, speakers of English were not likely to encounter this word in their everyday life.

Cognates such as *dish*, *diskette*, *discus*, *fame*, *infamy*, *infant* show traces of their origin, no matter what the manner of historical transmission is. The semantic relationships are quite intricate, however. *Fame* and *infant* preserve the idea of speaking, but the legal term *infamy* meaning "loss of rights as a consequence of earning a bad reputation" is less transparently linked to the original *fa-*. Then there are surprising cognates, such as *infantry* or *bandit*, where the semantic traces are fully obscured. *Bandit* was borrowed into English from an Italian form *bandetto* (1593), which itself was borrowed from earlier Germanic through Late Latin. This explains why the word is *bandit* rather than **fandit*, since in Germanic the Indo-European *bh-* had changed to *b-*, but in Latin, the ancestor of Italian, it changed to *f-*. In Italian, the form had come to mean not just "to speak," but specifically "to summon, to muster, to band together"; the meaning of *bandit* is derived from the activities of outlawed gangs. *Infantry* is an Italian word, *infanteria*, army units made up of youngsters who did everything on foot, hence the meaning "foot-soldiers." The word was borrowed from Italian into French, and from French into English (1579). Thus, whether or not cognates share the same form, their meanings can be far removed from each other and from the original. Figure 3.1 summarizes some of the changes of Indo-European **bha-* "speak" in its various daughter languages.

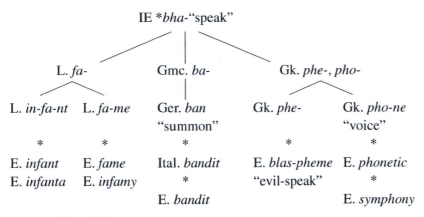

Figure 3.1

Etymology. Etymology is the study and recovery of formal and semantic links among words. Literally, etymology means "the study of *true* meanings," coming from the roots *etym* "true" and *o-log-y* "the study of" or "the theory of." An important point to understand in learning about etymology is that many semantic associations exist independently of historical cognate developments, and at the same time many cognate relationships exist (like *bandit, fame, infantry, euphemism*) in which the semantic connections are extremely remote and obscure. The historical (diachronic) relation between *dish* and *diskette*, or *infant, fame,* and *bandit,* would be lost upon us without the additional insight provided by these words' etymology. They have a common origin, yet, from a *synchronic* point of view, they are separate modern English words. The following chapters describe various ways in which the etymology of English words can become more transparent. Before we go on to the principles and methods of parsing and semantic change, here are some facts about the etymological composition of our present-day vocabulary.

The historical survey in Chapters 2 and 3 makes it clear why and how our language developed its rich and varied vocabulary, both in terms of numbers of items, and in terms of sources. The vocabulary of Old English was *homogeneous* (*homo* "same" + *gen* "origin"); as many as 97 percent of the words used by the Anglo-Saxons were Germanic words. The cultural changes following the Norman Conquest created conditions for the development of a *heterogeneous* (*hetero* "other, diverse") vocabulary. A modern speaker's awareness of the genetic diversity of the word stock depends on education, interests, familiarity with other

languages and many other highly individual factors. One perception we
all share, however, is that when we speak, read, or write, we encounter
words whose "foreignness" is beyond doubt. We may use them confi-
dently, or we may stumble at words like *blasé, glasnost, niño, pas de
deux*, or *echt*; in either case we *know* that these useful words are
somehow different from our garden variety English words. If one
thinks of the vocabulary as being distributed over a scale of
native↔foreign, obviously borrowed words such as *blasé, glasnost,
niño*, are at the "foreign" end of the scale. Many learned words with
which we are comfortable, we would probably still classify mentally as
non-native: *convalesce, deduce, exorcism, hermaphrodite, hibernation,
paradigm, polygamy*. For most people words such as *hesitate, machine,
neuter, pantry, supply*, would not carry any "foreign" associations,
though all of them are post-Conquest loanwords. Finally, words like
arrive, dinner, dollar, face, mountain, really, river, sky, very, will seem
"native"; time and frequent use have allowed these early borrowings to
blend with the genuinely native words, but for the etymologist, they
remain "outsiders."

The composition of the modern English vocabulary reflects the historical circumstances of its growth. Table 1 shows the percentages of
Old English and post-Conquest etymologies in the 10,000 most frequent words in English.[9]

Old English	French	Latin	Other Gmc.	Other Lgs.
31.8	45	16.7	4.2	2.3

Table 1

These numbers allow us to see how significant the turnover of vocabulary from Anglo-Saxon times to this day has been. Only one third of
the first 10,000 words we learn and use are *native*, i.e., Germanic words
which have been in continuous use since Old English times. The imbal-
ance between native and non-native sources becomes quite striking if
we take French and Latin together; the ratio then approaches two to
one in favor of Romance borrowings.

The figures in Table 1 should be treated with caution. They reflect
only the *immediate sources*, the languages from which a word was
directly borrowed into English. The *ultimate source*, the language where
the word first originated, is not recorded in these data. Thus *telegraph*,
which contains two Greek roots: *tele* "distant" and *graph* "write," is
counted as French; a predecessor of the telegraph, a contraption with

---

[9] The percentages are from A. H. Roberts, *A Statistical Linguistic Analysis of
American English*, The Hague: Mouton, 1965: 36.

movable arms sending signals at a distance, was invented in France in 1792, and that's the immediate source of the word in English. Similarly, a word like *agony* from the Greek *agōniā* "struggle to win an athletic contest" counts as French in this classification. The route of transmission is from Greek to Latin to French. The Romans borrowed the word in its more general sense of "any mental or physical struggle," and it was modified in Old French to *agonie*, "mental anguish," which is the meaning first recorded in English after 1382. *Draco* was an Athenian lawgiver in 621 B.C., known for having established the first rigorous code of laws in ancient Greece, 200 years before the classical period, but the word *draconic*, first recorded in English in 1680, comes to us via Latin. These are examples where the distinction between ultimate and immediate source is clear. Often, however, the boundaries between the sources can be very fuzzy: we can't tell whether *destructive*, *cooperation*, *position*, *solid*, come to English from Latin or from French.

Etymological classification is also hampered by mixed-language word formation. As pointed out in Chapter 2, Section 2.2.1, hybridization of the vocabulary in Middle English led to the formation of new items whose etymology is mixed. Native affixes modify the borrowed roots in *un-important*, *prince-ly*, *over-estimate*, *respect-ful*, while native roots combine with borrowed affixes in *woman-ize*, *re-fill*, *foresee-able*. *Clergyman*, *nobleman*, *superman* count as native, because of the key element *-man*, but *man-hour*, *manservant*, and *manpower* do not qualify as native because the key elements are *hour*, *servant*, and *power*.

The vocabulary of English is truly heterogeneous only in terms of its immediate sources. Ultimately, as many as 98 percent of the words in our language are of Indo-European origin. This is unsurprising in view of the geographical and cultural distance between English and non-Indo-European languages for most of the language's long history.

The percentages in Table 1 are somewhat problematic also because a blanket count of all 10,000 words obscures the important correlation between etymology, the frequency of a word, and the context and style in which it is used. More specialized contexts and more elevated styles rely heavily on borrowed or uncommon words. The most frequent words form the core of the vocabulary, shared by all adult speakers, but outward from that core lie layers of words of decreasing familiarity. Here is how the editors of the *OED* describe the situation:

> . . . the vast aggregate of words and phrases which constitutes the vocabulary of English-speaking people presents . . . the aspect of one of those nebulous masses familiar to the astronomer, in which a clear and unmistakable nucleus shades off on all sides, through zones of decreasing brightness. The English vocabulary contains a nucleus or central mass of many thousand words whose "Anglicity" is unquestioned; . . . but they are linked on every side with other words which are less and less entitled to this appellation and which pertain ever more and more distinctly to the

domain of local dialect, of slang, . . . of the peculiar technicalities of trades and processes, of the scientific terminology common to all civilized nations, and of the actual languages of other lands and peoples.[10]

Figure 3.2 is a graphic representation of the core-periphery distribution for the first four deciles; more layers can be added around the ones shown here.

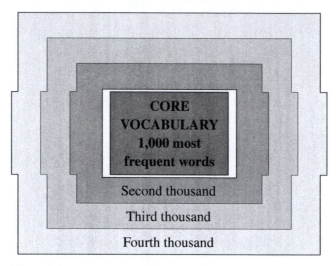

CORE VOCABULARY 1,000 most frequent words

Second thousand

Third thousand

Fourth thousand

Figure 3.2

The dividing lines between the layers, or deciles, are only approximate. Word frequency counts depend on the nature of the texts from which the data have been drawn. Still, large-scale vocabulary studies are quite informative about the etymological composition of English in relation to the relative frequency of words. Table 2 shows the results of one such study, based on more than fifteen million running words, over half of which were recorded in business and personal correspondence reflecting ordinary everyday activities.[11]

Possible individual variation aside, the figures in Table 2 prompt some interesting observations. The percentages in the first row bear out the assertion that the core vocabulary of English, the words which are indispensable in our daily life, such as *water* and *food*, *go*, *sleep*, *wake*, *sister* and *brother*, *green* and *yellow*, are most likely to be of native origin. The more complicated and abstract our notions become, e.g. *cognition*, *psychoanalysis*, *reverberate*, *telethon*, the more likely English is to turn to

---

[10] *OED*, 2nd edn., p. xxiv.
[11] The original results of the investigation were published in Roberts, *A Statistical Linguistic Analysis of American English*, pp. 35–38. The tabulation of the results used here is from Joseph M. Williams, *Origins of the English Language, A Social and Linguistic History*. New York: The Free Press, 1975: 67.

Sources of the most frequent 10,000 words of English					
Decile	*English*	*French*	*Latin*	*Norse*	*Other*
1	83%	11%	2%	2%	2%
2	34	46	11	2	7
3	29	46	14	1	10
4	27	45	17	1	10
5	27	47	17	1	8
6	27	42	19	2	10
7	23	45	17	2	13
8	26	41	18	2	13
9	25	41	17	2	15
10	25	42	18	1	14

Table 2

loanwords. The higher deciles include words from the realm of ideas, art, science and technology, specialized discourse; in these the proportion of borrowed words increases. Going from higher to lower frequency of usage, we notice a very significant drop: only 34 percent of the second layer of words are words that have survived directly from the time of King Alfred, about 1,000 years ago. In that same frequency range, the 1,000 to 2,000 decile, the proportion of combined French and Latin words jumps from 13 percent in the first decile to an impressive 57 percent. After that, the proportion of native words goes down more slowly, and remains approximately steady at 25 percent in the last four deciles. The share of French and Latin remains remarkably steady in the outer layers. Starting with the second decile, the percentages of "other" sources are on the rise. Since the study on which these figures are based does not separate Greek sources from any other sources, including words of uncertain and unknown etymologies, the increase in this column is largely due to the presence of Greek borrowings.

The correlation observed in English between frequency of usage and etymology is not necessarily true of every language. Some languages – German is a case in point, within Germanic – have traditionally turned to their own resources for enriching the vocabulary with words for more sophisticated notions or new products. For example, *Übersetzung* is equivalent to our word "translation," but it literally means "setting over." *Fernsehen* is equivalent to "television" but it literally means "far-seeing." *Lautlehre* is equivalent to "phonology," but it literally means "sound study." That is, in German, native roots are combined to form new compounds having the same meaning as the classical-based compounds. This method of vocabulary enrichment is familiar also in English: *doorbell*, *horseshoe*, *lighthouse*, *shorthand*, *stronghold* are all compounds containing native elements only. However, compared to

German, English has been less inventive in producing new words from its own roots; instead, it has added and creatively recycled roots from other languages. Chapters 5, 6, and 7 in this book address the mechanisms of borrowing roots and affixes from the classical languages in detail.

4   Summary of early British history and loanwords in English

The vertical centerline below is a time line, from earlier to later. Many of the dates have to be taken as approximate:

500 B.C. or earlier	Celts in Britain
from *c.* 200 B.C.	Roman contacts with Germans
56 B.C., final conquest after A.D. 43	Romans in Britain
by *c.* 430	Romans out of Britain
449 Germanic settlement of Britain	**Beginning of Anglo-Saxon period** **Old English**
450–600	Pre-Christian England
597	Christianity to England
from *c.* 700	First Old English texts
850–1066	The Danelaw
1066 Norman Conquest	**End of Old English**
1066 Norman Conquest	**Middle English**
1086	Doomsday Survey, 1.5 million population
1204–5	King John loses Norman estates
from *c.* 1150	Literature in English revives
until *c.* 1450	Laws written in Latin and French
1363	Parliament opens in English
1383	First will written in English
1400	Death of Chaucer[12]
1476	William Caxton introduces the printing press
1489	French no longer used in statutes of Parliament
	End of Middle English
1476–1650	20,000 titles printed
1500–1600	Translations of Classical books[13]
1564	Shakespeare born
from *c.* 1550	Literacy borrowings (dated below)

---

[12] About 12 percent of the words used by Chaucer are borrowed from French.
[13] Thucydides, Xenophon, Herodotus, Plutarch, Caesar, Livy, Tacitus, Aristotle, Cicero, Seneca, Ovid, Horace, Homer, Boethius.

Latin

1500–1600: *abdomen, aborigines, acumen, albumen, alias, animal, appendix, arbiter, axis, cadaver, caesura, caveat, cerebellum, circus, compendium, cornea, corona, decorum, delirium, folio, fungus, genius, genus, hiatus, innuendo, integer, medium, miser, multiplex, peninsula, pollen, radius, regalia, sinus, species, stratum, terminus, torpedo, vacuum, vertigo.*

1600–1700: *affidavit, agendum, album, alumnus, antenna, apparatus, arena, calbum, calculus, census, cerebrum, complex, copula, curriculum, data, desideratum, dictum, equilibrium, fiat, fulcrum, honorarium, impetus, imprimatur, insignia, lacuna, lumbago, minimum, momentum, nebula, onus, pendulum, plus, premium, query, rabies, residuum, series, serum, specimen, spectrum, squalor, stamen, status, stimulus, tedium, torpor, vertebra, veto, vortex.*

1700: *addendum, alibi, auditorium, bonus, deficit, extra, habitat, humus, inertia, insomnia, maximum, moratorium, nucleus, propaganda, prospectus, referendum, ultimatum.*

Greek through French before 1500: *academy, atom, bible, center, character, climate, diet, diphthong, dynasty, ecstasy, emblem, fancy, fantasy, frenzy, galaxy, harmony, horizon, idiot, ink, logic, magic, magnet, melon, mystery, nymph, pause, plane, pomp, rhetoric, rheum, scandal, schism, spasm, sphere, stratagem, surgeon, theater, tragedy, turpentine.*

Greek through Latin before 1500: *abyss, agony, allegory, artery, asphalt, centaur, chaos, chimera, comedy, crypt, cycle, demon, echo, halcyon, hero, history, hyena, mania, mechanic, meteor, paper, piracy, plague, siren, theme, thesis, thorax.*

Greek after 1500: *acoustic, acrostic, amnesty, basis, caustic, chasm, chemist, chord, chorus, climax, clinic, comma, crisis, critic, cube, cylinder, cynic, cynosure, despot, diatribe, dilemma, disaster, drama, elegy, energy, enigma, enthusiasm, epic, idea, irony, isthmus, larynx, machine, nausea, nomad, ode, orchestra, pathos, phrase, prism, python, rhapsody, rhythm, scene, scheme, skeleton, skeptic, stigma, strophe, theory, tome, topic, tragic, trochee, trope, trophy.*

4 Smaller than words: morphemes and types of morphemes

1 The smallest meaningful units

We think of words as being the most basic, the most fundamental, units through which meaning is represented in language. There is a sense in which this is true. Words are the smallest free-standing forms that represent meaning. Any word can be cited as an isolated item. It can serve as the headword in a dictionary list. It can be quoted. It can be combined with other words to form phrases and sentences. In general the word is the smallest unit that one thinks of as being basic to saying anything. It is the smallest unit of sentence composition and the smallest unit that we are aware of when we consciously try to create sentences.

But actually there are even smaller units that carry the fundamental meanings of a language. Words are made up of these units. Consider just the unit *gen* in Figure 4.1. It is clearly not a free-standing word, but rather some kind of smaller unit which goes into the make-up, the composition, of words:

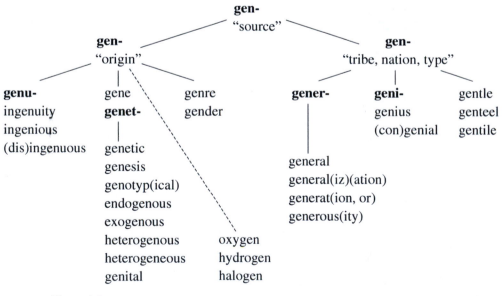

Figure 4.1

These smaller units are called **morphemes**. *Gen* is a morpheme. It has a basic single meaning "source" (at the top of the diagram) which has split into two now distinct meanings, "origin" and "tribe, nation, type." Looking at the words that appear under each of these meanings, one can readily see the difference. The meaning "origin" is most easily seen on the middle branch below it, in words like *genetic* or *genital*. The meaning "type" is most easily seen in words like "general." The meaning "gentle" is derived from the notion "belonging to a good tribe/family." There is some overlap: words like *generate* could just as reasonably be attached to the left branch ("origin"). *Gentile* originally, in the Vulgate translation of the Bible from Hebrew into Latin, simply meant "nations/tribes other than the Jews." A later, seventeenth-century re-borrowing of the same word, *gentil*, from French, originally also meaning "of good stock," resulted in our word *genteel*, which has changed its erstwhile positive meaning of "having proper breeding," "elegant, stylish," to its rather ironic and disparaging current meaning. *Genius* comes about through Greek mythology. It meant "The tutelary god or attendant spirit allotted to every person at his birth, to govern his fortunes and determine his character, and finally to conduct him out of the world" (*OED*). It is a short step from "attendant spirit" to "having a genius for music" to "being a musical genius." *Genre* is used by literary scholars to mean "a literary type." *Gender* refers to types, or categories, of nouns, in the usage of grammarians. In general usage it has recently become the accepted term, though it is an obvious euphemism, for two categories of humans, male and female, differentiated by virtue of their sex.

1.1   Morphemes and syllables

Since morphemes are the smallest carriers of meaning, each word must contain at least one morpheme. Some words are made up of more than one morpheme. The word *morpheme* itself is made up of two morphemes: *morph* "form, shape" and *-eme* "meaningful." So a *morpheme* is a meaningful unit of form. The essential point about morphemes is that they cannot be dissected further into smaller meaningful units: they are themselves the smallest ones. But one might challenge this claim by pointing out that *morph* itself consists of the sound <m> plus the sound <o> plus the sound <r> plus the sound <ph> (= <f>). Why are these not smaller units? The answer is that they are not units of **meaning**. They are units of **sound** (or spelling) which serve together to **represent** the morpheme. The relationships between sounds, morphemes, and meanings is like this, taking *gen* as our example.

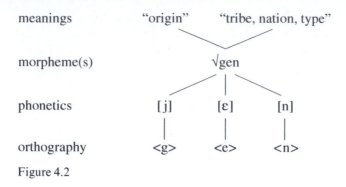

Figure 4.2

In Figure 4.2 we find some technical symbols. The checkmark in front of the morpheme *gen* simply means, "This is a morpheme." Although the common mathematical meaning of the symbol is "root," we use "√" for all morphemes, roots and affixes both. We could not write, for example, √genetic, because *genetic* is more than one morpheme. We would have to write something like √gen √et √ic, indicating that it is made up of three morphemes. The square brackets on the level below √gen indicate pronunciation. They are used for phonetic writing, also known as phonetic transcription. Don't worry if you don't recognize all the phonetic symbols: we will explain them later. Finally, in the orthography row, the angle brackets mean "This is a letter of the alphabet traditionally used to spell this sound in this word."

1.2   The properties of morphemes

We summarize below the properties of morphemes in an effort to show how they differ from other linguistic units like syllables, words, and individual sounds. The properties which uniquely differentiate morphemes from other linguistic units are these:

(1) A morpheme is the smallest unit associated with a meaning. As an example, consider the following words:

car	**car**e	**car**pet	**car**digan
carrot	**car**ess	**car**go	**car**amel
vi**car**	s**car**e	dis**car**d	pla**car**d

Each of these words contains the spelling <c a r>. How can we determine whether this fact is significant or not? Answer: Ask whether there is some constant meaning in each word that can be attributed to a morpheme having the form <car>. It is obvious that *care* has nothing to do with *car* – the meaning of *car* is completely independent of the meaning of *care*. Take *caress*: although superficially *caress* resembles *car* the way *princess* resembles *prince*, there is clearly no shared meaning in the first pair. *Carpet*, on the other hand, looks as though somehow (imaginably) there might be a connection: perhaps *carpet* could be a little *carp* (as *cigarette* is a little *cigar*), but of course it is not. So *carpet* is a single morpheme, and can be written √carpet. We can also write √care, √cardigan, √carrot, √caress, √cargo, √caramel, √scare, and √vicar, following the same logic in each instance. They merely "accidentally" contain <car>, but they do not contain the morpheme √car. (Why can we not do this also with *discard* and *placard*?)

(2) Morphemes are recyclable units. One of the most important properties of the morpheme is that it can be used again and again to form many words. The morpheme √care can be used to form *uncaring*, *careful*, *careless*, *caregiver*, and we saw in Figure 4.1 that √gen is used in forming dozens of words. If you did not know the meaning of the words *cardigan* and *caramel*, and if you thought that they might contain the morpheme √car, one way to test your conjecture would be to see whether the remaining material can be used in other words, – i.e., whether it is another morpheme. Obviously, -*digan*, and -*amel* do not meet our first definition of a morpheme, they are not contributors of independent meanings, nor are they recyclable in the way in which the morphemes √care + √ful, or √un + √care + √ing, or √care + √give + √er are. One should be careful, however: recyclability can be deceptive, as it was in the case of *carrot, carpet, caress, cargo*. Though all morphemes can be used over and over in different combinations, non-morphemic parts of words may accidentally look like familiar morphemes.

The test defined in (1) above, namely that what makes a sequence of sounds a morpheme is its ability to convey independent meaning, or add to the meaning of the word, should always be applied first. However, there are some interesting cases for which the decision on whether some part of a word is a morpheme or not requires a combination of tests (1) and (2). If we try to parse the word *happy*, we can easily isolate √-y as a morpheme: it adds to the grammatical meaning of the word by turning it into an adjective. But what about *happ-*? Taken in isolation, it does not mean anything to a speaker whose knowledge of etymology does not extend to Old Norse. In Old Norse there was a noun *happ*, meaning "luck, chance." The word was borrowed into English in the twelfth century. That morpheme is no longer likely to appear by itself, but it has kept its ability to turn up in various words and to form the core of their meaning: *mishap, happen, happenstance, hapless, unhappiness*. In other words, the recyclability of √hap(p)- in the language today confirms its status as a morpheme, even without the etymological information. As you will see, many of the classical morphemes we will be dealing with in this book are of the √hap(p)- type.

(3) Morphemes must not be confused with syllables. A morpheme may be represented by any number of syllables, though typically only one or two, sometimes three or four. Syllables have nothing to do with

meaning. Syllables are units of pronunciation. In most dictionaries, hyphens are used to indicate where one may split the word at the end of a line. Hyphens are also used to separate the word into syllables. A syllable is the smallest independently **pronounceable** unit into which a word can be divided. The number of morphemes in a word is very likely to differ from the number of syllables. √Car and √care are one syllable each; √carpet, √caress, √carrot, and √cargo are two syllables each; and √cardigan and √caramel have three syllables. But each of these words is a single morpheme.

Morphemes may be **less** than a syllable in length, too. Consider *car* vs. *cars*. *Cars* is one syllable, but two morphemes, namely √car + √-s, where √-s is the morpheme that means "plural," i.e., more than one. Other examples of morphemes which are not syllables include the √-ed of *cared*, *caressed*, and the √-th of *growth*, *warmth*. Generally, however, morphemes are independently pronounceable and are at least one syllable in length, like √gen, √morph, √hap(p), and √-y. In some (few) instances, a morpheme may be present only by inference. If we say *The sheep are grazing*, we have to infer that *sheep* is plural, even though its form is the same as the form of the singular. If we say *I cut some flowers yesterday*, we understand *cut* to be in the past tense because of *yesterday*, not because of any morpheme attached to *cut*. The longest morphemes tend to be names of places or rivers or Indian nations, like *Mississippi*, or *Potawatomi*, or *Cincinnati*. In the indigenous languages of America from which these names were borrowed, the words were polymorphemic, but that information is completely lost to us, as English speakers.

(4) One and the same morpheme may take phonetically different shapes. Different forms of the same morpheme are called "allomorphs" (which means "other forms" – √allo "other" + √morph "form"). This general property of allomorphic variation is called **allomorphy**. Recognizing different allomorphs of the same morpheme is one of the surest ways to extend one's vocabulary and to identify relationships between words. Any speaker of English will identify the nouns *cares*, *caps*, and *classes*, as sharing the plural morpheme √-s, though both the spelling and the pronunciation of the morpheme vary in the three words. That is, the morpheme has three allomorphs. But although the allomorphy of the plural √-s is part of everyone's core knowledge of English, there are many morphemes where this knowledge is not at all automatic. Consider the morpheme meaning "take" or "contain" whose most familiar allomorph is √cap, as in words like:

capable   **cap**sule   **cap**tive   **cap**acity

It also has the allomorph √cep in words like

accept   deception   intercept   perceptible   receptacle

It has a third allomorph √cip in words like

anti**cip**ate   eman**cip**ate   in**cip**ient   parti**cip**ate   prin**cip**al
re**cipe**   re**cip**ient

The fourth allomorph is √cup in a few words like *occupy* and *recuperate*. In Chapter 9 we will discuss the fact that the meaning of the morpheme *cap* is **transparent** in some of these words – e.g., *captive* is "one who has been taken," *capable* is "able to take," *participate* is "to take part." But it is **opaque** in others. For example, it is not obvious what *perceptible* has to do with the basic meanings "take" or "contain." Perhaps the association is something rather vague like "able to take in [through one of the senses]." It is even more opaque in *recuperate* – perhaps something like "to take back [one's health]," and *anticipate* "take beforehand." Finally, the connection between *recipe* and √cap is recoverable only with the help of an etymological dictionary: it is the imperative form of the verb "take" in Latin. That's how the word *recipe* acquired its first meaning of a "formula for a medical prescription." Later, it was extended further into cooking and, of course, today, into general transferred use as a "list of ingredients and a set of actions" in phrases such as "a recipe for success, a recipe for disaster" – a far cry from the basic meaning of √cap. The interplay of formal variation and semantic variation is very complex; we will be returning to these issues in the following chapters.

These, then, are the four essential properties of all morphemes: (1) they are packaged with a meaning; (2) they can be recycled; (3) they may be represented by any number of syllables; and (4) morphemes "morph," i.e., they may have phonetically different shapes.

2   Types of morphemes

2.1   Roots

Not all morphemes are equally central to the formation of a word. Morphemes are of two main types: **roots** and **affixes**. We turn our attention first to roots. Every word has at least one root. Roots are at the center of word-derivational processes. They carry the basic meaning from which the rest of the sense of the word can be derived. Morphemes such as *chair, green, ballet, father, cardigan, America, Mississippi*, are roots; these roots also happen to be free forms, i.e., independent words. But more often, roots are like *seg* in *segment, gen* in *genetics, card* in *cardiac, sequ* in *sequence, brev* in *brevity, pter* in *pterodactyl*. These cannot stand alone as words. They are called **bound root morphemes**, as distinct from **free root morphemes** (the ones that are also independent words).

Most bound roots found in the language today are of classical origin – i.e., they were borrowed into English from Latin or Greek during the Renaissance, or through French. Moreover, we usually borrowed words from these languages wholesale, i.e., the classical roots came into the language nested inside derived forms such as *segment, genetics, cardiac* etc. Sometimes, though not very frequently, borrowed roots do make their way into the inventory of free forms too: *contra* in the meaning of "counterrevolutionary" (1981), *graph* (1878), *phone* (1866) are some examples. As you can see from the dates of their first recorded appearance in English, such roots which are also independent words are fairly recent and formed by shortening of the classical words or phrases that contain them, i.e. their transition from bound to free roots has occurred on English soil. So, it would be fair to say that roots borrowed from classical sources are nearly always bound roots.

On the other hand, the number of bound roots of Germanic origin like *happ* "luck, fortune," as in *hapless, happy*, is comparatively small. Of Germanic origin are the bound roots of *feckless, reckless, ruthless, listless, uncouth, unkempt.* What has happened in all these cases is a straightforward historical change: a root, which used to be also a word at earlier times, became obsolete or disappeared completely, leaving behind only a derivative. Thus *feckless* is derived from a sixteenth-century Scots word *feck*, a shortened form of *effect*. Later *effect* was reintroduced into Scots, replacing the form *feck*, yet its derivative *feckless* "ineffective" is still around. We consider *ruth* in *ruthless* as a bound morpheme today, but it used to be a common word in English meaning "pity, sorrow" well into the eighteenth century. Though it appears as an entry in many dictionaries, the word is obsolete in present-day English, but note its connection with the verb "to rue," from which the noun was obviously derived originally. In any case, the historical processes we are illustrating here are not recoverable without the aid of specialized dictionaries. For the ordinary speaker of English *feck-, hap(p)-, ruth-* etc. are bound roots.

To be completed, bound root morphemes require that another morpheme be attached to them. This additional morpheme may be either another root or an affix. If it is another root, the result is a **compound**. Some issues related to compounds and compounding were discussed in Chapter 1: you will remember that words like *airship, birdcage, bookmark, flagship, hemisphere, hydrogen, phonograph, polymath, telephone* etc. are compounds. They all contain two roots. If a bound root is not attached to another root, as in **brevity, capable, cardiac, gentile**, etc., it must be accompanied by an **affix**.

Affixes carry very little of the core meaning of a word. Mainly affixes have the effect of slightly modifying the meaning of the stem – a stem is either a root or a root plus an affix, or more than one root with or without affixes – to which more affixes can be attached. The most common such modification is to change the word-class, the part of speech, to which the word belongs. Thus *child* (a noun) becomes an adjective in *childish*. That adjective can in turn be changed to an adverb: *childishly*, or to a different kind of noun – an "abstract" noun – by adding another affix, as in *childishness*. This process, known as *affixation*, is one of the two most fundamental processes in word formation (the other is compounding, discussed below). Let us therefore examine more closely the properties of affixes.

2.2   Affixes

All morphemes which are not roots are affixes. Affixes differ from roots in three ways.

(1)   They do not form words by themselves – they have to be added on to a **stem**.

(2)   Their meaning, in many instances, is not as clear and specific as is the meaning of roots, and many of them are almost completely meaningless.

(3)   Compared with the total number of roots, which is very large (thousands or tens of thousands in any language), the number of affixes is relatively small (a few hundred at most).

In English, all the productive affixes ("productive" in the sense that they do a lot of work) are either attached at the end of the stem – **suffixes** – or at the front of the stem – **prefixes**. Here are examples of common prefixes where the meaning is clear:

co + occur "occur together"	**peri** + meter "measure around"
mid + night "middle of the night"	**re** + turn "turn back"
mis + treat "treat badly"	**un** + filled "not filled"

And here are examples of common suffixes where the meaning is also clear:

act + **ion** "state of acting"	child + **ish** "like a child"
act + **or** "person who acts"	child + **hood** "state of being a child"
act + **ive** "pertaining to being in action"	child + **less** "without a child"

The majority of affixes are, unfortunately, less clear than these. We will provide more detailed information on them later, matching them to some of the possible meanings they may have.

All affixes, by definition, are bound morphemes. Historically it is quite normal for free morphemes to lose their independence and become "bound." One transparent example is the suffix *-less*: its origin in the adjective *less* "devoid of" and its connection with the word *less* do not require specialized knowledge. The suffixes *-dom*, *-hood*, and *-ship* once had independent meaning as nouns. *Dom* meant "doom, judgment, statute" and is the ancestor of the modern word *doom* as well as the suffix *-dom*. The suffix *-hood* meant "condition" or "state of affairs"; it has no modern independent counterpart, however, and is unrelated to our word *hood* "covering for the head." The basic numerals in the classical languages, which were free forms in Greek and Latin just as the corresponding numerals are in English, have provided the bound roots out of which many English compounds are formed: e.g., *penta-* in *pentagon* "having five angles," *sept-* in *septet* "a group of seven," *oct-* in *octagonal* "having eight angles"; *uni-* in *unilateral* "one-sided."

The opposite development, whereby a bound morpheme escapes into the list of free morphemes, is unusual. This is even more true of affixes than it is of roots. There has been a recent trend in the language to detach affixes and elevate them to the status of roots. A typical example is *anti*. We can say things like, "It doesn't matter what the principle is, he is so stubborn that he's bound to be anti." There are even a few forms, originally affixes, that have been detached to become independent words themselves: e.g., the form *pro* from the word *professional*, which originally meant "one who declares (*fess*) forth (*pro-*)." We no longer think of *pro* in a phrase like *pro golfer* as having anything to do with the prefix *pro-* that occurs in *process, provide, profess*. Since the mid-eighties, the negative prefix *dis-* has been used as a verb meaning "insult, show disrespect, criticize," as in *dissed, dissing*. "The Lady is a Trans," meaning "a transgendered person," was a 1996 musical hit.[1] The latter two examples are still considered "non-standard." Other examples of this kind, more or less acceptable, include *hyper, mini, maxi, stereo*. In any case, the status of these items is still in flux and their occasional encroachment into the realm of free roots does not change the basic norm that affixes are bound forms which must be attached to stems.

2.3   Functions of affixes

Affixes have two quite different functions. The first is to participate in the formation of new words. The affixes which do this are called

---

[1] Cited at p. 69 in the *Barnhart Dictionary Companion: A Quarterly of New Words*, vol. 10, no. 1, Summer 1997, Springfield MA: Merriam-Webster, Inc.

derivational affixes. We can think of the root as the **nucleus** of the derivation. The affixes are like satellites; furthermore, they have to circle the nucleus at different distances, vaguely like the solar system. As an example, consider the word *uninhabitableness*. The stem is *habit*. Now, can we add *un-* to *habit*? Of course not: *unhabit* is not a word. So in this derivation, *in-* must be added first. Again we ask: can *un-* be added to *habit*? Same answer.[2] And so on: we keep adding morphemes on the right-hand side until we get to *inhabitable*. Now, finally, we can put *un-* in front of the formation. Why is this? Because after we added *-able*, we had finally created an adjective. It is one of the properties of *un-* that it normally attaches only to adjectives. There are a few funny counterexamples like *uncola*, but precisely the reason why that formation is so effective is that it violates the normal rules of word formation in English. And of course we can't attach *un-* to just any adjective whatever: with few exceptions such as *unable*, *unkind*, *unwise*, simple adjectives can't take *un-*: *unbad, *unglad, *ungood, *unstrong are not possible. Derived adjectives, on the other hand, take the negative prefix freely: *uninteresting*, *unreliable*, *unimportant*, *unsympathetic*, etc. We can represent this hierarchical property of word formation by affixation in the tree-diagram in Figure 4.3.

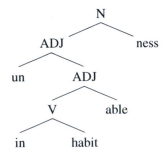

Figure 4.3

Note that the root *habit* can have the prefix *in-* attached first, followed by the suffix *-able*, because both *inhabit* and *inhabitable* are words. By the same logic, *-ness* can only be added after the word has become an adjective, or an adjectival participle. Thus the affix *-ness* is constrained in its use: it cannot be attached to roots with a clear verbal meaning, therefore *habitness*, or *inhabitness* are as impossible as *eatness, *jumpness, *sleepness. The isolated example of *forgiveness* is not really an

---

[2] Note that the *un-* which we are examining here has the meaning of "not, negation, contradiction," and it can only be attached to adjectives and participles which function as adjectives. The *un-* meaning "reversal" which can be placed in front of verb roots such as *unbutton*, *undo*, *unfasten*, is a different prefix which requires a verb with a special "reversible" meaning. The verb *inhabit* in our example is clearly not of that type.

exception because it is probably a simplification of the adjectival past participle *forgiven* + *-ness*, which would be a regular formation. Thus, with *-ness* too, in order to get to the proper form of the noun we have to attach the adjective suffix first.

The affixes which have the function of deriving new words, then, are called derivational affixes. The other type of affix, which does not participate in word formation at all, is called **inflectional**. Inflectional affixes, of which English has only a very small number compared with Latin or Greek or Old English are really part of syntax, though some inflectional affixes are the indicators of very broad semantic categories like tense (*plays*, *played*) or number (singular–plural, as in *girl*, *girls*). The most typical inflectional affixes, in most languages, serve to indicate which word is the subject of the sentence or which word is the object of the verb. Thus Latin:

Ama-t puer puella-m
"love-s boy–NOM girl–ACCUS"

NOM means "nominative," the case for marking the subject of the sentence. ACCUS means "accusative," the case for marking the object of the verb. The three words can be arranged in any order without changing the meaning – they all just mean "The boy loves the girl":

Puer puellam amat
Puellam puer amat
Puellam amat puer
Puer amat puellam

Since inflectional affixes are nothing more than markers of sentence structure and organization, they are not involved in the derivation of new words and hence of no further interest in the present context. It should be acknowledged, however, that this is a simplified picture: there are cases where the addition of an inflectional affix can result in the development of a new meaning, detached from the original semantic category represented by the affix, as in *customs*, *news*, *spectacles*. Similarly, the present and past participle affixes: *-ing* and *-ed*, lead a dual life: They can be purely inflectional as in "They were *building* the new dorm," "They *painted* the wall," or they can behave more like derivational affixes and produce new parts of speech: "The *building* on the corner, the *painted* walls."

3   Compounds

A compound is a word which contains two or more roots. It may also contain affixes, because a compound is a stem, just like a simple non-compound root. The roots in a compound may be either free or bound, but there must be at least two of them. Thus *orthodontist* is a compound consisting of two bound roots and a suffix:

√orth "right" + √odont "tooth" + √ist "one who"

Pterodactyl is a compound consisting of one bound root and one free root:

√ptero "wing" + √dactyl "finger"

Dactyl is a free root only in one special sense, having to do with poetic meter. The *OED* gives no current citations in any other sense, and the only sense listed in the *Merriam-Webster Tenth Collegiate Dictionary* is this one. So in the sense "finger," *dactyl* should be viewed as a bound root. Less controversial examples would be *stratosphere*, *hemisphere*, and *biosphere*, in all of which the second root is *sphere*, which is clearly a free root:

√strato "spread out"
√hemi "half"   + √sphere "round, ball"
√bio "life, living"

Airport, *backpack*, *getaway*, *leftmost*, and *killjoy* are familiar and transparent compounds in which both members are free morphemes. This is an enormously productive pattern: *downsize*, *laptop*, *shareware*, *trackball*, are all late twentieth-century compounds – speakers continue to create them on a daily basis.

Figure 4.4 summarizes all the types of morphemes discussed above.

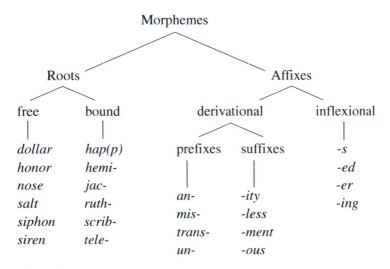

Figure 4.4

4 Hyphens

Throughout this book we have indicated the position at which an affix attaches to a stem by placing a hyphen either before or after it, depending on which side the affix is added to: thus *trans-*, *un-*, but *-ment*, *-ous*, *-ly*, *-ness*. Affixes have a fixed position: they are either prefixes or suffixes, and speakers are not at liberty to switch around their place in order to create a different meaning. There is very strict ordering of the morphemes in terms of types, i.e. what affix can attach to what kind of stem, and the strictness is applicable to their linear ordering too. A simple example: *un* + *happ* + *y* + *ness* is the only option we have for combining the morphemes in this word; any other combination is linguistic garbage: **y* + *happ*, **un* + *ness* + *y* + *happ*, **happ* + *ness* + *un* + *y*, **un* + *ness* + *happ* + *y*. The principle of fixed linear ordering is valid for all affixes, so note the position of the hyphen when you first encounter an unfamiliar affix.

If a morpheme is not marked with a hyphen, it may still be a bound morpheme that can occur only in compounds or with affixes. Even when root morphemes are bound forms, however, it is not possible to predict whether other forms will occur necessarily before, or necessarily after, them. This is true of all roots, native and borrowed, free and bound, compare *baby-sit* to *crybaby*, *crowbar* to *scarecrow*, *horsepower* to *racehorse*. Similarly, with borrowed and bound roots, *tele* generally occurs as the first root in a compound, but *phon* may occur in either position: compare for example *telephone* with *phonology*, *dictaphone* with *verdict*.

5 Cognates

In Chapter 3 we defined cognates as words which start out from the same ancestral root, but which develop into separate dictionary entries. Both roots and affixes can have cognate relations: historically *hyper* is cognate with *super*, *hemi-* is cognate with *semi-* in the same way that *bha-* is cognate with *fa-* and *phe-*. The word *cognate* actually contains a form of the root with which this chapter started, namely √gen. The word breaks down like this:

co- "together" + √gn (= √gen) "origin" + *-ate* "having"

or, roughly, "having a common origin." All root morphemes that can be traced back to a common origin are said to be cognate. Being cognate does not at all entail that such roots would today be viewed as examples of allomorphy. Being cognate is a historical relationship. Allomorphy is a synchronic relationship usually recognized by the speakers of the language as it is today. The two sometimes merge rather closely into each other, as we will see. First, let us remind ourselves of a fairly extreme example of obscured common origin where the divergence is so extreme that the relationship of allomorphy cannot be invoked without reference to sophisticated historical knowledge. This is the story of the IE *bha-* root which surfaces in a number of common words: *bandit*, *fame*, *infant*, *phonetic*, and *symphony* all contain this root (in the forms √ban, √fa, and √phon) and these roots are cognates. But would we invoke the relationship of allomorphy between them? Not automatically, and probably not at all for the ordinary speaker of the language, though it is always interesting to know what the relationship is. Let us reproduce here the family tree of the root *bha* which will be familiar to you from Chapter 3.

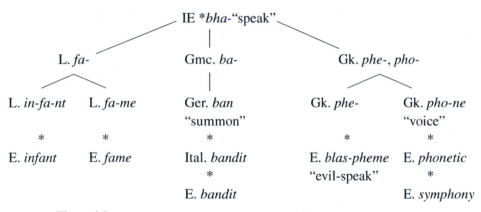

Figure 4.5

Looking at the "family tree" of the morpheme *bha-* in Figure 4.5 may give you the impression that there is a continuous line of inheritance from the older to the modern languages. But this is not always true, especially for words which have come into English more recently, say within the last four or five centuries. The Germanic form of *bha-*, *ban* "to summon, to proclaim, to band together" did not produce the word *bandit* directly. What happened was that first (Late) Latin borrowed the Germanic allomorph *ban*, in addition to its own allomorph *fa-*, then Italian used the new allomorph to create the word *bandit*, and finally English imported the word from Italian at the end of the sixteenth century. Thus, at a certain point, the line of transmission can break, a fact which we represent with an asterisk: *. What this means is that the link between the IE form and the form we use in English today is not a natural inheritance, but rather a borrowing. When borrowing takes place, it may easily happen, as here, that the borrowed form no longer resembles the cognate forms in the borrowing language. It is therefore no longer recognizable as related through allomorphy. It is just a different root altogether, from the point of view of the borrowing language. The "natural" root here is √ban. It does not look at all like √fam or √phon, and when the latter two are borrowed they are not associated with √ban in the minds of the speakers of English who borrowed them in the first place or learned them later.

For English speakers the most accessible and fairly rich account of cognate relationships among English roots is to be found in the Appendix of the *American Heritage Dictionary* (first edition 1973, and third edition 1992) entitled "Indo-European Roots." It is also available as a separate publication, but that version is extremely difficult to use because one needs the cross-references to the Appendix that are found in the regular dictionary entries.

5.1   Shared derivation

If several words share the same root, they are cognates, but what if words share a common derivation: that is, they are based on different roots but they share a common derivational affix or set of affixes? It is rather like saying, "All the members of this group have red hair, though they may differ in every other way." Consider the sets *childless*, *humorless*, *painless*, *timeless*, or *apologize*, *dramatize*, *digitize*, *terrorize*. These words are not cognates. They resemble each other because they contain a recognizable recurring part of the word, the affixes *-less*, and *-ize*. When a set of words shares an affix or even several affixes, they are said to have a shared derivation. Suppose we make a list of some of the words, or parts of words, that end in *-ology*. (There are hundreds of them including many "sportive nonce-words," as the *OED* describes them, such *as nothingology, commonsensology, keyboardology*.) It might look like this:

bio-	-ology	phil-	-ology
cosm-	-ology	phon-	-ology
herpet-	-ology	physi-	-ology
immun-	-ology	rheumat-	-ology
music-	-ology	robot-	-ology
neonat-	-ology	ur-	-ology
ornith-	-ology	vir-	-ology

It is clearly not the case that all of these words are cognates: they simply share a form, namely the form *-ology*, which is actually *-o-log-y*, that is, three affixes together. All of the suffixes are the same and therefore obviously cognate with each other (being identical is sort of an empty sense of being cognate). But the roots are not cognate. The part of the word which is important to establish a cognate relationship is the root – the part on the left, in this list. *Infant* and *fame* are cognate in this sense:

they share a root. But *biology* and *virology* are not cognates, even though they share a form -*ology*, because they are not descended from a common ancestral root.

5.2   Shared form and meaning

If two words contain a shared form with a constant meaning, there will necessarily be a semantic relation between them – the meanings will be similar in some clear way. In the list above, -*ology* means "the study of." These words mean, therefore, "the study of life," ". . . the cosmos," ". . . snakes," ". . . immune systems," etc. It is one of the curiosities of natural languages that a pair of words may actually be true cognates, and even have completely shared forms, yet still be, at least on the surface, quite different in meaning. Such a pair is *graceful* vs. *disgraceful*. Knowing pairs like *organized* vs. *disorganized*, where it is obvious that the entire difference in meaning depends on the negative polarizing sense of *dis-*, we should be able to infer that *disgraceful* is somehow the opposite of *graceful*. Even more dramatic is the difference between the cognates *ease* and *disease*; indeed, for most people the connection between these two words comes as a surprise. But such mismatched pairs are not typical: usually we can infer the meaning of the whole from the meanings of the parts.

6   Finding roots in a dictionary

Before we end the discussion of morphemes and the types of morphemes that make up the words of English, we should find out how roots and affixes are identified in dictionaries. All dictionaries mark words into syllables. The division into syllables is done mainly to enable the reader to decide where to hyphenate at the end of a line. Most dictionaries also indicate pronunciation, including especially marking where the accent falls in polysyllabic words. And of course they provide meanings and usage notes and all sorts of encyclopedic information. But curiously, most dictionaries do not divide up words into morphemes, and even if they do, they do not label roots and affixes as such. Rather, they give some etymological information from which the user is supposed to figure out what the root morphemes and other morphemes are. There is no dictionary, anywhere, in which the editors have neatly marked up the words of English into their constituent morphemes, though there are dictionaries of roots and dictionaries of affixes. Here is the relevant part of a dictionary entry (from the *Concise Oxford*) for *municipal*:

> **municipal** †pert. to the internal affairs of a state; pert. to local self-government, esp. of a town. xvi. -L *municipalis*, f. *municipium* Roman city of which the inhabitants had Roman citizenship, f. *municeps*, *-cip*, f. *munia* civic offices + *capere* take.

From this information how do we find the root(s)? We have to know what the abbreviations mean, first. They're all listed in the front of the dictionary. In this entry, the symbols and abbreviations we need to know are the dagger, "†" for "obsolete" (i.e. the first meaning is obsolete, not the word), the Roman numeral xvi, which tells us that the word appears in English for the first time in the sixteenth century, L for "Latin," f. for "formed on," and most important the hyphen which precedes the "L." The hyphen marks the beginning of the etymological information. This means "adoption of" – that is, the word was borrowed from the Latin form *municipalis*, with just a small change, namely we dropped the final syllable *-is*. Now we look at the etymology itself – the material that follows the hyphen. This is where we find the roots, but only indirectly. We must look at the ultimate source of the word – the very last entries in the etymology, where in this case it says "f. *muni-a* civic offices + *capere* take." This tells us, first, that this word is formed on two roots: the word is a compound, combining the root that means "civic offices" and the root that means "take." Now comes the hard part: we have to be able to subtract from the forms that are given here any part of these forms that are not themselves roots. In the case of *munia*, for example, we have to know that *-a* is a suffix. We don't have to know very much Latin to know this, but we do have to know this much. It doesn't matter what suffix it is, or what it means: it only matters that it is a suffix, and can be subtracted to find the root. In this case, then, the first root is *muni*. The second root is given as *capere* "to take." Once again we have to know a little Latin: we have to know that *-ere* is some kind of suffix. It happens to be the suffix that marked the infinitive in a certain class of verbs. One thing we can count on, in looking at etymologies that contain Latin sources, is that whenever we find *-are*, *-ere*, or *-ire* at the end of a word, and the word is translated as a verb, then it is an infinitive, and the *-are*, *-ere*, *-ire* can be subtracted to get the stem. That stem will also be the root if the whole word has been maximally broken down, as in this case.

5 Allomorphy, phonetics, and affixation

1 Morphological rules

Etymology is the study of the history of words. Over time, words may change both their form and their meaning. Knowing the etymology of a word requires familiarity with the ways in which its phonetic shape has evolved, and familiarity with the evolution of its semantic content. The following two chapters will deal with some regular changes in the phonological form of roots, affixes, and whole words. We will refer to these regularities as **morphological rules**.

1.1 Types of allomorphy

We can divide all the roots and affixes of English into three types of allomorphy:

(1) Unchanging – i.e., zero allomorphy.
(2) Irregular allomorphy: these are morphemes whose variant forms are not derived from one another by regular rules. These unpredictable allomorphs are said to be **opaque** because the relationship between them, though historically valid, is not apparent to the ordinary speaker of the language.
(3) Regular allomorphy: these are morphemes whose variation can be described in terms of regular rules; the allomorphs are predictable. Such allomorphs are said to be transparent because one can easily recognize that the two forms are variants of a single form.

1.1.1 Zero allomorphy

Morphemes belonging to this group preserve their **base form** in all the derivatives where they appear. Thus in the family of the root √phil "love," this morpheme remains unchanged in *Philadelphia, philanthropy, philology, philosophy, zoophilia*. Here are some additional examples of morphemes which illustrate zero allomorphy:

√lim "boundary"	√head	√loc "place"
limit	behead	local
eliminate	headway	locus
preliminary	headlong	locomotive
unlimited	warhead	dislocation

√ven "come, bring"	√morph "form"	√chron "time"
intervene	morpheme	chronic
invent	amorphous	anachronism
revenue	allomorph	chronometer
venture	geomorphology	diachrony
event	ectomorph(ic)	synchronize
convene	isomorph(ic)	chronicle

This stability of form is characteristic of many other roots and affixes in English. Zero allomorphy can be found among both native and borrowed morphemes: √air, √berry, √bitter, √liber "free," √mani "intense desire," √mim "copy, imitate," √nud "uncovered," √orth "straight, correct," √riv "shore, river," √son "sound," √soph "wise," √week, √vir "male, man," √de- "from, down," √dys- "bad, badly," √pro- "before, in space or time," √re- "back," to mention but a few.

In deciding whether a morpheme retains its base form or not, we will ignore those changes in pronunciation which are not reflected in the orthography. Because these changes in pronunciation are based on phonological rules known subconsciously by native speakers, the allomorphs created by the changes are not orthographically shown as allomorphs and do not need to be taught. Their identity in the orthography is sufficient to justify viewing them as unchanging base morphemes, for etymological and vocabulary-growth purposes. Thus we take it that in *anglo**phile*** and ***phil**osophy*, ***ven**ture* and *con**vene***, ***river*** and *ar**rive***, ***mime*** and ***mime**ograph* etc., the boldfaced roots are essentially one and the same unchanging morpheme. English has a large number of such differences which are indeed part of the allomorphy of the language, from a linguistic perspective, but which are not normally reflected in the orthography. Consider such pairs as *photograph–photography, telegraph–telegraphy, serene–serenity, duplicate–duplicity, resign–resignation, deprive–deprivation*, etc. Irrespective of the changes that such pairs exhibit, we will treat them as containing the same root morphemes.

1.1.2 Irregular allomorphy

There are two levels of unpredictability among the morphemes with irregularity. First, there are morphemes which are now irregular because some sound change took place years ago in one of them but not the other. In these instances, along with many regular alternations we will find a very large number of "exceptions." Such historical irregularities will be described in Chapter 7. They come under such headings as vowel gradation, rhotacism, Grimm's Law, and Latin–Greek correspondences. The second subgroup of morphemes with irregular changing allomorphs includes totally unpredictable forms. Even if such morphemes were, at some ancient stage in the history of the source language, subject to rules producing allomorphy, these rules have become completely obscured and it is pointless to try to recover them. Examples of this type of unpredictable allomorphy are not hard to come by: √ab = abs- "from, away," √dei = deo = theo "god, deity," √bene = bon "good, well," √can = cyn "dog",√ced = ceed "go, let go," √erg = urg = org "work," √st = stat = stit "stay, stand, make firm," and many more. We return to irregular allomorphy in Chapter 8.

1.1.3 Regular allomorphy

Regular variation may be illustrated by examining the allomorphs of √syn "together" in these words:

symmetry	[-m]	*symphony*	[-m]
syllable	[-l]	*synchronic*	[-ng] though spelled <n>

Note that the prefix √syn- "with, together" has changed its final sound in accordance with the initial sounds of the roots to which it is attached. In the vast majority of instances, a morpheme will have only two allomorphs, occasionally three. In the rest of Chapter 5 and Chapter 6 we summarize some rules to help one recognize morphemes which exhibit regular allomorphy.

1.1.4 Derivation

A root can be extended either by an affix or by another root (making a compound). The stem *derive*, for example, is itself derived by combining the prefix *de-* with the root √*riv*, which means "flow." (Is "river" derived from this root?) If we take the stem *derive*, we can form several other words like *derivative, derivation, derivational.* Are these all cognates? Yes, they are, but in a rather uninteresting way: they simply all contain the same form of the same root, to which different affixes have been attached.

1.2   Origins of allomorphy

Language change is inexorable. Many of the same processes that create dialects create allomorphy. Dialects come about mainly because of phonetic change and lack of contact between groups. If a particular change, say the introduction of a plural pronoun *youse*, spreads all the way through one dialect, but not in others, we will perceive dialect boundaries. The shape of morphemes may change due to their phonetic environment. If a particular phonetic change spreads part way through a cognate set of words but not all the way, we will perceive allomorphy, because the change will have occurred in some words but not in others. As an example, consider the words *compel* and *compulsion*. √pel is the root that means "push." If the [l] at the end of √pel comes to be followed by a suffix beginning with a consonant, as in *pulse* or *compulsion*, then the <e> changes to <u>. This change is the outcome of a **phonological rule** which came into the language as a result of a specific **phonetic change**. It is a completely regular process which has the effect of creating a new allomorph of the morpheme whose base form is √pel.

Another major source of allomorphy is borrowing related words from two different languages or from the same language at different times. From Greek we borrowed √onym "name," as in *pseudonym*, *anonymous*, *heteronym*, and from Latin we borrowed √nom, which also means "name," as in *nominal*, *nominate*, *nomenclature*, etc. As a result of this double borrowing we have a pair of allomorphs *onym* and *nom*.

1.2.1   Phonetic change

By definition, predictable allomorphy emerges as a result of phonetic changes. The operation of these phonetic changes and therefore the applicability of the rules of allomorphy may depend on a number of linguistic, historical, or social factors. Before we look into the details of individual rules, let us examine briefly five general principles which determine the way in which a particular phonological rule is likely to create allomorphy. These are:

(1)   Ease: some phonetic sequences are preferable to others because they are easier to pronounce.

(2)   Age: phonetic sequences are slowly modified by time. Metaphorically, erosion due to years of usage may show the age of an item.

(3)   Frequency: more frequent forms are more likely to be reduced by erosion than uncommon forms.

(4)   Origin: native words often behave differently from borrowed words, because different languages favor different processes of phonetic change.

(5)　　Transparency: some phonetic sequences are more transparent
to the ear than others, even though they are harder to articulate. Ease of perception may override ease of articulation.

Let us examine these five principles in more detail:

1.2.1.1 Ease of pronunciation. When morphemes come together
in sequence, it is frequently the case that the sounds at the point of
contact between the two morphemes are not compatible, or not very
natural for an English speaker. For example, sequences of two syllabic
vowels will be avoided. Thus √homo "same" + √onym "name" becomes
homonym, not *homo-onym*. Likewise consonantal sequences such as [n
+ p] are commonly changed to a more natural sequence (e.g. *in + pos'''
sible* becomes *im + possible*). In other words we can expect that there will
be rules which simplify or eliminate uncomfortable phonetic combinations whenever they arise in the course of deriving a more complex
word.

The principles which govern, for any given language, what sequences
are judged to be comfortable to pronounce, and what sequences are
uncomfortable or difficult or even impossible, are called **phonotactic
constraints** (√phono- "sound" + √tact- "arrange"). These constraints
vary from one language to another, and even between earlier and later
stages of a single language. In Old English the first two consonants in
words like *know*, *knee* were actually pronounced as [kn-], and there
were words beginning with [hn-], [hl-], [hr-], which we now consider
impossible word-initial consonant clusters. So, phonotactic constraints
may change with time. The constraints are sometimes violated when we
borrow from other languages. Thus we can force ourselves to pronounce successfully (though this is frequently accompanied by a substantial distortion of the original sound sequence), but still find
strange, combinations such as **Brno**, **Dniepr**, **Nkruma**, **Mbabane**,
Lhotse, **Tsangpo**, **Zw**eig, and many others.

1.2.1.2 Age or time of entry of the word into English. Roots
and words which were borrowed or coined at a relatively early stage in
the history of the language are more likely to have undergone a number
of changes which bring them in line with the regular phonetic structure
of the language. More recent borrowings or new coinages, on the other
hand, are likely to preserve the original form. This may happen because
the phonotactic constraints outlined above are specific to English, and
it takes the speakers of the language some time to adapt the borrowed
phonetic shape to the native patterns. Thus *problem*, first recorded in
the fourteenth century, has no vowel in √bol, "throw," but *parabola*
(first recorded in the eighteenth century) has a different shape of the

root; *autopsy* and *autarchy* contain √auto and have lost the final vowel of the root (the *-o-* in *autopsy* is from the second root, √ops "eye, sight"). Both entered the language in the seventeenth century, but more recently *autohypnosis* and *autoimmunization* retain the vowel under similar phonetic circumstances. They entered the language only after 1900. You can guess that *antagonist* and *Antarctic* are both early (four-teenth and sixteenth centuries) but the following words, with the second vowel of √anti- retained, are recent: **anti**-*orgastic* (first recorded 1880), **anti**-*attrition* (1833), and **anti**-*odontalgic* (1817), and the *OED* records two forms for some words in which the same vowel might be subject to loss: *anti-acid* and *antacid*, *anti-emetic* and *antemetic* and even *antodontalgic* (1880).[1]

1.2.1.3 Frequency of use. The correlation between frequency of use and the degree of change is not a straightforward matter, but for purely phonetically induced changes we can say that the more frequent a word is, the more likely it is to change. Speaking metaphorically again, as with any mechanism, excessive wear can be a factor in deter-mining how well the mechanism survives. Consider the variation in the form of √anti- noted just above, where the final vowel is sometimes retained, sometimes lost. Morphemes with relatively low frequency in colloquial English may even be completely unaffected by this vowel deletion process: thus √omni-, √peri-, √hypo-, √iso-, √neo-, √poly- keep their second vowel in all environments.

1.2.1.4 Origin. The etymological source of a morpheme is also important. The applicability and generality of the phonetic rules will depend on whether the word is of Germanic descent, or whether it is to be traced to a non-Germanic, non-Old-English source. Some rules are shared by native and borrowed morphemes. Thus we find [n] disappear-ing before a consonant in both the native √an (indefinite article, origi-nating in the Old English numeral *an*, "one"), and in the common negative prefix √an- "not" borrowed from Latin, so *an opportunity*, but *a perspective*, *an + arch + y → anarchy*, but *an + political → apolitical*. Other rules apply only to morphemes of classical origin. Thus a rule which changes [d] to [s] under certain conditions, discussed below, affects only non-native morphemes ending in *-d*: *pend + s + ive →* *pensive*, *de + fend + se → defense*, but *hand + some → handsome*, *road + ster → roadster*. The decision to label some morphemes native and some foreign will depend on how far back in history we want to go. The

---

[1] References to the age of borrowing are from *The Oxford Dictionary of English Etymology*, ed. by C. T. Onions (Oxford, 1966), and references to the year of borrow-ing are from *Chronological English Dictionary* by Finkenstaedt, Leisi and Wolff (Heidelberg: Carl Winter Universitätsverlag, 1970) and the *OED*.

accepted practice is to classify morphemes common to most Germanic languages as **native**; morphemes which have come into the English language from Latin or Greek, sometimes via French, Spanish, Italian, are lumped together as **Romance** borrowings (where "Romance" includes "classical," especially since many of the Latin borrowings are quite late, after 1500, from the European *lingua franca* of science and higher education, known as New Latin).

1.2.1.5 Transparency. Transparency is the opposite of **ease**. When we change pronunciation to make it easier, we often make it harder to understand. Consider the difference between *unfulfilled* and *emphatic*. The first would be easier to pronounce if it were *umfulfilled* (because [m] is more similar to [f]). But this would make the identity of the prefix √un- less transparent. The second would be easier to understand if it were *enphatic* (because the prefix √en- would be immediately recognizable). But this would make it harder to articulate. Pronouncing the last three consonants of *length* is not easy at all, but any shortcut which changes the cluster would also damage the transparent relationships of this word – with *long* and with a number of other nouns ending in *-th*: *depth*, *warmth*, *wealth*. It is not predictable whether ease will win – as in *emphatic*, or whether the need to maintain transparency will block the effect of ease as in *unfulfilled*, *midtown*, *midsummer*, *subclass*, *subsection*, where the prefixes resist phonetic change in favor of maintaining transparency.

1.2.1.6 The fossilization of allomorphy. At the beginning of this section we classified the possible types of allomorphy as regular, irregular, and zero. A question which might arise in this connection is whether allomorphic variation can produce forms which are so far apart in both sound and sense that they are no longer recognizable allomorphs. There comes a point, admittedly not easily defined, when some members of a word-family become unrecognizable as variants of a single morpheme. For the modern speakers, even for many highly sophisticated and well-educated speakers, such allomorphy is completely dead, or at least fossilized. In the same way that fossils tell us the story of earlier geological times, fossilized allomorphy takes us back to earlier layers of linguistic history. If we go into considerable time-depth, we can find cognate relationships which are not recognizable any longer: that is, forms which at one time were regular rule-governed allomorphs are no longer seen as being allomorphs at all. Good examples of fossilized allomorphy are provided by the cognates *bandit*, *infant*, *emphatic*, *monograph* and *monogram*, *glottis* and *glossary*, *vacant* and *void*, in which the etymological roots have appeared in alternate shapes for ages, but the reasons for the alternation are not recoverable. For us forms exhibiting such completely fossilized allomorphy are simply cognates, not allomorphs.

2   The sounds of English

Before we go on to the discussion of specific rules of allomorphy we need to survey briefly the inventory of sounds in English. Knowledge of the basic facts will help you understand and remember many of the rules governing allomorphy in English.

2.1   Phonetic notation systems

The sounds of all languages can be written reliably in phonetic notation systems, of which the International Phonetic Alphabet (IPA) is the most famous. However, there is not just one single phonetic notation system. Different dictionaries use different systems, and to discover the details of their systems one must check the introduction, and the bottom of the pages in the main part of the dictionary, where one will find a pronunciation key in most dictionaries. American phoneticians and lexicographers in general use a slightly different set of symbols from those used by European phoneticians. The important thing to understand is that phonetic symbols are arbitrary, codified, representations of language sounds. Any well-defined system is, in principle, as good as any other. However, because the IPA is used in the *OED* and its various derivative dictionaries, although it is not used in *Chambers* nor in any of the general purpose American dictionaries, we have used (a simplified version of) it here. We believe it is becoming more widely known in general education anyway, as it certainly should. Later in this chapter we provide a comparison between the symbols of the IPA, of *Chambers*, of *Merriam-Webster*, and of a very broad respelling system of the type that is commonly used in newspapers to indicate the pronunciation of unfamiliar words, so that you can see what the differences and similarities are.

2.2   Phonetic symbols in square brackets

When symbols of the alphabet are intended specifically to represent language sounds, they are enclosed in square brackets: [p t k] means the sounds at the beginnings of the words *pill till, kill*. Once a symbol is enclosed in square brackets like this, it no longer refers to the spelling, only to the sound. Thus the first letter of the word *philosophy* is *p*, but the first sound is [f]. The first letter of *pneumonia* is *p*, but the first sound is [n]. It is common in our highly literate western world to confuse the **sounds** of words with the **spelling**. We must seek to keep these two separate from each other, because many etymological statements (which are normally made about **sounds**) can be quite confusing if misunderstood as statements about spellings.

Most of the phonetic symbols of the IPA will be familiar to you from the standard spelling of English words. A few new symbols will have to be introduced, however, to avoid ambiguity, since the basic idea of phonetic writing is to use a single symbol for a single sound, and always to use the same symbol for the same sound. For example, we will use the symbol [θ] to represent the initial consonant sound in words like *thigh* and *think* (this symbol, the Greek "theta," is the standard IPA symbol), because the actual sound is a single sound (i.e., it is not *t* plus *h*).[2] The IPA symbol [ð], known as "eth" will be used to represent the initial consonant sound in words like *them* and *though*. If you are uncertain about the difference between these sounds, compare *ether* (like *thigh* and *think*) with *either* (like *them* and *though*) and you should hear it easily. To represent the initial sound in words like *shout* and *she*, we will use [š] "s wedge" instead of the IPA symbol [ʃ] "esh," simply because it is typographically easier. There is a similar, but not identical sound in the middle of the word *measure* and at the end of the word *garage*.[3] We will represent this sound with [ž], "z wedge," although the IPA symbol is [ʒ], "yogh." Four other deviations from standard IPA are not in principle damaging to the general utility or purposes of IPA phonetic writing. The first, [č], "c wedge," represents the initial and the final sound in the word *church*. A similar sound occurs as the initial and final consonant in the word *judge*. We will represent this sound as [ǰ], "j wedge." We write [ng] instead of IPA [ŋ] "eng" in words like *sing* and *singer*. Finally, we write [y] instead of [j] for the first sound of words like *year*, *yes*, because writing [j] is an unnecessary source of confusion for English speakers.

2.3   Consonantal parameters

When describing the articulation of the consonants of English (or any language), it is necessary to consider three parameters:

(1)   **Place of articulation**: precisely where does the tongue or lower lip – the two moveable "articulators" – make closure or near-closure with some point along the roof of the mouth? The possibilities are (a) the upper lip, (b) the upper teeth, (c) the area directly behind the upper teeth called the alveolar ridge, (d) the

---

[2] The names of the IPA symbols can be found in the very useful *Phonetic Symbol Guide* by Geoffrey Pullum and William Ladusaw, Chicago: The University of Chicago Press, 1986.

[3] In some people's speech, the word *garage* ends in the sound [ǰ].

hard palate, and (e) the soft palate, also called the velum. One can feel all five of these with a single sweep of the tip of the tongue from the upper lip to the furthest point back along the roof of the mouth that the tip can reach.

(2)   **Manner of articulation**: what is the degree of the closure or near-closure (i.e., some kind of hindrance of the airflow through the mouth) that is made between the articulator and the place of articulation?

(3)   **Voicing**: are the vocal cords vibrating or not during the production of a particular sound?

These three parameters are spelled out in more detail below.

2.3.1   Place of articulation

This parameter in the description of consonants refers to the parts of the vocal tract involved in the production of a given sound. For instance, the sounds [p, b, m, w], as in *pill, bill, mill, will*, involve both lips. We refer to these sounds as bilabial. The sounds [f, v], as in *fairy, very*, are articulated with the lower lip and the upper teeth, and are therefore referred to as labiodental sounds. There are six major places of articulation relevant for English consonants:

Bilabial [p, b, m, w]: articulated with both lips.
Labiodental [f, v]: articulated with the lower lip and upper teeth.
Dental [θ, ð]: as in *thistle, this*, articulated with the tongue touching the back of the teeth.
Alveolar [t, d, s, z, r, l, n]: as in *too, do, sue, zoo, rue, loo, new*, articulated with the tongue contacting or approaching the bony (alveolar) ridge behind the upper teeth.
Palatal [š, ž, č, ǰ, y]: as in *shoe, genre, chew, jew, you*, articulated with the tongue contacting or approaching the hard palate behind the alveolar ridge.
Velar [k, g, ng]:[4] as in *kill, guilt*, and the last sound in *sing*, articulated with the back part of the tongue raised toward the soft palate.

2.3.2   Manner of articulation

"Manner" of articulation is a reference to what happens to the air as it escapes from the lungs through the mouth and/or nose as the sound is produced. For example, during the production of the consonants [p, b, t, d, k, g], there is a brief period when the air is completely **stopped**, and so these consonants are called **stops**.[5] During the production of the consonants [f, v, θ, ð, s, z, š, ž], the air is allowed to flow out

---

[4] The sound [w] also involves a velar articulation, and is often classified as both bilabial and velar.
[5] Another name for the stops is *plosives*.

of the mouth, but there is some friction which results in a hissing sound, so these are called **fricative continuants**. In the production of the consonants [č, ǰ], the air is stopped for a brief period, and then is released with a certain degree of friction, and the consonants are called **affricates** (half stop and half fricative). In the production of [m, n, ng] the airflow is stopped in the oral tract but allowed to continue through the nose, so they are called **nasal sonorants** (sonorants are sounds which can be hummed). The other sonorants deflect the airstream in various ways: [l] is called a **lateral sonorant** because it deflects the airflow around the side of the tongue; [r] is called a **retroflex sonorant** because the airflow is redirected up over the curled-back tip of the tongue. There are thus five major manners of articulation relevant for English consonants:

Stop [p, b, t, d, k, g]: the air is completely stopped for a brief period – you should be able to feel this stoppage at the beginning of *town*, *down*, or in the middle of words like *upper*, *rubber*, *sucker*, *mugger*.

Affricate [č, ǰ]: the air is stopped, then released with a degree of friction – *pitcher*, *ledger*.

Fricative [f, v, θ, ð, s, z, š, ž]: the air passes uninterrupted, with a degree of friction[6] – *fan*, *van*, *through*, *this*, *sip*, *zip*, *sure*, *azure*.

Nasal sonorant [m, n, ng]: the air is released through the nose, rather than the mouth – *mom*, *nun*, *hung*.

Oral sonorant [r, l, y, w]: the air is allowed to flow more freely than for the other types of consonants, but with coloring introduced by tongue shape. [r, l] are called **liquids**, [y, w] are called **glides**. Examples: *rear*, *lull*, *yea*, *wow*.

2.3.3 Voicing

The final parameter relevant to the phonetics of consonants is voicing. In English, all consonants except the sonorants are either **voiced** or **voiceless**. When the vocal cords are vibrating during the articulation of a sound, we say that the sound is voiced. When the vocal cords do not vibrate during the articulation of a sound, we say that the sound is voiceless. You can feel your vocal folds vibrating by placing your fingertips on your larynx (Adam's apple) as you say the sound *zzzzzzzzzz*. You should be able to feel a vibration beneath the skin. Then try the same experiment, but instead say *sssssssssss*. You should feel no vibration beneath the skin this time. This is because the fricative [z] is voiced, whereas the fricative [s] is voiceless. Now try saying *s-z-s-z-s-z*. You should be able to feel the voicing turning on and off. The voiceless consonants of English are [f, θ, s, š, p, t, k, č]. The voiced consonants are [v, ð, z, ž, b, d, g, ǰ, m, n, ng, r, l].

---

[6] Another commonly used term for the fricative consonants is *spirants*.

2.3.4   English consonants: summary

All this information about consonants is displayed in Figure 5.1.

	LAB.	LAB-DEN.	DENT.	ALV.	PAL.	VEL.
STOP	p			t		k
	b			d		g
AFFR.					č	
					ǰ	
FRIC.		f	θ	s	š	
		v	ð	z	ž	
NAS.	m			n		ng
LAT.				l		
RETRO.				r		
GLIDE	w				y	

Figure 5.1 *English consonants*

In each box of Figure 5.1 where there are two symbols, the one on the left is voiceless, the one on the right is voiced. The only English consonant which is not listed in Figure 5.1 or discussed above is [h]. [h] is really a type of vowel: it is in fact a voiceless vowel. That is why in most of the phonetic rules which concern vowels, the rules work in the same way whether the vowel is preceded by [h] or not. A source of confusion for some readers may be the common assumption that there really is an [h] in the sounds represented by the spellings <th, ch, sh, ph>. The fact is that the orthographic symbols <th, ch, sh, ph> do not contain or represent an [h] at all, phonetically. The [h] in these instances is simply a diacritic mark used in conjunction with the symbol to which it is adjacent to indicate an altogether different sound, namely [θ, ð, č, š, f].

2.4   English vowels

Except for the diacritic spellings with <h> discussed above, English orthography represents the consonant sounds with a high degree of consistency and reliability: not perfectly, but still straightforwardly. There are jokes about it, like George Bernard Shaw's question, What does *ghoti* spell? – the answer, of course, is *fish*.[7] On the other hand, the main source of dismay on the part of foreigners learning English, and of English-speaking children learning to spell, is the

---

[7] For those who are not familiar with the joke <gh> spells [f] as in *tough*, <o> spells [ɪ] as in *women*, and <ti> spells [š] as in *revolution*.

extreme variability of English orthography in the representation of vowels. They are more difficult than consonants to characterize phonetically, partly because we don't have the same easy articulatory reference points as we do with the consonants, and partly because the manner in which our orthography represents them is erratic. When the spelling system of English is criticized, the basis of the criticism is usually this very fact, the inconsistency of the system. The sound represented by the letters *ee* as in *beet* is also spelled *ie* in *niece*, *ea* in *neat*, *i* in *machine*, *e* in *complete*, and so on.

Vowel sounds are maximally sonorant – there is no consonantal-type obstruction at all. All that happens is that the size and shape of the resonating cavities of the vocal tract, namely the upper throat and the mouth, are varied in such a way as to produce different vowel qualities. How may we represent those variations in a consistent manner? Since vowels play a less important role in what might be called "visual" allomorphy – i.e., the differences which turn up visually in the writing system (the ones we are mainly concerned about in looking at classical allomorphy), we will not attempt a full account of vowel sounds here. Rather, we lay out below the main parameters of vowel production but without the refinements needed to develop serious skills of vowel discrimination. Nonetheless, it is necessary to understand the rudiments of vowel articulation in order to interpret the phonetic indications of preferred pronunciation found in dictionaries, and in order to understand certain etymological processes described below.

2.4.1   Vowel variation

The precise details of how vowels are articulated varies strikingly across the English-speaking world, and any description of the vowel system will be correct only within some selected dialect area. In Britain, one of the widely accepted norms is usually referred to as "Southern British Received Pronunciation," though sometimes (especially in America) it is called "BBC English." It is this pronunciation which is recorded in the *Oxford English Dictionary* and in the many editions of Daniel Jones's *Everyman's English Pronouncing Dictionary*.[8] The one we shall use in this book is referred to as "General American," which means – by and large, though we shall simplify it somewhat – the pronunciation recorded in *A Pronouncing Dictionary of American English*.[9] What is recorded there is basically the variety of American

---

[8] Jones's first pronouncing dictionary was published in 1907. Its latest, 15th, version, appeared in 1997: Daniel Jones, 15th edn. edited by Peter Roach and James Hartman; pronunciation associate, Jane Setter. Cambridge, New York: Cambridge University Press, 1997.

[9] John S. Kenyon and Thomas A. Knott. Springfield: Merriam, 1953. See also *A Concise Pronouncing Dictionary of British and American English*, by J. Windsor Lewis, London: Oxford University Press, 1972.

English spoken west of the Appalachians and north of the Ohio River on a line extending westward at approximately the 40th parallel until the Rockies, and then the area spreads north and south like a great fan and there comes to be minimal variation throughout the whole area.

2.4.2   Vowel parameters

To understand the way vowels are produced and differentiated, you must become aware of some fairly subtle differences in the way your tongue is positioned in your mouth. Begin with the doctor's instruction: say AH. Why does the doctor ask anyone to say AH? Because if you say AH, you have to open your mouth wide, and your tongue will be lying along the very bottom of the jaw (on the inside). Only then can the doctor see your throat, since otherwise your tongue is in the way. The sound you make with your mouth wide open is called an "open" vowel. That particular vowel is the most open of all vowels. On Figure 5.2, you will find this vowel represented as [ɑ] in the box that shows the intersection between LOW on the vertical axis and CENTRAL on the horizontal axis.

	FRONT	CENTRAL	BACK
HIGH LOW HI	i (peat) ɪ (pit)		(boot) u (put) ʊ
MID LOW MID	e (pate) ɛ (pet)	ə (uh …)	(boat) o ʌ (putt)
HIGH LOW	æ (pat)		(paw) ɔ ɒ (pot Br.)
LOW		ɑ (pot)	

Figure 5.2 *English vowels*

Figure 5.2 is a schematic representation of the relative height and frontness of the tongue in producing these vowels. Think of the left side of the diagram as the front of the mouth, just behind the teeth, and the right side is the back of the mouth, where it turns down into the throat. You should be able to feel what is happening to your tongue if you say, in fairly rapid alternation, EE – AH – EE – AH. You should feel your jaw (and tongue) dropping in going from EE to AH and then closing as the tongue moves up high again for EE. Now try moving your tongue from the most open position, the doctor's AH position, very slowly up to the EE position. You should hear the vowel quality gradually change, going through the intermediate front vowels along the way.

Taking the doctor's AH (i.e., phonetic [ɑ]) in Figure 5.2 as the maximally open reference point in the system, we can establish two other such reference points, namely the vowels at the other extreme, maximally close. (1) The maximally close **front** reference point is the vowel represented by [i] (the intersection of HIGH and FRONT in Figure 5.2). This is commonly spelled with "double *e*" in English orthography, as in words like *geese, meet, beet, feet, keep*, but also *ea* as in *beat, bean, grease, flea*. The only English words which use the letter *i* to represent this vowel sound are relatively recent borrowings from French, like *machine, mystique, fatigue, regime*. The use of *i* to represent this sound phonetically is no doubt due to the fact that in most European languages the letter *i* is the regular representation of the sound we are discussing: consider French *oui*, Spanish *si*, Italian *si*. English is the odd language in this respect. (2) The maximally close **back** reference point is the vowel represented by [u] (the intersection of HIGH and BACK in Figure 5.2). This is commonly spelled with "double *o*" in our orthography, as in words like *goose, moot, boot, loop*.

You can feel these three reference points by saying *me–ma–moo* – i.e., phonetically [mi – mɑ – mu]. You'll find that the third vowel, [u], not only requires that you move your tongue to the high back position, but you must also pucker your lips, or as phoneticians say, you must "round your lips." This lip rounding is an additional parameter, but it is automatic in English and requires no special discussion.

Up to this point, we have listed only the **monophthongs** of English. That is, they are relatively "pure" vowels. We must also have a notation for certain combinations of two vowels, called **diphthongs**, which behave like single units but are in fact carriers of the height and frontness properties of two vowels. Diphthongal vowels are produced by starting with the first vowel and gliding quickly toward the second vowel. The four common diphthongs in English are [ɑi] as in *bite, lie, hide, might, dine*; [ɑu] as in *bout, bow, bowed, down, noun*; [oi] as in *boy, avoid, groin, coy*; and **[iu]** as in *beauty, cute, fume, dispute*. For many speakers **[iu]** appears also in *duty, dues, news, sue, tune*, but in America more often these words have the vowel **[u]** instead of **[iu]** whenever the vowel follows a consonant in the dento-alveolar series ([t d s z]) as in these words.

All of the points in the vowel space can be calculated from the three extreme positions [i u ɑ]. Working from the key words given in Figure 5.2, you can determine precisely what sounds are represented by which phonetic symbols. In Figure 5.3, we display these sounds in four notation systems:

(1)   Simplified IPA, discussed above (our system).
(2)   *American Heritage Dictionary* (3rd edition 1992).
(3)   *The Chambers Dictionary* (1998).
(4)   Newspaper "respelling."

Examples	IPA	Heritage	Chambers	Respelling
bead, see, niece	[i]	ē	ē	ee
bid, his, sin	[ɪ]	ĭ	i	i
paid, may, came	[e]	ā	ā	ay
bed, said, bread	[ɛ]	ĕ	e	e
bad, pack, jazz	[æ]	ă	a	a
pod, lot, father	[ɑ]	ŏ	o	o
pawed, caught	[ɔ]	ô	ö	aw
bud, was, rough	[ʌ] ([ə])	ŭ	u	u
hoed, coat, note	[o]	ō	ō	oa
good, would	[ʊ]	oo	oo	oo
boot, food, noon	[u]	o͞o	o͞o	oo
beauty, new	[iu]	ȳ	ū	yoo
eye, mine, pie	[ɑi]	ī	ī	igh
how, bout, loud	[ɑu]	ou	ow	ow
boy, loin, point	[oi]	oi	oi	oy
bird, hurt, fur	[ər], [ɝ]	û(r)	û(r)	ur
uh, a(bout)	[ə]	ə	ə	uh

Figure 5.3

2.4.3   Reduction of vowels

The distinction between full and reduced vowels depends on the presence or absence of prominence (we mark prominence with boldface type). Compare the different allomorphs of the morphemes *tele* and *graph*:

tele-graph – [tɛlə-græf] or [tɛlɪ -græf]

vs.

tele-graph-y – [təlɛ-grəfi]

Notice that the first syllable of *tele-* when accented almost rhymes with *belly*; when unaccented, its first syllable has the same vowel as the word *but.* This change in the quality of the vowel is called **vowel reduction**, and it is directly associated with loss of prominence. Vowel reduction replaces whatever the stressed vowel is by the most neutral and under-articulated vowel in the system, namely the one called *schwa*, represented by the upside-down e, namely [ə]. Notice that in Figure 5.3 the only symbol that is agreed upon by *IPA, Heritage*, and *Chambers* is this one. It is also used by *Merriam-Webster's*, starting with their great unabridged dictionary of 1961. Much of the phonetically-based allomorphy of the Romance vocabulary of English turns out to depend on the prominence-shifting of the type seen in this pair and thousands of other pairs like *photograph–photography, vary–variety, emphatic–emphasis, rheumatic–rheumatism.*

3   The affixes of English[10]

While by far the largest number of English morphemes are roots, the most frequently occurring morphemes are the affixes. Almost every word that has come down to us from the classical languages Greek and Latin, or that has been newly created from Greek or Latin roots (as is done these days as well as earlier in history in nearly all fields of learning), has one or more affixes. The same affixes occur over and over again, and they must be memorized.

Roots vs. affixes: how they differ. Roots have a clear meaning, in and of themselves. While some affixes are like that (e.g., *un-* means "not"), affixes do not usually have such clear meanings. They are also extremely subject to a process of "bleaching," in which their original meaning is bleached out completely and what is left behind is almost impossible to specify. In the lists below, meanings are given that reflect the basic sense of each affix, but you cannot count on that meaning as being the only sense that you will ever encounter. Historically roots frequently become affixes, as in *ambi, tele*, or conversely *ex, pro*.

3.1   Prefixes

Counting-prefixes: those which in some way quantify the root

a- or *an-* "lacking" as in *asymmetric, amoral, atonal*
ambi- "both, around" as in *ambidextrous, ambiguous, ambivalent, amphibious, amphitheater*
arch- "chief, principal, high" as in *archbishop, archduke*

---

[10] The main source of detailed information about English affixes, on which we have drawn freely, is Hans Marchand, *The Categories and Types of Present-Day English Word-Formation*, Munich: Beck, 1969.

bi- "twice, double" as in *bifocal, biennial, bipolar, bisulfate*

di- "two" as in *dioxide, ditransitive, dichloride*

mono- "one" as in *monograph, monosyllabic*

multi- "many" as in *multifaceted, multivalent, multiform*

oligo- "few" as in *oligarchy, oligotrophic*

omni- "all" as in *omnipotent, omniscient, omnidirectional*

pan- "all, comprising or affecting all" as in *panorama, pandemic*

poly- "many" as in *polychromatic, polyangular, polygamy*

tri- "three"[11] as in *triangle, tridimensional*

uni- "one" as in *unisex, unidirectional, univocal*

Involvement prefixes: those which say something about the kind of involvement of the participants in the action of the root

anti- "opposed, instead" as in *antidote, antisemitic, antacid*

auto- "self" as in *automaton, autobiography, automobile*

co-, con- "together, jointly" as in *coexistence, cooperate, concur*

contra- "against, opposite" as in *contradiction, contrary*

vice- "in place of, instead" as in *vice-consul, vice-president*

Judgment prefixes: those which make a judgment about the root

dis- used as an intensifier as in *disturb, disgruntle, disannul*

dys- "bad, badly" as in *dyslogistic, dyspeptic*

eu- "good, well" as in *eugenics, evangelical, euphoria*

extra- "outside the scope of" as in *extraordinary, extramarital*

mal- "ill, evil, wrong" as in *malfeasance, malodorant, malpractice*

meta- "transcending, changed" as in *metaphysics, metamorphosis*

mis- "badly, wrongly" as in *misspent, miscalculate, mislead*

pro- "on behalf of" as in *pro-British, pro-education*

proto- "first, chief" as in *protoorganism, protoplasm, prototype*

pseudo- "false, deceptive resemblance" as in *pseudonym, pseudo-prophet, pseudo-archaic*

Locative prefixes: those which say something about place or direction

ab- or *a-* or *abs-* "from, away" as in *abnormal, abstinence, abjure*

ad- "toward" as in *admit, advance, admonish*

ana- "back" as in *anatomy, analogy*

apo- "away, from" as in *apocryphal, apostasy, apology*

cata- "down, away, back, opposite" as in *catapult, catastrophe*

circum- "around" as in *circumnavigate, circumspect, circumcise*

counter- "against, opposite" as in *counterfeit, counterbalance*

de- "away from, down" as in *decay, debase, deny, depend*

---

[11] One might also list the prefixes for 4, 5, 6, 7, 8, 9 and 10, namely √quadri (quadrilateral) or √tetra (tetrahedron), √penta (pentagon), √hex (hexagonal), √sept (septuagenarian), √octo (octogenarian), √nov (November), √dec (December, decasyllabic).

dia- "across, through" as in *diameter, diachronic*

ecto-, exo- "external" as in *ectoplasm, ectoderm, ectophyte, exocentric, exocardial*

en- "in, into" (a form of *in-*) as in *encapsulate, enclose*

endo- "internal" as in *endodontic, endogenous, endocardial, endocrinology*

epi- "on, over" as in *epiglottis, epidermis, epicycle*

ex-, ec- "out from, away" *ex consul, ex-wife; eccentric;* in reduced form *educate, eradicate, emit*

in- "in, into, within" as in *inaugurate, inchoate*

infra- "below, beneath, within" as in *infrastructure, infrared, infraterritorial*

inter- "between, among" as in *interchange, interpose, intersect*

intra-, intro- "inside" as in *intracity, intramural, intracellular, introvert*

ob- "toward, against" as in *obdurate, obfuscate*

para- "beside, along with" as in *paramedic, parallel*

per- "through, thoroughly" as in *perspire, pernicious, pervade*

peri- "around, nearby" as in *perimeter, peristomatic*

pro- "in front of" as in *proposition, proscenium, propel*

pros- "concerning, towards" as in *prosody, proselyte*

retro- "backwards, back" as in *retrogression, retrospection*

sub- "under, below" as in *subdivision, subtraction, subtitle*

super- "over, above" as in *supernatural, supererogatory, superman*

sur- "over, above, beyond" as in *surtax, surrealistic*

syn- "with, together" as in *synthetic, synchronic*

trans-, tres-, tra-, "across, surpassing" as in *transalpine, transoceanic, transhuman, trespass, trajectory, traduce, tradition*

Measurement prefixes

crypto- "secret, hidden" as in *cryptography, cryptanalytic*

hyper- "over, to excess" as in *hyperactive, hypersensitive*

hypo- "under, slightly" as in *hypotactic, hypoglossal, hypotoxic*

is-, iso- "equal" as in *isochrony, isosceles, isotope*

macro- "large, broad scale" as in *macroeconomics, macroclimatology*

micro- "tiny, small scale" as in *microorganism, microscope*

mid- "middle" as in *midwinter, midlands, midnight*

semi- "half, partly" as in *semicolon, semifinal, semi-annual*

ultra- "beyond, extreme" as in *ultraliberal, ultramodest, ultraviolet*

Negative prefixes

dis- "apart, reversal, lacking" as in *displease, disallow, distaste*

in- "negative" as in *indiscreet, ineffectual, incredible, illegible*

non- "not" as in *nonsense, non-resident, non-intervention*

ob- "inverse, in the opposite direction" as in *object, obverse*

se-, sed- "apart" as in *separate, select* "chosen apart," *sedition, seduce*
un- "not" as in *unclean, uneven, unmindful, unbearable, uncouth*
un- "opposite" as in *untie, unlock, uncoil*

Temporal prefixes: those which say something about time or duration

ante- "preceding" as in *antechamber, ante-Norman*
fore- "before" in time or space, as in *forecast, forefinger, foreskin*
neo- "new, recent" as in *neonatal, Neolithic, neotype*
post- "after, behind" as in *postpone, postnasal, postposition*
pre-, pro- "before, in front of" as in *preconceive, preposition, progress, professor*
re-, red- "anew, again, back" as in *regenerate, rehearse, reward, restore, redaction, redeem*

3.2   Suffixes

The last suffix of a word always determines what part of speech the word belongs to: i.e., whether it is a noun, verb, adjective, or adverb. Very often it seems that that is **all** the suffix is doing: just converting a noun into an adjective (*friend→friendly*) or an adjective into a verb (*final→finalize*), for example. Some suffixes, then, have more specific meanings than others: in the list below, we have been as specific as possible, and some of the meanings are probably too highly specified. You should treat the meanings given as elastic and in need of fitting to any particular context.

Suffixes which form adjectives from nouns or verbs

-able "fit for doing, fit for being done" as in *agreeable, comfortable, incalculable*
-al (-ial, -ical, -ual) "having the property of" as in *conjectural, fraternal, dialectal, sensual, comical, analytical, ministerial*
-an, -ian "belonging to, resembling" as in *reptilian, Augustan, plebeian, patrician*
-ary "having a tendency or purpose" forms adjectives, and then secondarily nouns, as in *secondary, discretionary, rudimentary, tributary*
-ate "full of" forms adjectives from nouns, pronounced [ət], as in *passionate, affectionate, extortionate*
-ese "belonging to a place" forms adjectives from locative nouns, as in *Japanese, New Yorkese, journalese*
-esque "having the style of X" forms adjectives usually from nouns, as in *Romanesque, lawyeresque, statuesque*
-esc "become" as in *tumescent, coalesce*
-ful "full of X" forms adjectives from nouns, as in *peaceful, powerful, skillful*

-iac "pertaining to the property X" as in *elegiac, hypochondriac, maniac*

-ic "having the property X" forms adjectives, as in *alcoholic, atheistic, naturalistic, romantic.* *-ical* is an occasional variant, as in *comic/comical*

-ish "to become like X" forms adjectives from nouns, as in *churlish, boyish, Irish, modish*

-ive "characterized by" forms adjectives from most stems, especially verbs, as in *abusive, contradictive, retrospective*

-less "without, free from" forms adjective from noun, as in *faultless, keyless, fearless*

-ly "appropriate to, befitting" as in *friendly, timely, shapely, fatherly*

-oid "having the shape of, resembling" as in *humanoid*

-ory "connected with, serving for" forms adjectives as in *obligatory, inflammatory, illusory*; also forms nouns with the meaning "place where," as in *dormitory, lavatory, refectory*

-ose "full of, abounding in" as in *verbose, morose, jocose*

-ous "of the nature of X" forms adjectives, as in *virtuous, torturous, glorious, grievous*

-some "like, characterized by, apt to" forms adjectives from almost any kind of stem, as in *cumbersome, awesome, bothersome*

-y "full of, characterized by" forms adjectives from nouns, as in *mighty, moody, healthy*

Suffixes which form abstract nouns

-asy, -acy "state or quality" as in *advocacy, intricacy, accuracy, ecstasy*

-age "condition, state, rank, office of" as in *anchorage, postage, coinage*

-ance, -ence "state, act, or fact of" forms abstract nouns from verbs, as in *repentance, perseverance, emergence*

-ad(e) "general noun" *accolade, brigade, cannonade, ballad, salad, parade, lemonade, comrade, sonata, armada*

-al "act of" forms abstract nouns from verbs, as in *renewal, revival, trial*

-ation "state of being X-ed" forms abstract nouns from verbs of four types: those ending in *-ify, -ize, -ate*, and a few without endings (like *damn, inform*). Examples: *purification, organization, contemplation, information*

-ery, -ry "collectivity" forms abstract nouns from concrete nouns, as in *masonry, carpentry, slavery, savagery*

-hood "state of, condition of" forms abstract nouns from concrete nouns, as in *childhood, womanhood, priesthood*

-ia "condition of" as in *euphoria*

-icity "abstract noun from *-ic*" as in *historic/historicity, electric/electricity*

-ism "doctrinal system of principles" as in *communism, realism, romanticism*

-ity "state, quality, condition of" forms abstract nouns from adjectives, as in *agility*, *diversity*, *actuality*

-ment "condition of being X" forms abstract nouns from verbs and adjectives, as in *advancement*, *treatment*, *abandonment*, *aggrandizement*, *amusement*, *merriment*

-ness "state, condition, quality of" forms abstract nouns usually from adjectives, but not verbs, as in *bitterness*, *fairness*, *idleness*, *deafness*

-ship "state, condition" forms abstract nouns usually from concrete nouns, as in *dictatorship*, *trusteeship*, *workmanship*

Suffixes which form agentive nouns

-ant, *-ent* "one who" forms agentive nouns from verbs, as in *agent*, *defendant*, *participant*

-arian "member of a sect, holding to a doctrine" forms nouns or adjectives, as in *utilitarian*, *egalitarian*, *authoritarian*, *septuagenarian*

-ast "one associated with X" as in *enthusiast*, *pederast*

-er "agent" forms agentive nouns from verbs, as in *baker*, *thriller*, *worker*, *sweeper*, *retriever*

-ist "one connected with, often agent" as in *socialist*, *perfectionist*, *dentist*, *pugilist*, *ventriloquist*

-ician "one skilled in some art or science" as in *physician*, *musician*, *magician*, *mathematician*

Suffixes which form verbs from roots and stems

-ate "cause X to happen" pronounced [et], as in *create*, *contaminate*, *frustrate*, *terminate*

-en "to become" forms verbs from adjectives, as in *darken*, *chasten*, *cheapen*, *deafen*

-ify "to cause to (be) X" forms a causative verb, as in *purify*, *denazify*, *sanctify*, *verify*, *amplify*

-ize "to cause to be X" forms a causative verb from almost any stem, as in *popularize*, *legalize*, *plagiarize*, *miniaturize*, *weatherize*

Miscellaneous suffixes

-arium, *-orium* "locative, a place for or connected with" as in *aquarium*, *vivarium*, *honorarium*, *auditorium*, *crematorium*

-ess "feminine of X" as in *tigress*, *laundress*, *stewardess*

-let "diminutive" as in *leaflet*, *driblet*

6 Replacement rules

This chapter and the next deal with rules which account for predictable allomorphy. The rules of predictable allomorphy are of three types:

replacement rules – replace one sound by a different sound in a certain position in the morpheme;
deletion rules – account for the loss of a sound, or sounds, from a morpheme;
expansion rules – expand a morpheme by inserting a new sound within the existing structure of the morpheme.

This classification exhausts the logical possibilities of what can happen to one phonetic segment. It can be replaced, deleted, or some sequence of sounds can be expanded.

1   Assimilation and types of assimilation

Assimilation rules are replacement rules which have the effect of making one vowel or consonant more similar to, or even identical with, another. In principle, assimilation can affect both vowels and consonants; most instances of assimilation discussed below, however, are cases of consonantal assimilation.

The process of assimilation can be described in terms of the target, the direction, and the scope of the resulting similarity. Assimilation can target some or even all of a sound's features: voicing, place, or manner of articulation. Depending on the direction of the influence between the sounds we find **right-to-left** assimilation, when the influence is from the second to the first sound, i.e. A ← B, also known as *regressive assimilation*, and **left-to-right**, when the first sound influences the second, the A → B type, known as *progressive assimilation*. The majority of the consonantal assimilations presented here are instances of right-to-left assimilation. However, left-to-right assimilation is also a familiar process in English – some such instances will be mentioned when we come to the section on voicing assimilation. In terms of scope, assimilation can result in the replacement of a feature in one of the contiguous sounds by a feature of the sound with which it has come into contact (i.e., one gesture less). This kind of change is **partial** assimilation – the two consonants preserve their identity as distinct sounds, but become more similar to each other. The ultimate case of assimilation, **full** assimilation, involves the elimination of all differences between the contiguous sounds; full assimilation is in essence a replication of one of the sounds, also known as **gemination**. The types of assimilation that we will be referring to in what follows in this chapter are shown in Figure 6.1.

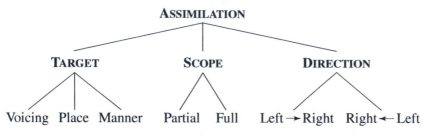

Figure 6.1

The principle which governs assimilation is the principle of ease defined in Chapter 5, 1.2.1. Stripped to their essence, assimilation rules simply say:

Prefer the easier articulation.

As a feature spreads from one sound to another, it replaces an existing feature in the assimilating sound. The two sounds end up sharing a gesture; the resulting articulation is easier because it eliminates one gesture from the overall articulatory process. The next two sections cover two types of partial assimilation; the target is either the place of articulation, or the voicing of adjacent segments.

2   Labial assimilation

The essence of labial assimilation is:

Prefer labials before labials

```
-n + [p-, b-, m-, f-]
↓
-m
```

This formula is read, "When -n occurs at the end of a morpheme, followed by a morpheme beginning with [p-, b-, m-, f-], the -n changes to

-m." The consonant [m] is labial, and therefore it is more similar to [p, b, m, f] than [n] is, since [n] is alveolar.

Labial assimilation affects the place, but not the manner, of articulation of the input consonant (the "input consonant" is the one in the top row: the "output consonant" is the one below the arrow in the second row). Although in principle labial assimilation may be a much broader process, we have narrowed it down to the change of [n] to [m] because all morphemes affected by labial assimilation discussed in this section are prefixes which end in [-n]. All instances of labial assimilation in English are instances of right-to-left assimilation, i.e. a non-labial consonant becomes labial in anticipation of the "labiality" of the initial consonant of the second morpheme. Here is how it works:

con + bat "strike"	→ combat
con + pater "father" + iot	→ compatriot
en + bell "beautiful" + ish	→ embellish (*en-* is intensifying)
en + ploy "fold"	→ employ
en + pha "speak" + t + ic	→ emphatic
in + ped "foot" + e	→ impede
in + bib "drink" + e	→ imbibe (but: inbred, inborn)
pan + pleg "stroke" + ia	→ pamplegia
pan + phag "eat" + ous	→ pamphagous
syn + path "feel" + y	→ sympathy
syn + bol "throw"	→ symbol
syn + phon "sound" + y	→ symphony

Labial assimilation affects the prefixes *con-*, *en-*, *in-*, *pan-*, and *syn-*. The triggers of the change, the consonants [p-, b-, m-, f-] in the second morpheme, share the articulatory feature labiality.

Not all labial consonants have an equally strong effect on the preceding [-n]. The bilabials [p, b, m] are stronger in this respect, while [f] seems to be weaker. The prefix *in-* does not change to *im-* before [f], compare *infant, infect, infinite, influence*. On the other hand, *pan-*, *syn-*, and *con-* are open to assimilation to *pam-*, *sym-*, and *com-* before a following [-f]: *pamphagous, symphony, comfit, comfort*. It is *con*fusing and *con*founding to be *con*fronted with a whole group of common words which have resisted the change for no obvious reason: *confidence, confirm, conflate, conflict*. The n- is preserved in the more recent formation *synfuel*, a blend from the first syllable of *synthetic + fuel*, a formation which entered the language in the early 1970s. Both the assimilated and the unassimilated forms are found with some items. Thus the seventeenth-century Greek borrowing *panpharmacon* "universal remedy, panacea," is also recorded as *pampharmacon*, and unassimilated forms *confit, confort*, and even *conmit, conpetent* are earlier forms recorded in the *OED* for the items *comfit, comfort, **commit**, competent*. In the assimilated words ease of articulation has won over transparency. Sometimes, however, the effect of the assimilation is reversed by the need for greater transparency: the *OED* records a now obsolete form *pambrittanick*, but the same adjective today is *pan-Britannic*, the form *comfect* was reversed to *confect* (as in *confectionery*).

The change of [-n] to [-m] before another [m-] is quite pervasive: earlier forms such as *inmaculate, inmaterial, inmovable, inmortal*, all on record in the *OED*, have changed to *immaculate, immaterial, immovable, immortal*. Such assimilation is both an instance of labial assimilation, and of total assimilation. In pronunciation, one of the identical consonants is lost; such words are pronounced with a single [m]. Only the spelling preserves the trace of the total assimilation.

2.1   Exceptions to labial assimilation

An apparent exception to the rule of labial assimilation is provided by the unchanged form of the native prefix *un-* meaning "not" or "reversal." The alveolar nasal in this prefix does not change into a labial nasal in the environment of other labials, so: *unbridled, unbalanced, unmistakable, unmanageable, unprepared, unprofitable, unfair, unfathomable*. Although this prefix has been in the language since Old English times, and it has been steadily productive, the phonetic rules of relaxed spoken English have not produced forms with orthographic labial assimilation in such words. It must be acknowledged, of course, that connected speech combinations of [un-]+[p-, b-, m-, f-], as well as other apparently "unassimilated" sequences such as *inbred, inbuilt*, often show assimilation in casual or fast speech and sound like *umbridled, ummanageable, umplanned, imbred, imbuilt*.[1] Labial assimilation occurs in rapid speech occasionally also when the final [-n] of one word is in contact with initial [p-, b-, m-] of the next word: *pen pal, ten boys, bran muffin* may change the [-n] of the first word to [-m], thus [pem-, tem-, bram-].

One reason for this stability of n- forms may be in the highly recognizable semantic individuality of this morpheme, which often correlates with stress, as in *unforeseen, unforgiving, unmistaken, unprepared*. Thus we can attribute the behavior of *un-* with respect to labial assimilation to the fact that among the prefixes likely to undergo this change, *un-* normally bears half stress, and is usually attached to free roots, unlike the prefixes listed above. It once carried main stress. It is the oldest negative prefix in the language: it was a very productive negative prefix in Old English, and it exists in all Germanic languages. On the other hand, *in-*

---

[1] The morpheme *in-* in *inbred, inbuilt, inmost, is* different from the negative *in-*. The adverbial *in-* has the status of a root morpheme, so that *inbred, input*, etc. are treated as compounds.

(with its variant *en-*), *syn-*, *con-*, *pan-* have had a shorter life in English, and the derivatives they produce are also newcomers, mostly from the classical word stock; they usually precede bound roots. In the majority of cases of attested assimilation, the process took place in the donor language, and not in English, and English borrowed the words whole-sale, ignoring the principle of transparency. We can therefore think of the rule of labial assimilation as a rule reflected in the spelling and con-sistently affecting the pronunciation of mostly non-native prefixes.

3   Voicing assimilation

Voicing assimilation changes the voicing parameter from "plus" to "minus" under the influence of the voiceless segments [t], [s], [θ]. The voiced velar stop [g] becomes a voiceless velar stop [k], the voiced labial stop [b] becomes a voiceless labial stop [p], and a voiced labial fricative [v] becomes a voiceless labial fricative [f]. [t] affects [g-, b-, v-] in the same way. In addition, [g] assimilates before [s], and [v] assimilates before the voiceless dental fricative [θ]. Clearly, it is easier NOT to turn the vibration of the vocal cords off and on rapidly. This is all that the rule really says:

Voicing assimilation: prefer steady-state voicing

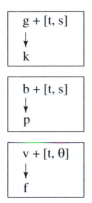

If we refer just to the voicing feature, instead of symbols for fully spec-ified segments, we can collapse the three rules into one:

$$
\begin{array}{l}
[+\text{VOI}] + [-\text{VOI}] \\
\downarrow \\
[-\text{VOI}]
\end{array}
$$

This more general description of the process says that voiced segments become voiceless in front of voiceless segments, as shown below:

ag -t	→act	nub "marry" -t-ial	→nuptial
se – leg -t	→select	scrib – t	→script
in – seg -t	→insect	give – t	→gift
syn – tag "touch" -s	→syntax[2]	five -th	→fifth

3.1   Sound versus spelling

When learning about replacement rules, it is important that there should be no confusion between sound and spelling. As in labial assimilation, right-to-left voicing assimilation is reflected in the spelling. However, the voicing assimilation of [g] to [k] does not correspond to a shift of the letter <g> to the letter <k>. Instead, <c> is conventionally used for the voiceless velar stop [k] when followed by back vowels and other consonants. <c> can have other values as well, as in *city, Alice, recede, discern, cycle*, etc. The sound [k] may appear in spelling also as <k>: *keep, kitchen, cook, kid*, as <ch>: *ache, monarchy*, as <ck>: *smack, trick*, <qu>: *picturesque, quote*, British *cheque*.

3.2   Left-to-right voicing assimilation

Most of the consonantal assimilations in English derivational morphology occur from right to left. However, in English inflectional morphology, the directionality of change is from left to right. Consider the difference between *racks* and *rags*. In *racks*, the allomorph that marks the plural is *-s* in the spelling and indeed it is also phonetically [s]. But in *rags*, the consonant that precedes <-s> is a voiced consonant [g]; its voicing creates a different allomorph of the plural morpheme, namely [-z]. The assimilation progresses from left to right, from [g] to [z]. The same is true of verbs taking the third person singular present tense inflection -s, compare *taps, sits, tucks* with [s] to *blabs, bids, lugs* with [z]. A third possibility, which voices [s] to [z] across an inserted vowel, is the pronunciation of the plural and the third person singular inflexions as a separate syllable, [-ɪz] or [-əz]. The syllabic allomorph appears after alveolar and palatal fricatives and affricates [s, z, š, ž, č, ǰ]: *masses, quizzes, dishes, garages, batches, ledges*.

Assimilation from left to right affects also the morpheme that represents past tense, usually spelled *-ed*. Thus *racked* ends with [-kt], but *bragged* ends with [-gd]. A third allomorph of the past tense morpheme requires that the orthographic vowel be kept to make <-ed> pronounceable after the alveolar stops [t, d]: *wanted, corroded*. Notice that

---

[2] The replacement of the sequence [ks] by <x> is a spelling convention. It has no effect on the pronunciation of the consonant cluster. This replacement practice has given rise to attention-getting facetious spellings like *thanx, truxtop, thumb tax.*

the realization of the vowel in the articulation of *-es* and *-ed* is not motivated by ease, as in labial and voicing assimilation. Rather, the vowel in [-ɪz] or [-əz] or [-ɪd] or [-əd] is a response to the need for transparency; without the intervening vowel the sequences [s + s], [z + z], [t + t], [d + d] would not be heard well. Historically, *-es* and *-ed* were separate syllables in all instances; the vowel was lost only in cases where the transparency was not endangered, and assimilation occurred simultaneously with the vowel loss.

4 Total assimilation

The transfer and replacement of features in adjacent sounds can alter completely the phonetic nature of the original consonant in a morpheme. When assimilation renders an input sound identical to the sound which follows it, we talk of total assimilation. The change of [-n] →[-m] before [m-] is due to labial assimilation, but it also represents a case of total assimilation:

con + memor + ate	→commemorate	in + mort "die" + al	→immortal
en + mesh	→emmesh[3]	syn + meter + y	→symmetry

In these examples the labial gesture happens to be the only difference between the adjacent nasals [n] and [m]. In many other instances, however, total assimilation involves more gestures; it amounts to copying the second consonant over the first one. The word *assimilation* is itself an example of the process:

    ad - simil - ate - ion   →assimilation

4.1 Total assimilation of prefixes

Total assimilation occurs most frequently in borrowed words in which prefixes ending in consonants are attached to roots beginning with a non-identical consonant. To highlight the transparency of the root, its initial consonant was probably pronounced with sufficient force to trigger regressive, or right-to-left assimilation. Among the frequently used morphemes subject to total assimilation are the prefixes *ad-*, *sub-*, *ob-*, *in-*, *con-*, *syn-*:

ad - "to, towards, against":

ad - cur-ate "care"	→accurate	ad - rive "shore"	→arrive
ad - firm	→affirm	ad - sent "feel, agree"	→assent
ad - grav- ate "heavy"	→aggravate	ad - tribute	→attribute

---

[3] The unassimilated form *enmesh* is also standard in all varieties of English.

A special case of total assimilation of the prefix *ad-* occurs before roots beginning with [st-, sp-, sk-]:

        ad - **sp**ir - ation "breathe"   →a∅**sp**iration
        ad - **st**ring - ent   →a∅**st**ringent
        ad - **s**cribe   →a∅**s**cribe

The total assimilation of the [d] to the initial consonant of the following morpheme in these words results in both phonetic and orthographic deletion. Only a consultation with the dictionary and some semantic reasoning can help us recognize the compositionality of items such as *aspiration, astringent, ascribe.*

The [-d] in the prefix *ad-* is extremely susceptible to total assimilation in front of other consonants. The **only** consonants to which it does not assimilate are the voiced [m, v, j]; in front of these consonants the prefix keeps its shape.

        ad - **v**enture "come, bring"   →a**dv**enture
        ad - **m**ixture   →a**dm**ixture
        ad - **j**ective   →a**dj**ective

The prefix *ad-* remains unchanged also if the morpheme following it begins with a vowel or [-h]. This pattern repeats itself: as noted in Chapter 5, vowels or initial [-h] frequently behave in the same way with regard to the operation of various phonetic rules.

        ad - **o**re "speak"   →a**do**re
        ad - **u**mbra "shadow" + ate   →a**du**mbrate
        ad - **h**ere "stick"   →a**dh**ere

The final consonant of the prefix *sub-* "down, under" undergoes total assimilation in more restricted environments: [-b] in *sub* is assimilated to [k, g, f, p, r, m]:

sub - **c**umb "lie"	→su**cc**umb	**sub** - **m**on "warn"	→su**mm**on
sub - **f**er "bear, bring"	→su**ff**er	**sub** - **p**ort	→su**pp**ort
sub - **g**est "carry"	→su**gg**est	**sub** - **r**og "ask"	→su**rr**ogate

Like *ad-*, the prefix *sub-* can lose its final consonant altogether before roots beginning with [sp-, st-, sk-]:

        sub - **sp**ect   →su∅**sp**ect
        sub - **st**enance →su∅**st**enance

More often, however, we will find the <b> in this suffix intact in that environment: *subscript, substance, substratum, subspecies, subspecific.*

The prefix *ob-* "to, towards" undergoes total assimilation only when followed by three voiceless consonants: [k, f, p], and sometimes when followed by [m] (when it undergoes orthographic loss as well):

ob - **c**ad-s-ion "fall"	→o**cc**asion
ob - **f**er "bring"	→o**ff**er
ob - **p**os "place, put"	→o**pp**ose
ob - **m**it "send, go"	→oØmit

We have already noticed that the prefixes *in-* (both with the meaning "in" and with the meaning "not"), *en-*, *con-*, and *syn-* undergo total labial assimilation when followed by the labial nasal [m-]. The consonant [n-] in *in-*, *con-*, *syn-* is also fully assimilated to the liquids [l, r]:

in - **l**eg-al "law"	→i**ll**egal
in - **r**eg- ular "rule"	→i**rr**egular
con - **l**egt "choose"	→co**ll**ect
con - **r**upt "broken"	→co**rr**upt
syn - **l**og "speak" -ism	→sy**ll**ogism

One peculiarity of the prefix *con-* is that while the [n] assimilates to some consonants in the following morpheme, it can also lose the [n] completely before vowels and <-h>. We will discuss this along with other cases of n-loss in Chapter 7.

4.2   Double consonant spellings

Total assimilation is a very old change whose traces can often be recovered from a word's orthography. In such instances the spelling preserves the slot for the assimilated sound, so that there is a **double consonant letter** at the point of contact between the two morphemes: the word *assimilation* parsed above is an example of total assimilation with the input consonant position reflected in the orthography.

There is an important difference between doubling consonants in the spelling and pronouncing double consonants. English is a language which does not make use of long consonants in pronunciation, except very marginally. Words like *furry* and *fury*, *masses* and *races*, *sappy* and *soapy*, have identical middle consonant sounds. Occasionally, we get doubling of the consonants at the morpheme juncture in compounds and syntactic phrases: e.g. *pen-knife*, *unnamed*, *big garden*, *midday*. Although the sequence of identical consonants is pronounced with only one onset and one release, the actual duration of these "long" consonants may be as long as that of a cluster of two separate consonants. The extra length is useful because it identifies the boundary between the morphemes, which is immediately clear to any speaker of the language. This is not automatically true for words of classical origin whose components are not part of every speaker's basic knowledge of English. In spite of the spelling <-ss-> in *assimilation*, the pronunciation is as though it were spelled with a single <s> as in *aside*. The added knowledge from this chapter is that *<-ss->* *does* signal what the etymological composition of the word is. Total assimilation is therefore a two-step process:

(1)   the input consonant becomes identical with the contact consonant – the stage reflected by the spelling of the word, and

(2)   the "double" consonant is shortened phonetically to a single consonant. Step (2) involves the loss/deletion of the totally assimilated sound from the phonetic structure of the word.

5   Other replacement rules

Another set of morphological changes affects the sounds of morphemes without the clear and overt signals of labial and total assimilation. Some of these changes occur on consonants, some only on vowels. One of these processes, the process of T-Lenition, is extremely common, even though it takes place only when the input consonant is adjacent to a small number of affixes. In this change, a stopped consonant, [p t k b d g], becomes a fricative, [s, z, š, ž]. This process is called **lenition**, or weakening.[4] Stops have more pronounced consonantal properties; they are viewed by phoneticians as being "stronger" than consonants in which the airstream is modified in some way without actually being stopped. Consonants produced without complete blockage of the air stream are called "continuants"; this group includes all the fricatives, the lateral [l], the retroflex [r], and the glides [w, y]. Since stop consonants require slightly more effort to produce than continuants, and the manner of articulation of continuants is closer to that of vowels, lenition is yet another instance of the principle:

Prefer the easier articulation.

The following two sections discuss lenition of the stops [t] and [d] before vowels; in both instances the stops are replaced by sounds whose consonantal properties are weaker.

5.1   T-Lenition

> t + {-y, -e, -is, -ia} (vocalic suffixes)
> ↓
> s

T-Lenition affects both roots and suffixes ending in [-t] and followed by the suffixes *-y*, *-e*, *-is*, "abstract noun," and *-ia* "condition."

---

[4] The term is derived from the Latin adjective *lenis* meaning "soft, mild."

Although all four suffixes causing T-Lenition begin with a front vowel, that is not a sufficient condition for the operation of the rule, since other suffixes beginning with a front vowel do not trigger the same change, e.g. *democratic, democratize, importer, active*. Nevertheless, it is correct to think of the "frontness" of the following vowel as a facilitating factor since when [-t] is followed by a suffix beginning with a back vowel the rule never applies: cf. *important, auditorium*, etc. We will see below that the correlation of the lenition with the feature "frontness" continues to be important after the initial change of [t] to [s], producing additional changes due to the principle of ease.

5.1.1   T-Lenition and spelling

T-Lenition may or may not be recognizable in the spelling. The [s] sound which is the immediate result from this change is spelled both <s> and <c>; it can also remain unchanged, thus:

$$
<\text{-t-}> + \{\text{-y, -e, -is, -ia}\}
\begin{cases}
<\text{s}> & \text{stat "stay"} + \text{is} \longrightarrow \text{stasis} \\
<\text{c}> & \text{grat "kind"} + \text{e} \longrightarrow \text{grace} \\
<\text{i}> & \text{dict "speak"} + \text{ion} \longrightarrow \text{diction}
\end{cases}
$$

Unfortunately, there are no rules which can predict which of these letters will appear in the spelling of a particular form – it is a matter of orthographic conventions which started four centuries ago. Further examples of T-Lenition manifested in different spellings are:

eu "good" + than at + **i**	→ euthanasia	in + port + ant + **e**	→ importance
gen + et + **is**	→ genesis	milit + **ia**	→ militia
demo + crat + **y**	→ democracy	in + tuit "watch" + ion	→ intuition

5.1.2   T-Lenition, palatalization, and affrication

Historically, the [s] resulting from T-Lenition can undergo a second change called **palatalization**. This is an assimilation process which changes the alveolar consonant [s] to [š] or [ž] when the next morpheme begins with the palatal glide [y]. The appearance of the voiced palatal fricative [ž], probably through an intermediate [z] stage, is restricted to post-stress environments (immediately following a stressed syllable). Thus, *euthanasia* has palatalization but *genesis* does not. The change shows up only in the pronunciation; the spelling remains <s>, <c>, or <t> as in other instances of T-Lenition.

In front of <-ure> [t] palatalization often goes a step further and produces the **affricate** [č]:

```
t- + -u(r)e [-yu(r)]
↓
č
```

This change, which is not inherited from the classical languages, but occurred after the borrowing of these words into English, has an easy parallel in our speech. We produce affricates in casual pronunciation of word sequences like *You betcha, I wancha to do it*. Affrication is another instance of palatal assimilation. Though the trigger, the palatal [y], does not appear in the spelling, it is nevertheless the correct basis for understanding why the <-t> is pronounced [č] in *bet you, want you* and in such Romance words as *culture, literature, mature, nature, statue, virtue.* (The vowel spelled <ue> in Early Modern English words borrowed from French, as in *virtue*, was understood as [yu].) Affrication, too, is related to the presence of stress – historically the syllable in which the affrication occurred carried the main accent of the word (they were pronounced *literaTYUR, naTYUR*, etc.).

5.1.3   Summary of palatalization and affrication after T-Lenition

Four distinct changes can take place at the intersection of a morpheme ending in [-t] and a morpheme beginning with [i] or [y]. We can get simple lenition from [t] to [s], as in *secrecy, apostasy, genesis, importance.* In addition, within English, i.e. after the borrowing took place, we can get palatalization to [š] in addition to lenition, as in *patient, derivation, segregation, secretion, vacation, action;* or palatalization to [ž] as in *euthanasia, anesthesia.* Finally, we can get affrication to [č] as in *nature, literature.*

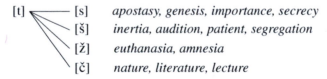

[t]   [s]   *apostasy, genesis, importance, secrecy*
       [š]   *inertia, audition, patient, segregation*
       [ž]   *euthanasia, amnesia*
       [č]   *nature, literature, lecture*

5.2   D-Lenition

A rule very much like T-Lenition turns the voiced alveolar stop [d] to [s] before the suffixes *-ive, -ion, -ile.*

> d + {-ive, -ion, -ile}
> ↓
> s

Like T-Lenition, D-Lenition can go through several stages. The simplest result is the one in the boxed rule: [d] changing to [s] as in:

pen**d** "consider" + ive → pensive

In words ending in *-ion* and other [y-] suffixes borrowed from French, the lenited output [s] can undergo further palatalization to [š], palatalization and voicing to [ž], or affrication to [-ǰ-]:

pend "pay" + ion   →pension [-š-]
ad + lud "play, touch lightly" + ion   →allusion [-ž-]
pend "hang" + ulum   →pendulum [-ǰ-]

When affrication to [ǰ] takes place (as in *module, verdure*), the rule of D-Lenition is not involved, properly speaking. Affrication does not occur before *-ive*, *-ion*, *-ile*; it requires a following [yu-], which causes affrication of both [t] and [d] (*nature, verdure*).

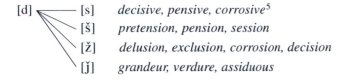

[d] ——— [s]   *decisive, pensive, corrosive*[5]

[š]   *pretension, pension, session*

[ž]   *delusion, exclusion, corrosion, decision*

[ǰ]   *grandeur, verdure, assiduous*

5.2.1   Summary: palatalization and affrication of dental stops

Simple lenition of the dental stops [t] and [d] before suffixes beginning with a front vowel produces [s]. Further, in the environment of [-i, -y], [s] can develop into the palatal fricatives [-š-] or [-ž-]. In the narrower environment of the glide [-y-], affrication rather than palatalization is the more common result, with [t] developing into the corresponding voiceless affricate [č], and [d] developing into the voiced affricate [ǰ].

PALATALIZATION   AFFRICATION

[-t-y-], [-d-y-]   [-t-y-], [-d-y-]

[-š-]   [-ž-]   [-č-]   [-ǰ-]

diction   *euthanasia*   *nature*   *verdure*

pension   *corrosion*   *statue*   *residue*

instruction *derision*   *spatula*   *module*

ratio   *vision*   *fortune*   *dune*

Some of the changes shown above are "young," historically speaking; they are not fully established in all words which contain the relevant phonetic sequences. There exist, therefore, alternative pronunciations, no doubt influenced by the spelling, as *amnesia* with [-z-], and not [-ž-], *habitual, fortune, literature* with [-ty-] and not [-č-], *grandeur, module* with [-dy-] and not [-ǰ-]. Although such pronunciations may appear to be more accurate representations of the spelling of the words, they violate the phonetic naturalness of the palatalized and affricated pronunciations, and can therefore sound pedantic and even affected.

---

[5] From *rod* – "gnaw," as in *rodent.*

5.3   v-Vocalization

The last consonantal replacement change is the most drastic one: it converts the voiced labio-dental spirant [v] into a vowel when another consonant, usually [t], follows it.

$$v + C$$
$$\downarrow$$
$$u$$

(Note that here the letter <v> is used in its normal alphabetical meaning, unlike capital V, which denotes any vowel sound.) Once again, ease of pronunciation is the principle involved in promoting this change. Combining [v] with other consonants produces clusters which are difficult to pronounce: [-vt-, -vf-, -vs-]. The remedy is to convert the voiced labio-dental spirant [v] into a vowel when another consonant, usually [t], follows it. The rule of v-Vocalization is restricted to six morphemes which are all of classical origin: *av* "bird," *ev* "good," *nav* "sail, boat," *salv* "safe, healthy," *solv* "loosen, unbind," and *volv* "turn, roll."

astro - nav - **t**	→ astron**au**t, but na**v**y, na**v**igate
a**v** - spic- ious	→ a**u**spicious, but a**v**iator, a**v**iary
con - vol**v** - **tion**	→ convol**u**tion, but revol**v**e, invol**v**e
e**v** - **ph**on - ic	→ e**u**phonic, but e**v**angelical
sal**v** - **te**	→ sal**u**te, but sal**v**ation, sal**v**age
sol**v** - **tion**	→ sol**u**tion, but resol**v**e, sol**v**ent

There are some interesting possibilities for multiple replacements within this small group of roots. If the [-v] of the root is followed by a [-t], then the derived word may show more than one change, e.g. *salute*, with the [t] preserved, but *solution, convolution, revolution*, showing T-Lenition and palatalization. One set of words, namely *nausea, nauseous, nauseate* show both v-Vocalization and a variety of options for T-Lenition: [s], [š], [z], and [ž].

6   Vowel replacements

Our final set of replacement rules covers changes of the vowels <a> and <e> when the morphemes containing them appear in the second syllable or later, never in the first syllable. These vocalic changes are also instances of lenition or weakening. The phenomenon of vowel lenition should be distinguished from **vowel reduction**, which turns vowels in unstressed positions to the neutral vowel schwa [ə]. Vowel lenition here is the progressive raising, or closing of the affected vowel. Everything else being equal, low vowels have greater sonority than high vowels; the lowest vowels are also the strongest, therefore the replacement of a lower vowel by a higher one can be described as a weakening of the sonority of the vowel.

6.1 A-Lenition

The first type of lenition affects the vowel spelled <a> if it appears anywhere but in the first syllable:

The boxed rule represents the change and the condition for it by the convention that "$" means "any syllable." By that convention, the <a> in the formula has at least one syllable to its left. If <a> were in the first syllable, it would not change. Examples:

art	→**art**istic	→in**ert** "without skill"
cand "shining white"	→**cand**id, **cand**idate[6]	→in**cend**iary
cap "seize"	→**cap**tive	→de**cep**tive
fac "make, put"	→**fac**t	→in**fec**t "put in"

This rule is very useful in explaining the morphological link between cognates. It is not an exceptionless rule, but, fortunately, the exceptions are words in which the original form of the root has been preserved intact; therefore the morphological relatedness between a root and its derivatives is transparent. Thus, the roots √fac in *manufacture*, or √cap in *recapture* are easy to recognize although the words are technically exceptions to A-Lenition.

6.2 E-Lenition

A second rule of vowel lenition changes <e> to <i>, hence the name E-lenition. In this instance, too, lenition is manifested as a raising of the vowel, from mid to high. This change is more complex than A-Lenition because there are more conditions on its application:

---

[6] In ancient Rome candidates for official posts wore white togas.

The formula should be read as follows: <e> becomes <i> if:

(1)   the morpheme ends in a single consonant,
(2)   it is not in the first syllable of the word, and
(3)   it is followed by a vowel.

Here are some examples of E-lenition:

leg "choose"	→**leg**ion	→di**lig**ent
sed "sit"	→**sed**iment	→pre**sid**ent
spec "look, see"	→**spec**tacle	→con**spic**uous

As in the case of A-lenition above, E-lenition is not exceptionless. It does not affect morphemes ending in [r, l, m, n]: √dem "people" remains unchanged in *endemic*, √del "erase" is unchanged in *indelible*, √her "stick" is the same in *inherent*. Here too, "no change" means preservation of transparency, easy recognition of the root in its derivatives.

6.3   Multiple lenition

Multiple lenition is not a rule; it is the application of A-lenition first, then E-lenition. Note that the intermediate stage, A-lenition, need not be represented by a surviving vocabulary item. However, since <a> cannot change directly to <i>, an <i> output has to be the result of unrecorded A-lenition:

ROOT	A-LENITION	E-LENITION
agent	vari**eg**ate	intrans**ig**ent
capture	rec**ep**tive	in**cip**ient
habitation	→	in**hib**it
de**cad**ent	→	in**cid**ent
fact	de**fect**	de**fic**ient

7   Backness assimilation

Backness assimilation applies only to a small number of morphemes, all of them highly productive and common roots. It involves the following change:

$$\{^0e\}\ 1 + C$$
$$\downarrow$$
$$ul$$

The formula reads: the sequence <el> or <ol> changes to <ul> whenever [l-] is followed by another consonant. Here is how this works:

cel "cover"	→cellar	→occult
col "live, grow"	→colony	→culture
mel "strong, great"	→ameliorate	→multitude
pel "thrust"	→propel	→propulsion
sel "jump"	——	→exult

The reasons for backness assimilation are not entirely clear. One possible factor for the preference for <u> could be sought in the combination of [l] + consonant, in which the [l] is "dark," a "backness" property, perceived as something close to [u], to which the preceding vowels are assimilated. Our pronunciation of words like *folk*, *old*, *help*, *silk*, in which the <1> of the spelling is closer to the vowel [u] than to the consonant [l] in *lip*, *last*, provides a phonetic parallel of the trigger of backness assimilation.

7 Deletion rules and other kinds of allomorphy

This chapter turns to deletion rules, as well as other kinds of allomorphy, some of which can be recovered only historically. The first set of changes to be considered produces allomorphic variation due to the dropping of one or more phonemes from the edges of the original forms of roots or affixes. Like replacement rules, deletion rules must be defined in terms of both the phonological environment and the type, position, and number of morphemes involved in the change.

1 Consonant deletion

No double consonants. The general principle which governs the simplification of double consonants to single ones, phonetically, is that English, unlike Italian, Finnish, and many other languages, does not allow "long" or "double" consonants within a word. Our discussion of double consonant spelling in section 4.2, Chapter 6, pointed out the important distinction between double consonants in the spelling, which can arise as a consequence of total assimilation, and "long" consonants in the pronunciation. Word-internal double consonant letters are not pronounced "long": *irrational* and *eradicate* have the same [r], *symmetry* and *cemetery* have the same [m].

English allows real long, or geminate, consonants, only at clear morpheme/word boundaries: *file log, roommate, bus-schedule, bookcase, letter writer*, etc. In such instances longer duration is a phonetic phenomenon only; it is unrelated to spelling. Nevertheless, there is a parallel between real long consonants and the double letters resulting from the total assimilations of Chapter 6: both are signals of morpheme boundaries. The spelling of *accurate, affirm, arrive* indicates the historical point of contact between morphemes which have now merged. A geminate consonant at the left edge of a morpheme is also a boundary signal: thus for example, the "long" consonant [s-s] marks the difference between *pass south*, and *pass out*, with a single [s].

Affixes which act like words. Most cases of genuine geminate consonants occur at the juncture of two root morphemes: *car race, room-*

mate, hip pain. Some affixes, however, namely the affixes *-ful, -less, –ness, counter-, dis-, inter-, mis-, -un-* etc., can show a strong degree of morpheme identity which preserves the phonetic gemination in *shelfful, soulless, sternness, counterrevolution, dissatisfy, interracial, misstate, unnamed.* With respect to gemination, these affixes are often treated as if they were independent roots. (Consonant gemination with affixes is not obligatory, however: *disseminate, dissent, interrogative, interrupt,* etc., are pronounced with single consonants.) On the other hand, the boundaries in common compounds such as *home made, bus stop, Van Nuys, grand daughter* may be sufficiently fuzzy to justify pronunciation with a single [m], [s], [n], [d], respectively. The realization of the geminate consonant depends also on the rate of speech: in slow and careful speech we are likely to prolong the [s] in *bus stop*, while the geminate will be simplified in fast and casual speech

1.1   S-Degemination

Naturalness. The simplification of consonant clusters across morpheme boundaries is a frequent and natural phenomenon. The process of S-Degemination drops one of two [s] sounds at the juncture between the prefix *ex-* "out of, from, off" and a morpheme beginning with [s-]:

Orthographically:	<ex-+s>	→<ex->
Phonetically:	[eks+s-]	→[eks-]

```
┌─────────────┐
│  eks + [s]  │
│      ↓      │
│      Ø      │
└─────────────┘
```

S-Degemination

ex	+	spir "breathe"	→	*expire*
	(cf. in + spir → *inspire*)			
ex	+	sequ "follow"	→	*exequies* "funeral rites"
	(cf. con + sequ, as in consequence, consecutive)			
ex	+	sta "stand" + nt	→	*extant*
	(cf. ob + sta, as in *obstacle*)			
ex	+	cep "take, contain" + t	→	*except*
	(cf. in + cep, as in *inception*)			

Note that the last example does not have an orthographic <-s> in the second morpheme, *cep*, yet the principle of dropping the redundant consonant remains the same. This is also true of words such as *excess* < *ex* + ced "go," *excel* < *ex* + cel "rise," *eccentric* < *ex* + center + ic (note the spelling change accompanying S-Degemination in this case).

In some historical instances of S-Degemination, the resulting single [s-] may get voiced to [z] as in:

ex	+	sample	→	*example*
ex	+	sequ "follow out" + te	→	*executive*
ex	+	sud "sweat" + e	→	*exude*

It is not just the [s] that gets voiced in these words: the whole sequence [-ks-] is voiced to [-gz-]. Often, the motivation for the voicing is the absence of stress in the first syllable which weakens, or "lenites" the strongly consonantal voiceless [k] in [eks-] to [g], which then spreads its voicing forward to the following [s]. The pattern is familiar from the pronunciation of pairs such as *Alex*, with [-ks], but *Alexander*, with [-gz]. Voicing of [-ks-] to [-gz-] is restricted to cases in which the cluster is to the left of a vowel or a silent <h->, as in *exaggerate, exaltation, exhaust, exhibit*.

1.1.1 Spelling exceptions

S-Degemination was an active process in classical Latin. Later Latinate words, words which came into English through Neo-Latin, however, may appear to violate the rule. Words in which S-Degemination occurs in the pronunciation, but does not affect the original spelling of the second morphemes, can be regarded as "spelling" exceptions:[1] *exsanguine*(1661), *exscind*, (1662), *exscribe* (1607), *exsert* (1665) (also *exert*), *exsiccate* (1545), *exstipulate* (1793), *exsudation* (1646) (side by side with *exudation*). These are all rare and specialized words, and keeping the original spelling of the second morpheme in them is clearly an attempt to safeguard the transparency of the two parts of the learned formation. Normally, they would be pronounced with a single [s], though some of them, e.g. *exsanguinate, exsolve, exstipulate* allow the same "long" [s] at the morpheme boundary that exists in *mass suicide, crass sound, less salt*. The geminate calls attention to the morphemic composition of such words; the independent status of *ex-* remains transparent to the speakers who choose to use that pronunciation.

1.1.2 Exceptions to S-Degemination

S-Degemination does not apply when the morpheme *ex-* means "a person out of a formerly held position or office" – a medieval Latin specialization of the original spatial meaning of *ex-*. Originally, the prefix *ex-* in the meaning of "former" was attached only to borrowed roots, but towards the end of the eighteenth century, it became a

---

[1] The list is based on the entries in *Webster's Third New International Dictionary*, Springfield MA, 1961 unabridged. The dates are based on the *OED*, 2nd edition.

productive element within English: *ex-wife*, *ex-mate*, *ex-lord*. Orthographically the *ex-* in this meaning is distinguished by a hyphen between the *ex-* and the second root, and it leaves intact the phonetic shape of the second root, irrespective of the phonetic environment: *ex-convict*, *ex-president*, *ex-husband*, *ex-actress*, *ex-senator*, *ex-service*, *ex-spouse*. In these words, *ex* has a status closer to that of a free root than to a prefix, it is an ex-prefix. Since the nineteenth century, *ex* has been used as an independent noun, usually with reference to an ex-spouse, though it may be used for any person or persons who formerly held some contextually defined position or rank.

The morpheme *ex-* triggers the S-Degemination rule only when it is used as a prefix and attached directly to a root to produce a derivative in which the prefix-root boundary is obscured. *Ex* does not participate in S-Degemination when it is a preposition in borrowed phrases, or phrases coined on the Latin model, such as *ex officio* "by virtue of the office," *ex warehouse* "sold directly." Its status as an independent word is in accord with the geminate consonants in *ex silentio* "from silence, from absence of evidence," as well as in the phrases of mixed etymological origin *ex ship*, *ex store*.

Having learned about S-Degemination, one might be tempted to look for it in *any ex-* initial forms. To avoid overgeneralizations, one should establish the exact form of the root. By definition, the rule is triggered only by s-initial roots, and *degemination* implies the historical adjacency of two [s] sounds. Latinate words such as *expedite*, *exculpate*, *explicate*, *exquisite*, *extemporize* preserve the original forms of the adjacent morphemes, and though they may look like *expire*, *except*, their histories are different.

1.1.3   Other affixes in -s

The principle of S-Degemination extends to two other affixes which end in [-s]: *dis-* and *trans-*. As with the prefix *ex-*, when they are combined with s-initial morphemes, the resulting "long" [s] is simplified. A blurring of the semantic morpheme boundaries can also occur in some cases, e.g. *disperse* (dis + sperse), *dispirited* (dis + spirit + ed), *distant* (dis + sta + nt), *distinct* (dis + sting + t). In these examples the rule is carried to its completion, both in spelling and in pronunciation. More frequently, however, our conservative spelling still preserves the clue to the composition of such prefixed words, as in:

dis + **cern** "separate, decide"	→ *discern*
dis + **cip** (< **cap** "take") + le	→ *disciple*
dis + **ser** "join" + t-at-ion	→ *dissertation*
dis + **sid** (< **sed** "sit") + ent	→ *dissident*
dis + **son** "sound" + ant	→ *dissonant*

In these examples the etymological trace of the two [s]'s in contact is only orthographic, not phonetic or semantic; *discern, dissertation*, etc. are pronounced with only one [-s-]. When the meaning of the prefix *dis-* is recognizably negative, meaning "reversal," the geminate [-ss-] is still pronounced in American English: *dissatisfy, disservice, dissimilar*. The fuzziness of the morpheme boundaries may result in optional phonetic gemination: words such as *dissemble, dissociate* can be pronounced either way. Also, the prefix *dis-* displays a strong tendency to drop the [-s] when it abuts voiced consonants: [g, v, l, r, m]. Examples of this change are *digest* (dis+ger+t), *digress* (dis+grad+s), *diverge* (dis+verge), *dimension* (dis+mens "measured" +ion). Occasionally, the [s] of *dis-* will be voiced to [z] under the influence of a following voiced sound: dis+aster "star" →*disaster*, dis+ease →*disease*, dis+dain (deign) →disdain (British), all with [z]. Finally, the spellings *dissyllable*, and even *trissyllable*, were adopted from French where an unetymological second *-s* was added to the numeral prefixes. These spellings were frequent from the sixteenth century onwards, but are now only a historical curiosity.

The prefix **trans-** also triggers S-Degemination:

trans+scend (< scand. "climb")	→ *transcend*
trans+scribe "write"	→ *transcribe*
trans+sect "cut"	→ *transect*
trans+sept (< L. septum "enclosure")	→ *transept*
trans+spir "breathe" +e	→ *transpire*

Recent coinages such as *trans-sexual* (first recorded 1953), or freely coined derivatives such as *Trans-Siberian, Trans-Silesian* (as in the railway lines), are pronounced with geminate consonants. The fate of some words is still undecided: The *Random House Webster's Collegiate Dictionary*, 1991, records both *trans-sonic* and *transonic, transship* and *tranship*. Notice also that in pronunciation most words with the prefix *trans-* allow its [-s] to change to the alveolar [-t] instead of degemination, so that we pronounce it as if it was spelled <tran(t)->: [træn(t)sɛpt], [træn(t)spɑir], etc.

As in the application of all other rules, overanalysis is a danger: while *transpire* undergoes S-Degemination, a potential false cognate *transparent* (trans+par "show" +ent), does not. Familiarity with the words' etymology, or a consultation with a good dictionary, will reveal that *disperse, distant* have undergone S-Degemination, while *display, distort* preserve the original consonants at the juncture of the two morphemes.

1.2   X-drop

More simplification. S-Degemination simplifies the phonetic sequence [ks-+-s] to [ks], i.e. a potential "double-s" [ss] surfaces as a single [s]. Yet another process which can affect the phonetic [-ks] sequence of the prefix *ex-* is X-drop, the complete disappearance of both consonants from the prefix *ex-* when it means "out, out of."

Unlike S-Degemination, which affects also *dis-* and *trans-*, X-drop is restricted to a single morpheme. When *ex-*, phonetically [eks-], is attached to a morpheme starting with a voiced consonant, the cluster [ks] is simply deleted. In the previous section we mentioned instances in which *dis-* can drop the [-s] when it precedes the voiced consonants: [g, v, l, r, m], as in *digest, digress, diverge* etc. A similar phenomenon, only more pervasive, applies to *ex-*. Both the dropping of the [s-] in *dis-* and X-drop are a consequence of what is called a **phonotactic** constraint. A phonotactic constraint prohibits the arrangement of certain sounds in sequence: a cluster of a voiceless stop followed by a voiceless fricative followed by a voiced consonant is not a possible word-internal sound sequence in English. In other words, the language disallows *-ksǰ-*, *-ksr-*, *ksl*, *-ksg-*, etc. morpheme-internally (but not across word boundaries: *likes jam, lacks rigor, packs luggage, tax goals*, etc. are all okay).

> Orthographically: **ex-** + voiced consonant   →<e->
> Phonetically: [eks] + voiced consonant   →[ɛ-] ([ɪ-] or [i] if the prefix is unstressed)

Here is how X-drop works:

> [e<u>ks</u>-] + [+ CONS, +VOI]
> ↓
> [Ø]

X-drop

ex + bull "boil" + ient	→ eØbullient	ex + lev "light" + ate	→ eØlevate
ex + duc "lead" + e	→ eØduce	ex + merge "dip"	→ eØmerge
ex + ges "carry" + t	→ eØgest	ex + ras "scrape" + e	→ eØrase
ex + jac "throw" + t	→ eØject	ex + vapor + ate	→ eØvaporate

The formulation of X-drop implies that if the prefix *ex-* precedes a morpheme starting with a voiceless consonant (other than [-s] or [f], see below), or a vowel, it will be preserved. This indeed is the case; see *exhale, extol, expose, excursion, exit, exonerate* etc. In this meaning of the prefix *ex-* too, in words in which the voiceless consonants [(k)s] precede a stressed syllable, voicing is likely to occur. Thus, with stressed roots which begin with a vowel (or *h*), we notice voicing of the [-ks] of the prefix to [-gz]: *exacerbate, exact, exaggerate, exalt, exhaust, exhibit, exhort, exist, exuberance, exude, exultation.* However, if the *ex-* is stressed, the cluster [-ks] may or may not be voiced: *exercise, exile, exit, exodus.* With some words in this group both [ks] and [gz] are acceptable: *exhume, exile, existential, exit*, etc.

1.2.1   Exceptions to X-drop

Like S-Degemination, X-drop is blocked when the morpheme *ex* preserves its status as an independent word, a preposition, as in the Latinate phrases *ex gratia*, *ex libris*, *ex nihilo*.

When it is attached to a root beginning with [f-], X-drop proceeds in a manner identical to the rule described above, namely the cluster [ks-] is dropped. Not surprisingly, the sequence *[-ksf-] is avoided within the word: English has a phonotactic constraint prohibiting three voiceless consonants in a row word-internally. However, in front of [f] the rule of X-drop looks different because in spelling, it leaves a trace – a doubling of the initial <f> letter of the root: *efface*, *effect*, *effeminate*, *effigy*, *effort*, *effusive*, etc.

1.3   N-drop

Limitations. The rule of N-drop applies only to the *-n* of the negative morpheme *an-* "not, without, less" and to the English indefinite article *an* (originally meaning "one" in Old English). The rule deletes the *-n* when the following morpheme (or word, in the case of the indefinite article) begins with a consonant. For both the negative morpheme and the indefinite article the rule operates without exceptions, so much so that in the case of the negative *an-*, the variant *a-* before consonants is described by the *OED* as a "living prefix of negation" in its own right.

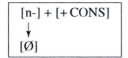

[n-] + [+CONS]
↓
[Ø]

N-drop

an +	**ch**romat "color" + ic	→ a∅chromatic
an +	**m**or "manner, custom" + al	→ a∅moral
an +	**gn**os "know" + tic	→ a∅gnostic
an +	**ph**a "speak" + sia	→ a∅phasia
an +	**p**ath "feeling" + y	→ a∅pathy
an +	**th**eo "god" + ism	→ a∅theism

Phrasal scope of N-drop. Unlike the other changes surveyed here, N-drop does not occur only at morpheme edges in derivational processes, that is, within the confines of a single word. The dropping of *-n* in the indefinite article applies within a whole noun phrase. When a noun or its modifier is preceded by an indefinite article, the article carries no stress and is prosodically attached to the following word. The linguistic term for the unstressed satellite of a stressed host word is *clitic* (the morpheme *clit* means "lean," "depend on"). Clitic and host together form a clitic group; a noun phrase containing an indefinite article contains by definition at least one clitic group. The noun phrase *a sore point* contains the clitic group *a sore* and it is within this group that the deletion takes place. Today, most speakers take the English indefinite article to be *a*, though the original historical form of this word is *an*. As with the *a-* of the negative *an-*, the allomorph *a* of the indefinite article is now considered an independent living form. Were it not for its history and the parallel between the two morphemes, we could consider the *an* form of the article as a synchronic variant of *a*, in which the consonant *-n* is inserted before vowels.

1.3.1   Pronunciation and boundaries

When the *-n* of the negative morpheme is deleted, the remaining vowel can be fully unstressed, pronounced like the indefinite article *a*, [ə] (schwa): *aphasia, amorphous* etc. When the prefix is stressed, or when we want to emphasize the article *a*, the vowel remains the unreduced full vowel, [e] (the vowel of *late, they*): *asymmetry, atheist, apolitical*, or "*Give me a* [e] *coin, not the contents of your pocket*." In some rare instances, e.g. *apathy*, the vowel is stressed and therefore not reduced to schwa, but it surfaces as the lower front vowel [æ].

The prefix *an-* remains unchanged before a vowel or *h-*:

an "not"	+	esth "perceive" et + ic	→ anesthetic
an	+	alg "pain" + es + ic	→ analgesic
an	+	hem "blood" + ic	→ anemic (with drop of initial h-)
an	+	hydr "water" + ous	→ anhydrous
an	+	onym "name" + ous	→ anonymous

The preservation of [-n] in the indefinite article before <h->-initial words is subject to some variation and speaker uncertainty. This is due to the historic instability of initial [h-] in words borrowed from the Romance languages. In late Latin and in Old French the [h-] sound was lost in the pronunciation of words such as *able* (compare to *habilitation*), *(h)istory, (h)erb, (h)onor*. The letter <h-> was frequently preserved, however, and under the influence of spelling and the model of native words such as *house, horse* which kept their first consonant, the [h-] was reinstated in many Romance loanwords in late Middle and Early Modern English. This accounts for the variant pronunciations of *herb, humor*, and for the allomorphy in pairs like *able–rehabilitation, heir–heritage, hour–horoscope, odometer–hodograph*. Therefore, for words borrowed from French (and ultimately "Classical"), the drop of *-n* before *h-* is not fully established yet. It is acceptable standard English to say both *a historic event*, and *an historic event*, though the second choice sounds somewhat stilted and academic today, and is usually seen in writing, not heard in speech. For native words the rule of N-drop operates without exception even before [h-]: *a house, a horse, a hot day*.

One curiosity of N-drop is that it can reset the boundaries within a clitic group. Historically, when the numeral *an* began to lose [-n] before consonant-initial words, the largely illiterate speakers of the language had to make difficult decisions about the word boundaries in some clitic groups. The problem must have been similar to the problem we have in interpreting *an aim* vs. *a name, an ice cube* vs. *a nice cube* without reference to spelling or a larger context. Consequently, the boundaries within some such groups were misinterpreted: the Old English article–noun groups *a(n) napron, a(n) nadder* became *an apron, an adder.* Conversely, *an ewt* and *an eke name* "substitute name," became *a newt, a nickname.* Such resetting of boundaries gives rise to popular jokes: "Be *alert*: your country needs *lerts!*"

Finally, we should be careful not to overidentify N-drop. The prefix: *an-* "not, without, less" should not be confused with *ana-* "back, again" as in *anachronism* ("back in time"), *anapest* ("reverse, turned backward,") referring to the fact that an anapest (*de-de*-DUM) is a reversed dactyl (*DUM-de-de*), as in *Cantonese* vs. *Italy.* Nor should the negative allomorph *a-* (after N-drop) be confused with words containing initial morphemes which accidentally begin in *a-*: *apo-, ad-, ab-, ag-* – thus *agent* is not someone who does not belong to the *gentility*, nor is *account* the reverse of *count*.

1.3.2   N-drop in other prefixes

While the more general rule of N-drop before consonants affects only the two morphemes *an*, N-drop across morpheme boundaries affects also two other prefixes: *con-* and *syn-*. Unfortunately, the conditions for the loss of the [-n] in these prefixes are different from the conditions for N-drop in *an*; they are also different from one another.

The prefix *con-* loses its [n] if the following morpheme is vowel-initial, or if it begins with [h-]:

$$[\text{n-}] + \{\,\text{V}\ldots,\ \text{h}\ldots\}$$
$$\downarrow$$
$$[\varnothing]$$

N-drop in *con-*

con + ag "drive, do" + ulate	→ co∅agulate
con + erc < arc "keep in" + e	→ co∅erce
con + it "go" + ion	→ co∅ition
con + oper "work" + ate	→ co∅operate
con + habit "abide"	→ co∅habit
con + hort "enclosure"	→ co∅hort (> court)

In addition to dropping [-n] regularly before vowels and [h-], the prefix *con-* becomes *co-* before the root *gn* "birth, origin," as in *coØgnate*, or *gn* "know," as in *coØgnition*. Before the voiced labiodental fricative [v] the prefix behaves inconsistently: con + ven "come" produces *convent*, *convention*, but the [n] is deleted in *coØvenant* "agreement," *coØven* "an assembly, gathering (especially of witches)." The *CoØvent* of London's *Covent Garden* retained the pronunciation of the word *convent* until the seventeenth century.

Like the post-N-drop status of the negative *a-* and the indefinite article *a*, the allomorph *co-* has acquired independence and can now be freely attached to any roots or bases. A set of three cognate words: *consign* (1430), *coØsine* (1635), and *co-sign* (1900), illustrates the historical possibilities for the development of new meanings out of *con-* allomorphs. The N-drop variant *co-* is equally productive with borrowed and native roots: *co-owner*, *co-father*, *co-founder*, *co-driver*. Moreover, the *co-* can be prefixed to words beginning with *con-*: *co-conspirator*, *co-constituent*, *co-conscious*.

The situation with the prefix *syn-* is simpler. When not subject to labial assimilation, *syn-* surfaces intact: *synchronic*, *synergy*, *synthesis*. When it attaches to a morpheme which begins with [s] followed by another consonant, the [n-] is deleted:

> syn + **st** "stand" + (e)m   → syØstem
> syn + **st**ol "place, draw" + ic   → syØstolic

The deletion in these examples, as well as the deletion in the only combination in English (borrowed from Greek) of *syn* followed by [-z]: *syzygy* "conjunction" (syn + **z**yg "yoke"), results in the simplification of consonant clusters which might have been hard to pronounce, another manifestation of the principle of ease.

2   Vowel deletions

This section describes processes which delete a vowel from a morpheme when that morpheme becomes part of a new word.

2.1   V-drop in hiatus

Hiatus. The word "hiatus" is a Latin borrowing meaning "a gap, opening." As a linguistic term, hiatus refers to a kind of phonetic opening which occurs when two vowels are directly adjacent across a syllable boundary, with no consonant in between. It is important to distinguish between vowel letters that are written next to each other, but belong to the same syllable, and vowels which are adjacent, but belong to two different syllables. The words *coat*, *sea-lant*, *prai-rie* have no vowels in hiatus, while *co-act*, *Se-attle*, *na-ïve* do.

Words like *reality*, *naïve*, *embryo*, which contain vowels in hiatus, are fairly rare in English. Hiatus within words or within clitic groups is disfavored in English and indeed in many languages; various "hiatus-avoidance" mechanisms are developed to repair hiatus. One such mechanism is the deletion of a vowel when the second (unstressed) vowel of a disyllabic morpheme, is adjoined to a vowel-initial morpheme. We can call this **V-drop**. (Read "vowel-drop"; we continue the convention of using a capital letter V to mean "any vowel.")

$$\boxed{\begin{array}{l} \$\,v + \{V\ldots, h\ldots\} \\ \quad\downarrow \\ \quad \emptyset \end{array}}$$

V-drop

an + th**eo** "god" + ism	→ athe∅ism, but theosophy, theology
di**a** + orama "view"	→ di∅orama, but dialysis, diagram
ep**i** + en "in" + thesis "placing"	→ ep∅enthesis, but epigraph, epidermic
hom**o** "man" + **age** "office of"	→ hom∅age, but *Homo sapiens*
hom**o** "same" + **onym** "name"	→ hom∅onym, but homograph, homophone
hyp**o** "beneath" + **alg** "pain" + ia	→ hyp∅algia, but hypothesis, hypotoxic
met**a** "beyond" + **onym** "name" + y	→ met∅onymy, but metabolism, metaphor
par**a** "beside" + **en** "in" + thesis	→ par∅enthesis, but paralegal, parameter
tel**e** "far" + **ex** (change)	→ tel∅ex, but telegraph, telephone, telescope

As the examples show, V-drop deletes the first of two consecutive vowels at the morpheme boundary. It affects both roots and affixes. The change can be attributed to the preference for an alternation of vowel – consonant – vowel across syllable boundaries rather than a sequence of two syllabic vowels appearing back-to-back within a word.

2.1.1   Exceptions

V-drop is not an exceptionless change. The application of the rule before <h-> is inconsistent. The orthographic preservation of <h-> in Romance words often reinstated the [h-] in the pronunciation of these words in English, see 1.3.1. V-drop before orthographic <h-> occurs in words such as *method* < meta + **h**od "way," *ephemeral* < epi + **h**emer(a) "day" + al. Side by side with such forms, we find forms like *parhelion*, *telharmonium*, in which the V-drop rule applies and [h-] is preserved phonetically. Finally, a third type of forms: *epihyal, homohe-dral, telehydrobarometer, parahypnosis*, all of them recent scientific coinages, preserve the [h-] and resist V-drop. Many disyllabic mor-phemes, such as *anti-, poly-, semi-, neo-, macro-*, and *iso-*, resist V-drop altogether, as attested by words such as *antiemetic, antioxidant, polyan-drous, semiautomatic, neoembryonic, macroanalysis, isoelectronic, iso-octane*, etc.

Also, the V-drop rule covers only the unstressed vowels in disyllabic morphemes; monosyllabic morphemes ending in a vowel are not subject to vowel drop. Thus *de-, bi-, re-* will not change their form, even if the morpheme attached to them begins with a vowel or h-: *deodorize, dehydrate, reinstate, rehabilitate, biennial*. Sometimes, however, V-drop applies to the prefix *con-*, after N-drop has created hiatus conditions across a morpheme boundary:

INPUT	N-DROP	V-DROP
con + ag "drive" + ent	→ co + ag + ent	→ cogent
con + ag(it) "put in motion" + ate	→ co + agit + ate	→ cogitate
con + hort "enclosure, yard"	→ co + (h)ort	→ court

Finally, it should be noted that V-drop within a clitic group is a change which accounts for the history of some Anglo-Saxon words, thus *no + one > none*, *do + off > doff*, and *do + on > don*. Hiatus avoidance accounts also for the contractions such as *she's, we're, I'm, we've*.

2.2   Syllable syncopation

Syllables are the smallest free-standing pronounceable units. When you say a word as slowly as possible, or when you yell it, you can count the syllables in it. Usually, there is a vowel at the nucleus of every syllable. However, the retroflex sonorant [-r-] is very commonly also the nucleus of a syllable, as in the unstressed syllable of *water, meter, matter, feather*, etc. The lateral [l] and the nasals [m, n] behave simi-larly: *little, rhythm, button*. In the case of [-r-], our spelling usually rep-resents syllabicity with the letters <e> or <o> in front of the <-r>. When the [r] becomes non-syllabic, the loss of syllabicity is accompa-nied by dropping the vowel in the spelling. We can think of the rule, therefore, as "Syllable Syncopation."

Syncopation is defined as "contraction of a word by omission of one or more syllables or letters in the middle" (*OED*). Like V-drop, Syllable Syncopation requires that the morpheme (or stem) in which the omis-sion occurs be at least disyllabic. When we attach a derivational mor-pheme to a morpheme or stem whose non-initial syllable is <-er> or

<-or>, the unstressed vowel is lost from the pronunciation (and the spelling) of the word.

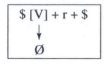

Syllable Syncopation

meter + ic	→ metØric	executor + ix	→ executØrix
cylinder + ical	→ cylindØrical	aviator + ix	→ aviatØrix
anger + y	→ angØry	actor + ess	→actØress
equi + liber + ium	→ equilibØrium	bisector + ix	→bisectØrix

However, syllable syncopation is not always reflected in the spelling. Consider the relaxed pronunciation of such words as *dangerous, federal, history, factory, natural, preferable.* The same type of syncopation in speech occurs with other syllabic consonants: consider the pronunciation of *bachelor, specialist, rhythmical, botany, scrivener.* The boldfaced unstressed vowels in these words are heard only in very slow and careful speech, probably only in citing the words in isolation, emphasizing them, or singing them so that each syllable corresponds to a separate note. Normally, however, the medial syllable in such words is not pronounced. The only difference between the spontaneous syncopation in speech today and the change occurring in historical derivational processes is that the historical syncopation of the sequence <-er-> and <-or> is reflected in the spelling, while other syncopations are not.

2.2.1   Preservation of <-er> and <-or>

Syllable Syncopation affects only unstressed syllables. Syncopation is blocked if the derivation of a new word involves shifting the stress onto the syllable containing [-r-], e.g.: *victórious, metaphórical, matérial, supérior, ultérior.* Also, even without stress shift, the need for transparency of the root or stem can prevent the operation of orthographic Syllable Syncopation: *sorceress, motorist, mastery, liberate,* although these words will lose the [r-] syllable optionally in speech. The presence of an adjacent unstressed syllable is also a factor: in *caliber -calibØrate* the dropping of the internal syllable is prosodically harmless, the syllable *-lib-* separates the two stressed syllables, whereas in words such as *liberate,* v. and *operate,* syncopation would result in stress clash. Fortunately, non-syncopation will not create parsing problems: if the rule does not apply, we parse the word directly from the surface form, not worrying about undoing the rule to get to the original morpheme.

3   Expansion rules: vowel or consonant epenthesis

A third group of rules in which recognizable phonetic factors cause predictable allomorphic variation are the *expansion* or *epenthesis* rules. Epenthesis (epi + en "in" + thesis "placing") is the technical term for inserting a sound between two other sounds. Both vowels and consonants can be inserted within an existing morpheme. Unlike deletions, epenthetic processes occur less often, affect a relatively small number of morphemes, and show numerous exceptions. In principle, however, they are similar to the deletion rules in that both types have parallels in the spoken language, and in both cases the changes are triggered by the avoidance of phonetically undesirable sound sequences.

3.1   U-Epenthesis

U-Epenthesis affects clusters made up of a velar stop ([g], [k]), or a bilabial stop ([b], [p]), plus the sonorant [l] where it is syllabic. When a morpheme ends in a syllabic [l] and is followed by a suffix beginning with a vowel, the cluster is broken up by the insertion of [yu], (spelled <u>), which turns the original sequence of consonants into a clearly defined syllable.

```
{- gl-,  -kl-,  -bl-,  -pl-} + V
   ↓      ↓      ↓      ↓
{-gul-   kul    bul    pul }
```

U-Epenthesis

single + ar	→ singular
particle + ar	→ particular
table + ate	→ tabulate
couple + a	→ copula

The final -e in words such as *single*, *particle*, *table*, *couple*, etc. merely indicates that the [l] is syllabic. In one exceptional case, namely the form *nucular (nuclear)*, the predictable, though not obligatory, U-Epenthesis has yet to achieve full respectability. U-Epenthesis occasionally appears in an environment not shown in our rule: *title*, but *titular*, *epistle* (pronounced with [-sl]), but *epistolary* – in the last word the epenthetic vowel is exceptional. The pronunciation [nyu.kyə.lr] is described by the 1992 *Random House Webster's College Dictionary* as "somewhat controversial . . . and disapproved of by many, although it occurs among such highly educated speakers as scientists, professors, and government officials." There is no rational basis for the disapproval: the new pronunciation is a normal analogical development based on the model of U-Epenthesis found elsewhere in English. Actual usage by the majority of speakers is the only coherent basis for choosing one pronunciation over another.

A parallel to this change can be found in the alternative forms of pronunciation of words such as *athlete*. A widespread pronunciation, sometimes considered non-standard, has a schwa inserted between the dental and the liquid, [-th(ə)l-]. A similar insertion of (parasitic) schwas can occur also between the sonorants in *film, firm*, etc. Not surprisingly, schwa insertion can be found in some varieties of American English in similar environments, i.e. before the syllabic sonorant [l] in a very wide range of environments:

ba**ffl**e	→baffling [f(ə)l-]	mu**ddl**e	→ muddling [d(ə)l-]
ba**ttl**e	→ battling [t(ə)l-]	o**gl**e	→ ogling [-g(ə)l-]
bede**vil**	→bedeviling [v(ə)l-]	to**ppl**e	→ toppling [p(ə)l-]
embe**zzl**e	→ embezzling [z(ə)l-]	tri**ckl**e	→ ticklish [k(ə)l-]
gar**bl**e	→garbling [b(ə)l-]	tu**ssl**e	→ tussling [s(ə)l-]

The rule of U-Epenthesis does not apply to all potentially eligible words. Some exceptions are: *cycle–cyclical*, *single–singly*, *simple–simplex*, *bible–bibliophile*, etc. Non-morpheme-final velar-labial consonant clusters do not undergo U-Epenthesis: *diglossia, inclination, medulloblastoma, implication.*

3.2   P-Epenthesis

This change has very limited scope, since it covers the avoidance of only one specific consonant cluster, *-mt-*, which is not particularly common. P-Epenthesis resembles the other allomorphy rules in that it is phonetically motivated and can therefore also be observed in the spoken language. The effect of the change is to ease the transition between the voiced bilabial [m] and the voiceless stop [t]. The epenthetic stop [p] shares the bilabial articulation with [m], the first segment in the cluster, and has the same manner of articulation and the same voicing value as the following [t].

P-Epenthesis

assu**m**e	→ assumption
tem-[2]	→ tempt
redee**m**	→ redemption

---

[2] **tem** is an unpredictable allomorph of **ten** "touch, try," as in *tentacle, tentative.*

A parallel phonetic change occurs in the pronunciation of some native English forms, though in such instances the spelling does not reflect the epenthetic [p]. English speakers find the cluster -*mt*- difficult, even if the -*m*- and the -*t*- belong to separate morphemes. The form *dreamt*, pronounced [drem(**p**)t] is unique; compare also *something*, often pronounced [səm(**p**)θɪŋ]. These examples mirror the historical process of P-Epenthesis in derivation, reflected in the spelling. A similar phonetic phenomenon is observed in English in the sequence *n* + *s* which is broken up by an epenthetic [-t-], so that *prince, tense, mince* sound the same as *prints, tents, mints*.

8 Fossilized allomorphy: false cognates and other etymological pitfalls

Unlike allomorphy resulting from phonetically motivated replacement, deletion, or epenthesis, the allomorphy discussed in this section cannot be attributed to the operation of an active and transparent phonetic rule. "Fossilized" allomorphs can be deceptively unlike each other in form, yet they are historically related – they *are* cognates. The morpheme variants in this group arose as a consequence of systematic changes in pre-Old English times, going all the way back to Proto-Germanic and even to Indo-European. Within English, i.e., after the fifth century, the conditions for these early changes became obscured, and their results can no longer be seen as regular or highly predictable. If we set up a scale of predictability for allomorphic variation, allomorphs due to assimilation or vowel weakening will rank very high; mostly, the conditions for these changes are transparent and recoverable. At the low end of the scale would be the non-productive allomorphic variation described in historical terms, for which the conditions have ceased to exist. At the bottom of the scale are completely unpredictable alternate forms of cognates, the subject of Section 5. Historical, or fossilized, allomorphy tends to follow several general patterns; familiarity with those can help us discern etymological cognates in spite of their overt differences.

Two such fossilized processes are *gradation* and *rhotacism*. Originally they affected root morphemes, and occurred regularly in conjunction with specific grammatical changes within a *paradigm*,[1] e.g., the present vs. the past-tense form of one and the same verb, the nominative vs. the genitive case of the same noun. Thus generated, the allomorphy then carried over into various derivative words, where the selection of one or another of the alternative phonetic forms of the root became largely accidental. Gradation and rhotacism could accompany the formation of a noun from an existing verb root or vice versa, or in general could

---

[1] *Paradigm*: a set of inflectional forms, a conjugation, or a declension. Unlike the simple paradigms of Modern English, verbs, nouns, and adjectives in Indo-European, Latin, Proto-Germanic, and Old English had rich paradigms with different forms for different grammatical functions and meanings.

mark off one word class from another. Only a small part of the rich gamut of grammatical alternations and word formation patterns of more than a millennium ago has come down to us, yet what remains is sufficiently coherent and interesting to make it worth understanding.

2   Gradation

Gradation, also known by its German name *Ablaut*, is a term characterizing the way in which the Indo-European vowels *e* and *o* once alternated with each other and with **zero** in different grammatical forms or word classes. Traditionally, the allomorph containing the vowel *e* is described as exhibiting the **e-grade**, the allomorph containing the vowel *o* shows the **o-grade**, and the allomorph with no vowel in it is labeled the **zero-grade**. Here are some examples of the alternations resulting from gradation:

Root	E-Grade	O-Grade	Zero-Grade
kel "hollow, cover"	**cel**lar	**col**or	**cl**andestine
gen "birth, origin"	**gen**etic	**gon**orrhea	co**gn**ate
men "think, warn"	de**men**ted	ad**mon**ish	**mn**emonic
pher "carry, bear"	Christo**pher**	eu**phor**ia	—
pel "skin, fell"	**pel**lagra[2]	—	sur**pl**ice
bol "throw, reach"	—	hyper**bol**e	para**bl**e

The horizontal arrangement of the *e-grade*, *o-grade*, or *zero-grade* is simply alphabetical; the *e-grade* which appears in most of the entries in the first column has no special status in our context, though some grammars may refer to it as "the normal" grade. In many instances of historical gradation only two of the three possible qualitative allomorphs have survived and are attested in our vocabulary. The gaps indicated by the dashed line in the last three rows in the chart are accidental. Other roots in which gradation is incompletely attested are: *cere, cre* "grow" (**cere**al, in**cre**ase), *gel, gl* "jelly, ice, solidify" (**gel**atin, **gl**acial), *leg, log* "gather, read, study" (**leg**al, apo**log**y), *mel, mol* "honey" (**mel**lifluous, **mol**asses), *men, mon* "lead, project, threaten" (**men**ace, **Mon**tana), etc.

Another type of frequent Indo-European gradation is *quantitative* gradation, where short vowels alternate with long or reduced vowels to produce paradigmatic and derivational allomorphs. An example of fossilized quantitative gradation in English is the paradigm of the verb *stand* with its past-tense form *stood*; such is also the historical relationship between *sit* and *soot*, *writ* and *write*.

---

[2] A disease marked by dermatitis, inflammation of the mucous membranes, gastro-intestinal and nervous system disorders.

2.1   Gradation in Germanic

The exact phonological and grammatical reasons for the existence of gradation are largely unknown. It is possible that the variation between *e* or *o* in the root is due to variation in the placement of the accent, while absence of stress correlates with the zero-grade. In the classical languages and in Germanic, gradation often signaled change from one word-class to another; it also regularly accompanied paradigmatic change. The major function of gradation within the Germanic languages was to mark person, number, and tense of a large class of verbs, traditionally referred to as *strong verbs*. Without familiarity with the phonetic changes from Indo-European to present-day English, through Germanic, Old, and Middle English, the original *e-*, *o-*, and *zero* grades of the verbal allomorphs are not recognizable today; we have come to label these verbs "irregular."[3]

Gradation in word derivation was also a common Germanic pattern which became less and less productive in English, but not in the other Germanic languages. Still, there are some fossils of this pattern in Modern English, as in the verb–noun pairs: *do–deed, sing–song, break–breach, bind–bond, bundle.* Historical phonetic processes have changed the initial vowel grades beyond recognition, though the semantic relationship between the members of these pairs is obvious to every speaker of English.

3   Rhotacism

Rhotacism is a philological term coined on the basis of the root *rho*, the Greek name of the letter and sound [r], Greek <ρ>. The term describes the change of the consonant [s] through its voiced counterpart [z] to [r] when paradigmatic alternations placed [s] between two vowels. Rhotacism is found both in words of classical origin and in Germanic words, though the conditions under which it applies are slightly different.

3.1   Rhotacism in Latin

In Latin rhotacism accompanied the addition of vowel-initial suffixes (*-is, -a, -um, -ere*) to words ending in a vowel followed by [-s],

---

[3] There are sixty-eight strong verbs in English, plus another thirteen which can be conjugated as both weak and strong (Baugh and Cable, *A History of the English Language*, 4th edn., 1993: 160). Strong verbs are, on the whole, frequently used verbs of native origin: *bite, choose, drive, eat, fight, fly, hang, lie, ride, run, see, write,* etc. Some verbs have alternative weak forms, though the strong forms are still used: *light, stave, thrive, wake.*

producing the sequence <-VsV->. Flanked by vowels, the consonant [-s-] was subject to weakening of its consonantal nature: first [-s-] was voiced to [-z-], and subsequently [-z-] developed into the sonorant [-r-]. The process accounts for the allomorphy in pairs such as *os* "mouth," gen. sg. *oris* "of the mouth"; *rus* "the country," gen. *ruris* "of the country"; *opus* "work," pl. *opera*; *ges* "bear, carry," verb *gerere* > *germ*, but *gesture* "bearing." Historically, the appearance of a rhotacized or an unrhotacized form was predictable: [-s-] changed to [-r-] in <-VsV- > sequences, otherwise the [-s] remained unchanged.

$$
\boxed{
\begin{array}{c}
V + [\text{-s-}] + V \\
\downarrow \\
[r]
\end{array}
}
$$

Rhotacism

flos "flower" + **al**	→ **floral** "of or relating to flowers"
flos + **cule**	→ **floscule** "little flower, floret"
ges "carry" + **t** + ure	→ **gesture** "mode of carrying, way of action"
ges + **und**	→ **gerund** "carried, verbal noun"
opus "work" + **cule**	→ **opuscule** "small work"
opus + ate	→ **operate** "work, produce"
os "mouth, speak" + ate + ion	→ **oration** "speech"
os + **cit** "move" + ant	→ **oscitant** "gaping," **oscitancy** "yawning"
rus "open land" + **al**	→ **rural** "of the country"
rus + **tic** + ate	→ **rusticate** "retire to the country"

In spite of the clearly defined conditions for the operation of rhotacism, some Latinate words appear to violate the above rule. Often an [-r-] or an [-s-] form will spread throughout the paradigm and will even be taken as the stem producing new words without further regard to the phonetic environment. Thus, we find an unchanged [-s-] allomorph between two vowels in the second words in pairs such as *adhere–adhesion*, *acquire–acquisition*. By the beginning of classical Latin, around 100 B.C., rhotacism was no longer an active process; analogy from the more frequently used forms of the root and historical accidents have subsequently produced almost as many "irregular" pairs as there are regular ones. In order to recognize etymologically related sets, special note should be taken of both the unrhotacized *and* the rhotacized forms of the roots.

Further complications may arise from unrelated allomorphy. The Indo-European form of the root "to know," *gn, gnos, gnor*, for example, preserves [-s-] predictably in *agnostic* and undergoes regular rhotacism in *ignorant*. However, derivatives such as *diagnosis, cognizant, gnosis, prognosis*, may contain -*gn*- rather than *gnos*. This cognate set points to a problem in the description and labeling of allomorphy. On the one hand, the [-s-] / [-r-] alternation of *agnostic* vs. *ignorant* is certainly "fossilized allomorphy." On the other, the *gn* – *gnos* allomorphy cannot be described in systematic terms at any historical period. Thus, in spite of the fact that a rule can be formulated to cover some of the cases, it is by no means as general as the rules we covered in the previous two chapters.

3.2   Rhotacism in Germanic

Voicing of [s] to [z] and a subsequent change to [r] in a vocalic environment could occur also in early Germanic, where there were additional prosodic conditions restricting the process. As with gradation, subsequent phonetic processes in English have eliminated, or greatly obscured, the results of Germanic rhotacism. Some pairs of cognate words which preserve traces of this ancient allomorphy are the past-tense forms of the verb *to be*: sg. *was* vs. pl. *were*, and the present tense and the adjectival participle of the verb *lose* – *(vor)lorn* (from earlier *(vor)loren*). The historical relationship between *rise* and *rear*, *sneeze* and *snore* can also be traced back to rhotacism, with some additional changes of the vowels.

4   Metathesis (transposition)

Metathesis (**meta** "change, beyond" + **the** "put" + **(s)is** "process") is a term describing the transposition of sounds, and sometimes syllables, in a word. Although metathesis occurs commonly in many languages, the phonetic conditions for it can be identified only in very general terms: certain sound combinations, often involving [r], are more susceptible to metathesis than others. Metathesis is the fossilized residue of a rather erratic alternation; we separate it from the fully "unpredictable" allomorphy in the next section because unlike full unpredictability, the allomorphs resulting from metathesis retain the same consonants, only reordered, or scrambled. Metathesis may have originated in slips of the tongue; evidence of the process is found both in borrowed classical roots and in native roots. Some frequently quoted examples of metathesis are:

[ks]	↔	[sk]:	mix – promiscuous
[pek]	↔	[kep]:	spectacle – skeptic
[ri]	↔	[er/ir]:	triad – ternary – third
[rt]	↔	[tr]:	nurture – nutrition

Sometimes metathesis combines with other processes and obscures otherwise transparent historical allomorphy. Thus the *e-* grade of the

Indo-European root (ə)gre(g) "to gather, flock" is recognizably related by gradation to the allomorph √(ə)gor only if we reverse the order of [-re-] to [-er-]:

Gradation:	*gregarious*	(ə)**ger**(g)	*agora*	(ə)**gor**
Metathesis:	*egregious*	(ə)**gre**(g)	*allegory*	—
	aggregate		*category*	

(Metathesis in pronunciation should not be confused with the alternative spellings for stem-final [(ə)r] written <-re> in British English vs. <-er> in American English as in *centre–center, metre–meter, theatre–theater.*) Finally, within the native vocabulary, Modern English dialect forms such as *apsen, waps, aks,* for *aspen, wasp, ask,* have their origin in an alternation which dates back to Old English: the Old English words were *æpse, wæpsa,* and *acsian.*

5   Obscure cognates: completely unpredictable allomorphy

Mastery of the rules of allomorphy still leaves a residue of obscure cognates. By "obscure" we do not mean words whose etymologies are "unknown" or "disputed" – those we can't even begin to discuss. By "obscure" we mean that the formal relationship between the allomorphs has become non-transparent, or that the semantic and logical link between the two allomorphs can no longer be reconstructed.

An example of phonetically obscure allomorphy comes from a small number of roots of classical origin: *spec, plec, fac, neg, lig.* They undergo simultaneous deletion of the vowel **and** the following velar consonant [k, g], when followed by the verb-forming suffix *-y.* Verbs formed in this way are *spy, ply, (de)fy, (de)ny, (re)ly.* One of these obscured derivatives, *-fy,* has developed into an extremely productive suffix in its own right: *signify, mortify, terrify, typify,* to say nothing of more recent coinages such as *countrify, Frenchify, fishify,* even *speechify* and *happify.* Most dictionaries just list *-(i)fy* as a verb suffix based on the root *fac* "do, make." Similarly, the derivative of *plec, ply* "fold, bend" has been quite productive: *apply, comply, imply, multiply, supply.* Notice also the productivity of *plex,* the past participle of the Latin verb with the root *plec: complex, duplex, perplex, simplex.*

The opacity of words which look and sound like Latin words has some interesting consequences for word-creation and spelling in English. The word *absquatulate* "to scram, decamp," is a nineteenth-century humorous pseudo-Latinism prompted by the existence in the language of words with *ab-* (**ab**breviate, **ab**dicate) and *-(ul)ate* (*articulate*, *matriculate*). The words *doubt*, *debt*, *advance*, *advantage*, *adventure* show what can happen when there is some real or putative discrepancy between the existing form of a word and its etymological history. *Doubt* and *debt* were borrowed into English from French at a very early date – between 1175 and 1225. The consonant <-*b*-> in these words (from Lat. *dub-* and *deb-* respectively) at that time had already been lost both in pronunciation and in spelling. This explains the absence of [b] in the pronunciation of these words. During the Renaissance, classical scholars became concerned about the "proper" form of these words and gradually reintroduced the -*b*- in their spelling on the analogy of newer borrowings and forms such as *dubious*, *debit*. *Advance*, *advantage*, *adventure* are examples of the *ad*- prefix resisting assimilation before [-v] (Chapter 6). This, however, was not true in Old French, from where these words were initially borrowed; loanwords such as *avenue*, *avenge*, *aver*, etc. indicate that the combination of *ad*- + a [v-] initial root in French borrowings normally ends up as [av-]. In Middle English the words *advance*, *advantage*, *adventure* had no -*d*- in the prefix. The -*d*- came in later, reintroduced by overzealous classicists on the model of Latin; presumably it is here to stay in the pronunciation as well as in the spelling.

Examples of opaque etymologies are quite numerous: the very first root listed in the "Indo-European Roots" section of the *American Heritage College Dictionary*, is the root *ag* "to drive, draw, move." The root is phonetically and semantically transparent in *act*, *agile*, *agitate*, *ambiguous*, *intransigent*. Somewhat more complex, but still possible, is the phonetic connection between *ag* and the derivatives *axiom* and *cogent*. However, without the help of the dictionary one could not guess that *essay*, *embassy*, and even *squat* (!!!) belong to that root phonetically. Nor is it in any way semantically possible to extract the wildly divergent current meanings of *ambassador*, *synagogue*, and *podagra* from the basic meanings of the morpheme *ag*.

Finally, there is some completely unpredictable allomorphy where the variation of sounds is apparently random and defies generalizations. The best we can do with these is to take notice of the variants and the words in which they appear. Specialized etymological dictionaries are quite helpful in this respect. Here are some examples of unpredictable allomorphy:

circ, curv, cor "round, around": *circle, curvaceous, cornice*
cli, cliv, clin "lie, bed, lean": *clinic, decline, inclination, proclivity*
cub, cumb "lie, hollow": *incubate, recumbent, succumb*
dei, div "god, augury": *deity, deism, divine, divinity*
don, dat, dot, dor, dos, dow "give": *donor, data, anecdote, Dorothy, dose, dowager*
vid, id, ed "see": *evident, idea, eidetic*

vac, van "empty, vain": *evacuate, vacancy, evanescent, vacation, vacuum, vanish, vanity*

6   False cognates

Knowledge of allomorphic changes and the basic techniques of parsing will help you discover and verify the real identity of cognates. The misanalysis of unfamiliar material is always a danger, however. Homophony can lead to the wrong division of a word into its components; reconstructing a word's semantic history and associations is also treacherous. The following sections will alert you to some of the ways in which parsing and interpretation of the meaning of an unfamiliar word can go astray.

6.1   Boundary misplacement

New words. Our first concern when we encounter an unfamiliar word is to decide where exactly to draw the boundaries, if any, within that word. The decisions can be hard, especially in the context of exposure to so much new information about morphemes whose existence we had been unaware of. Often a string of morphemes or words can be interpreted in more than one way, especially out of context. The placement of boundaries then will depend on what is on our minds at the moment, or the greater familiarity of one interpretation over another. Parallels to boundary misplacement in borrowed vocabulary are found in the everyday errors, deliberate puns and *double entendres* we seek and hear in *syntax* vs. *sin tax*, *ice cream* vs. *I scream*, *sly drool* vs. *slide rule*, *fast ring* vs. *fa string*, and names like *Polly Glott, Eileen Forward, Sarah Bellum.*

Encountering a familiar-looking morpheme in a complex word can trick us into an erroneous parse. In the following example, an asterisk means that the analysis is wrong:

> *anathema*:   ← **a(n)* "not" + *nat* "be born" + *hema* "blood"

Though phonetically plausible, this misanalysis computes the meaning of *anathema* as some weird and absurd "bloodless birth." In fact, the real meaning of this word is a semantic extension of different components: "back" + "place," i.e. "away (from mainstream society), and therefore accursed and loathed":

> *anathema*:   ← *ana* "back" + *the* "to place" + *ma* – noun suffix

Let us take another example. In the derivatives **mon***itor*, **pre*mon***ition, etc., the root *mon* "think" is the *o-grade* allomorph of *men, mn*, as in *demented*, *admonish*, *mnemonic*. However, it would be wrong to parse the words *monarch*, *Monday*, *month* into *mon* + the recognizable end of these words: a *mon* + *arch* is not a "thinking ruler," *Mon* + *day* is not a day (or at least *the* special day) for contemplation, a *mon* + *th* is not wisdom. *Monster*, on the other hand, is derived from the same root, where it has the meaning "warn": a *monster* is something that you need to be warned against.

Predicting or memorizing all possible combinations of roots and affixes is an inhuman task, and over-enthusiastic etymologizing can lead to errors in boundary identification. Usually, the proper context will provide fairly reliable clues as to the correct parse. Imagine encountering the word *neotenic* in a biology book in the sentence "These animals are *neotenic* and retain their larval character throughout life." Technically, there are several ways to divide the word:

neotenic   ← *ne* "not" + *ot* "ear" + *en* "verb" + *ic* "adj."
            ← *ne* "not" + *ot* "ease" + *en* "verb" + *ic* "adj."
            ← *neo* "new, young" + *ten* "hold" + *ic* "adj."

Since the word appears in a context describing the retention, the *holding* of larval, or *young, prior to maturity*, characteristics, logic dictates that only the last parsing will produce the combination of meanings that fit the context. Or, having just learned the root *via* "way, road," and knowing that *ad-* is subject to total prefixal assimilation (Chapter 6, 4.1), as in *avenge* (< L. *ad vindicare*), *avenue*, you want to know what the origin of the word *aviation* is. Since it has to do with transportation, one would be tempted to seek a connection with "way, road." Yet the word *aviation* is not composed of *ad* + *via* + *ation*. Its etymology is more poetic than that: *aviation* contains the root *av(ia)* "bird, fly" + *ation*. Parsing is useful and revealing, but it should be done with utmost care and regard for form and context; if in doubt, consult the dictionary.

6.2   Homophony in roots and affixes

The dangers of misanalysis persist beyond assigning the morpheme boundaries in the right places. Root and affix **homophony** ("sounding alike") is another potential source of confusion. Chapter 9 will discuss the phenomenon of word homophony: *caster–castor*, *seen–scene*, *sole–sole* in greater detail. Misidentification due to root or affix homophony is easy to avoid if one is already familiar with a parsable word: no one will associate the *ped* of *pediatrician* with taking care of people's feet, or the *ped* of *orthopedic* with a correctional facility for children. We know that *genuflection* will not alter the hereditary features of an organism, and that *gene therapy* is not a procedure specific to injured knees. But then, most of us would be puzzled if some keen observer of the features of our language asked us why **invisible** should be something that cannot be seen, while **invaluable** is something *very* valuable. Is a **seditious** person really **sedentary** (actually it's one who "goes apart")? If you are unduly doting or submissive to your wife, Latin *uxor*, you are **uxorious**, but does **nefarious** suggest that you are unquestioningly devoted to your nephew, Old English *nefa*?

Targeting the wrong association of identically or similarly sounding words is the stuff **puns** are made of. The humorous exploitation of the ambiguity arising from homophony can be amusing and clever. The character in the daily cartoon B.C., consulting *Wiley's Dictionary* for the verb *to deliberate*, came up with the meaning "to throw a parolee back in the slammer," capitalizing on the homophony of the roots *liber* "free," and *liber* "weigh, scales." Healthy lifestyles have rendered this familiar joke old-fashioned, but the pun: "Is life worth *living*? It depends on the *liver*," still evokes a smile. A famous pun, attributed to Dr. Johnson, is that when asked about the difference between men and women, he responded: "I can't *conceive*, madam, can you?"

On a serious note, before we can either parse or pun with confidence, especially on classical words, we must be alerted to the most frequently encountered homophonous morphemes. The rest of this chapter is intended to increase your awareness of root and affix homophony and help you avoid involuntary puns and socially embarrassing blunders.

6.2.1   Root homophony[4]

art "skill" as in **art**istic vs.
art(h) "segment" as in **arth**ritis

aus "ear" as in **aus**ral vs.
aus "gold" as in **aus**reate

cap "take, contain" as in **cap**sule vs.
cap "head" as in **cap**itulate

cit "put in motion" as in in**cit**e vs.
cit "civic" as in **cit**y, **cit**izen

col "filter" as in per**col**ate vs.
col "live, grow" as in bu**col**ic

cur "care" as in **cur**ator vs.
cur "run" as in re**cur**

dec "ten" as in **dec**ade vs.
dec "fitting" as in **dec**orum

fer "wild" as in **fer**al vs.
fer "bring, bear" as in **fer**tile

fil "offspring" as in **fil**ial vs.
fil "thread" as in **fil**ament

gen "origin" as in **gen**esis vs.
gen "knee" as in **gen**uflection

ger(on) "old" as in **ger**iatric vs.
ger "carry" as in belli**ger**ent

gn "origin" as in co**gn**ate vs.
gn "know" as in co**gn**ition

---

[4] Some of the homophonous pairs start out as semantic and morphological variants of the same root and are listed under the same head entry in *The American Heritage Dictionary of Indo-European Roots*, ed. by Calvert Watkins, Boston: Houghton Mifflin Co. 1985. The semantic divergence in such instances (e.g. IE *ar "to fit together" producing both *artistic* and *arthritis*) is so extensive that it justifies the separate treatment under the rubric of "etymological pitfalls."

gon "origin" as in **gon**ad vs.
gon "knee, angle" as in ortho**gon**al

her "inherit" as in in**her**it vs.
her "stick, hold" as in in**her**ent

homo "human being" as in **homo**cide vs.
homo "same" as in **homo**nym

hum "earth" as in **hum**us vs.
hum "moist" as in **hum**id

lab "seize" as in syl**lab**le vs.
lab "lip" as in **lab**ial

lat "carry" as in col**lat**e vs.
lat "side" as in col**lat**eral

leg "choose" as in e**leg**ant vs.
leg "law" as in **leg**al

liber "free" as in **liber**ty vs.
liber "weigh" as in equi**libr**ium

lign "wood" as in **lign**eous vs.
lign "line" as in a**lign**

med "middle" as in **med**iate vs.
med "attend" as in **med**icate

mel "song" as in **mel**ody vs.
mel "dark" as in **mel**anoma vs.
mel "honey" as in **mel**lifluous.

men "month" as in **men**struate vs.
men "think" as in **men**tal vs.
men "lead" as in a**men**able

mon "think" as in pre**mon**ition vs.
mon(o) "one" as in **mon**arch

mor "custom" as in **mor**ality vs.
mor "stupid" as in **mor**on vs.
mor(t) "die" as in **mor**ibund

nat "swim" as in **nat**ant vs.
nat "be born" as in **nat**ive

nom "law" as in astro**nom**y vs.
nom "name" as in ig**nom**iny

od "journey" as in **od**ometer vs.
od "song" as in pros**od**y

or "speak" as in **or**acle vs.
or "appear" as in **or**iginal

ot "ear" as in **ot**ology vs.
ot "ease" as in **ot**iose

pal "cover" as in **pal**liate vs.
pal "pale" as in **pal**lor

par "show" as in ap**par**ition vs.
par "produce" as in **par**ent vs.
par "setup" as in pre**par**ation

ped "child" as in **ped**iatrician vs.
ped "foot" as in bi**ped**

pen "tail" as in **pen**is vs.
pen "punish" as in **pen**alty vs.
pen "almost" as in **pen**insula

pha(n) "show" as in epi**phan**y vs.
pha "speak" as in a**pha**sia

pol "pole" as in **pol**ar vs.
pol "city" as in **pol**ice

prec "pray" as in de**prec**ate vs.
prec "worth" as in de**prec**iate

rad "scratch" as in ab**rad**e vs.
rad "root" as in **rad**ical vs.
rad(ius) "ray" as in **rad**ial

sal "jump" as in **sal**ient vs.
sal "salt" as in **sal**ine

sen "old" as in **sen**ile vs.
sen "feel" as in **sen**sual

ser "arrange" as in **ser**ial vs.
ser "fluid" as in **ser**um

serv "work for" as in **serv**itude vs.
serv "keep" as in con**serv**e

sol "sun" as in **sol**arium vs.
sol "alone" as in **sol**itude vs.
sol (hol) "whole" as in con**sol**idate

spir "breathe" as in re**spir**ation vs.
spir "coil" as in **spir**al

ten "stretch" as in *extend* vs.
ten "hold" as in *tenure*

ter "frighten" as in *deterrent* vs.
ter "earth" as in *terrestrial*

via "way" as in *trivial* vs.
via "live" as in *viable*

vir "male" as in *virility* vs.
vir "poison" as in *virulent*, *virus*

The list is not exhaustive, but it provides a good start. It differs from all other published alphabetical root lists where only the homophony of invariable forms is evident, as *vir* "male" and *vir* "poison." In many of the pairs collected here only one of several possible allomorphs is involved in the homophony, e.g. *cit* "put in motion" has the allomorphs *kin/cin*, as in **kin**etic, **cin**ematography, and *cit* "civic" has an allomorph *civ*, as in **civ**il. Similarly, the allomorphs *men*, *mon* "think" show homophony with *men* "month," *men* "lead," and *mon*(o) "one," but the allomorph *mn* "think" has no homophone.

Awareness of the possibility that two or more identical forms may have different meanings should lead to more informed etymological guesses. The allomorphy information in the preceding chapters can be useful in keeping homophonous pairs apart. The root *ped* "foot" has an *o*-grade allomorph *pod*: **ped**al, **ped**estrian, and **pod**ium are clearly related. The homophonous *ped* "child" has no allomorphs, and it can be spelled *paed*-. The boundaries can blur, however. The word **ped**ology is both the "study of what is under**foot**, "the study of soil(s)," and it is also "study of children." Quite surprisingly, the word **ped**igree is **not** etymologically related to "offspring," but comes from the Old French *pie de grue* "foot of a crane," through its Anglo-Norman form *pe de grue*, used to denote genealogical branching by association with the branching / | \ mark left by the foot of a crane. The adjective **de**cid*uous* parses correctly into *de* "down" + *cad* "fall" + *ous*, with multiple lenition of the root vowel. However, a parse such as *de* "down" + *ced* "go, let go" + *ous* (with E-Lenition) makes equally good sense, and *de* "down" + *cid* "cut" + *ous* would also be quite acceptable semantically. Knowing about homophony is only the first step; often there will be no sure and reliable way of disambiguating homophones except to check your derivations in a dictionary.

6.3   Affix homophony

Full affix homophony is rarer than root homophony. Nevertheless, homophonous affixes do exist, and awareness of the different meanings of one and the same affix can help us avoid misanalysis. For example, the most frequent meaning of the prefix *con*- is "jointly, together," but it also means "altogether, completely," and in that second sense it merely intensifies the meaning of the root to which it is attached. Thus **con** + *rupt* "burst, become unsound" turns into *corrupt*, which does mean **very** unsound, but has nothing to do with "together-ness." Similarly, *comfort* goes back historically to the sense of having greater *fortitude*, greater strength; it is not derived from the "together-ness" of *con-*, though perhaps in our understanding of human psychology the two notions can be related. A *complaint* comes from someone who is in a **very plaint**ive mood, but the "togetherness" of a complainer and an audience is not required. The prefix *dis-* means "apart, reversal, lacking" in *distend, disseminate, disallow, disrepute*. In *disannul, disgruntle, disturb*, however, the meaning of the prefix is simply "more," i.e. it is an intensifier. The prefixes *in-, for-, per-* can also be used as intensifiers: *incandescent, inflammable, invaluable* denote objects that are **very** *candescent*, **very** *flammable*, **very** *valuable*. The most *con-spicuous* examples of prefix homophony come from prefixes which have an intensifying meaning in addition to their other meanings.

6.3.1   Phonetic rules and homophony

Like root homophony, affix homophony can result from one of the phonetic changes discussed in the previous chapters. In the examples below, there are instances of N-drop, Prefixal Assimilation, Vowel-Drop, as well as homophony without homography. The affixes to the right of the arrows in the following sets are homophonous:

an- "not"	→ **a-** (**a**gnostic, **a**moral)
ad- "to, towards"	→ **a-** (**a**scribe, **a**venue, **a**venge, **a**ver)
on (Old English)	→ **a-** (**a**fire, **a**float)
an- "not"	→ **an-** (**an**archy, **an**omaly)
ad- "to, towards"	→ **an-** (**an**nihilate, **an**notate)
ana- "back, again"	→ **an-** (**an**ode, **an**odyne)
ad- "to, towards"	→ **ap-** (**ap**posite, **ap**pease, **ap**pend)
apo- "from, off"	→ **ap(o)-** (**ap**ogee, **ap**ology, **ap**oplexy)
bi- "two, twice"	→ **bi-** (**bi**cycle, **bi**ennial, **bi**weekly)
by- "near"	→ **by-** (**by**stander, **by**pass, **by**law)
dia- "through"	→ **di-** (**di**optric, **di**orama)
dis- "apart, asunder"	→ **di-** (**di**ffer, **di**rect, **di**vide)
di- "away from"	→ **di-** (allomorph of **de-**) **di**lapidate, **di**minish
di- "two"	→ **di-** (**di**lemma, **di**syllabic)
dis- "deprive, reverse"	→ **dis-** (**dis**robe, **dis**regard, **dis**establish)
dys- "badly"	→ **dys-** (**dys**lexia, **dys**pepsia)
-oid "form, like"	→ **-oid** (anthrop**oid**, human**oid**, ov**oid**)
-id "noun"	→ **-(o)id** (fibr**oid**, polar**oid**, cellul**oid**[5])

---

[5] *Polaroid* and *celluloid* are recent trademarks coined by analogy either to the *-id* in words such as *orchid*, or to the suffix *-oid*, as in *humanoid*.

par- "thoroughly"	→ **par-** (**par**don, **par**boil)
para- "along, beyond"	→ **par-** (**par**enthesis, **par**ody)

Some affixes which are similar but not totally identical in form, may also be difficult to parse:

-(i)a "plural of *-um*"	→ me**dia**, gang**lia**, rega**lia**
-ia "condition"	→ ane**mia**, insom**nia**, pho**bia**[6]
hyper "over, above"	→ **hyper**critical, **hyper**tonic
hypo "below"	→ **hypo**critical, **hypo**tonic
infra- "beneath"	→ **infra**red, **infra**sonic, **infra**structure
inter- "between"	→ **inter**cede, **inter**lude, **inter**national
intra- "within"	→ **intra**cranial, **intra**venous, **intra**uterine
per- "through"	→ **per**ception, **per**secute, **per**chance, **per**fume
peri- "around"	→ **peri**od, **peri**phery, **peri**scope

6.3.2 Homophony of grammatical suffixes

Suffixes can change both the lexical and the grammatical meaning of a word. The suffix *-ory*, for example, has two distinct meanings: one from the Latin *-orium* "place where," as in *auditorium*, which forms nouns, e.g. *conservatory*, *repository*, and an adjective-forming suffix meaning "connected with, serving for," as in *illusory*, *laudatory*, *mandatory*. Knowing this, we will not gloss *repository* and *dormitory* as "inactive" and "sleeping," or *amatory* or *satisfactory* as the places where one finds love or satisfaction. The suffix *-ose* forms adjectives from nouns, and has the meaning "full of," thus *jocose*, *verbose*. In the specialized language of chemistry, however, the suffix *-ose*, which arose as a nineteenth century *pseudo-suffix* (see below, Section 7) from a French pronunciation of the word *glucose*, is attached to a special group of carbohydrates: *fructose*, *dextrose*, *cellulose*. In its chemical function, *-ose* forms nouns.

Conversion from one grammatical class to another within English can create suffix homophony. In the nouns *divid**end***, *rever**end***, the *-end* started out as an adjectival suffix. A similar shift occurred with the suffixes *-ant* and *-ent*, as in *eleg**ant***, adj., but *account**ant***, noun. The dual nature of *-ant* and *-ent* is seen in adjective-noun pairs such as *conson**ant***, *irrit**ant***, *migr**ant***, *vagr**ant***, *convalesc**ent***, *cresc**ent***, *pati**ent***. The homophony of these suffixes is an accident of the way in which words of classical origin were adopted into English. In many words the duality never developed; there are two words each with the form

---

[6] The suffix *-ia* is used also for plants, zoological classes, country names: *wisteria*, *amphibia*, *Rhodesia*. The suffix *-a* by itself is used in borrowed words to denote feminine gender – *alumna*, *Chicana*.

astringent, *dependent*, *resident* in the language, while *client*, *ingredient*, *president*, *regent* are only nouns, and *evident*, *benevolent*, *urgent* are only adjectives. Some other suffixes used to derive words of different grammatical classes are:

-al (adjective):	→ medicinal, seminal, torrential
-al (noun):	→ denial, refusal, reprisal
-ate (adjective):	→ delicate, desolate, Latinate, ornate
-ate (verb):	→ designate, elongate, intimidate, negate
-ate (noun):	→ cognate, duplicate, predicate, primate
-esque (adjective):	→ gigantesque, picturesque, statuesque
-esque (noun):	→ burlesque, humoresque
-ic (adjective):	→ kinetic, patriotic, pediatric, Socratic
-ic (noun):	→ colic, heretic, metric, rhetoric, tonic
-ite (adjective):	→ apposite, favorite, contrite, Clintonite
-ite (noun):	→ parasite, retinite, granite
-ite (verb):	→ expedite, ignite, unite
-ive (adjective):	→ derisive, expensive, oppressive
-ive (noun):	→ executive, locomotive, missive
-oid (adjective):	→ paranoid, fibroid, tabloid
-oid (noun):	→ alkaloid, celluloid, steroid, fibroid
-ute (adjective):	→ absolute, destitute, minute
-ute (noun):	→ attribute, institute, statute, substitute
-ute (verb):	→ attribute, institute, distribute, substitute

The original affix homophony can be obscured by changes in the pronunciation of nouns, verbs, and adjectives, as in *coordinate*, *delegate*, *duplicate*, *postulate*. The placement of stress can also serve as the marker of grammatical class, as in *present*, *attribute*, *minute*. When affix homophony persists, the context is usually sufficient to disambiguate the grammatical properties of the word.

6.3.3   Mixed homophony: affixes and roots

Some affixes and some roots may have the same form, either inherently, or accidentally, as a result of some derivational process. They may be pronounced and spelled in the same way (*id*, *it*, *par* etc.), they may differ in the positions allowed for them in the word, as *id* "that one, particular" vs. *-id*, a suffix for adjectives and nouns. Mixed homophony may involve different spellings, but identical pronunciation, as *poli* "city" vs. *poly-* "many." We can't list all variant forms that might produce the appearance of root-affix homophony. The examples below are only intended to alert the reader to this source of potentially erroneous parsing.

id "that one"	→ **id**entity, **id**em, **id**iom
-id "adj., noun"	→ cand**id**, flu**id**, liqu**id**, orch**id**
it "go"	→ **it**inerary, ex**it**, in**it**ial, trans**it**
-it "adj., noun"	→ pos**it**, Jesu**it**, aud**it**, herm**it**, also -ite
par "give birth"	→ **par**ent, post**par**tum, multi**par**ous
par(a)- "along, beyond"	→ **par**affin, **par**ody
par "thoroughly"	→ **par**boil, **par**don
poli "city"	→ metro**poli**s, Minnea**poli**s, cosmo**poli**tan
poly- "many"	→ **poly**clinic, **poly**gamy, **poly**morphous
re "thing, affair"	→ **re**public, **re**alism, **re**ify, **re**bus
re- "back, again"	→ **re**plica, **re**pose, **re**produce
sed "sit"	→ **sed**entary, **sed**iment
sed- "without, apart"	→ **sed**itious, **sed**ulous

7   Pseudo-suffixes

Burgers and the like. Misanalysis is bound to happen to the speakers of any language at some time, no matter how well educated they are. One of the interesting consequences of misanalysis is that it enriches the inventory of formative elements. The story of the *burger* is a famous example of how the composition of one word was misinterpreted. The ground meat patty sandwich we all know as a *burger* was called originally a *Hamburger steak*, after the German city of Hamburg. For speakers of English the adjective *Hamburger* would have been unparsable, but the first syllable must have looked treacherously reminiscent of *ham*. Removing *ham* from *Hamburger* leaves the -*burger* part looking like a separate recyclable unit. And, indeed, *burger* did develop into a root meaning "a sandwich," now combining freely with adjectives and other roots that carry information about the ingredients: *double-* and *triple-burger, cheeseburger, steakburger, fishburger, oysterburger, veggieburger.*

The story of the -*buster* words is similar: it started out as a bound second element of a compound and became very productive in the twentieth century: *blockbuster, broncobuster, crime buster, doorbuster,* etc. – one dictionary lists seventy-two words ending in -*buster.*[7] Similar to -*buster* are the formations with -*cast* and -*caster: telecast,*

---

[7] Martin Lehnert's *Reverse Dictionary of Present-Day English.* VEB Verlag Enzyklopädie, Leipzig, 1971.

simulcast, sportscast(er). Less obvious are cases in which the wrong parsing of borrowed words has produced morphemes that are either non-existent in the source language: *-cade*, *-(a)thon*, or that have acquired a form different from that in the original language, as in *-(a)holic*.

-cade   → *aquacade, cavalcade, motorcade*
-(a)thon   → *walkathon, telethon, jogathon, strollathon, bikeathon*
-(a)holic → *chocoholic, workaholic, sexaholic, shopaholic*

When borrowed compounds are misanalyzed, one of the components can take a new life within English as a separate and productive root. In the late 1940s misanalysis gave us the word *copter*, where the first element of the word *helicopter* was wrongly associated with the sun, Greek *helios* (compare *helium, heliotropic*), rather than with *helix*, the spiral that keeps the flying object up in the air. The word *doxy* is a purely English creation based on borrowed items such as *orthodoxy* and *heterodoxy.* It still has a facetious ring about it, probably perpetuated by J. Q. Adams' famous 1778 quip that "Orthodoxy is my *doxy*, and heterodoxy is your *doxy.*" This did not deter the *LA Times* from publishing a serious piece on religion which contained *flexidox* in its title. Clever misanalysis can be catchy, amusing, and useful: *prequel* is the opposite of *sequel*, and *prebuttal* is the opposite of *rebuttal.*

8   Semantic variation

The existence of different meanings for one and the same root (**polysemy**) sometimes results in the separation of homophonous roots, as in the case of *art* "skill" and *art(h)* "segment," but more frequently various related meanings continue to reside within the same form. A serious study of classical roots means also taking note of the possible range of meanings that they carry. The root *arch(aeo)* "foremost, begin, rule" provides a good example of polysemy. The set of its derivatives includes words such as *archaeology, archbishop, archetype, matriarch, archipelago, architect.* On the surface, these are vastly different words. However, knowing the range of meanings of *arch(aeo)* helps us detect the common semantic denominator among them. The shift from "beginning" and "foremost" to "rule" is logical, the semantic connections are transparent. Matching the right meaning to the right word is as important as knowing the range of meanings. *Archaeology* is not "the study of ruling systems," *matriarchy* is not "the beginning of motherhood," *archetype* is not "a domineering type." These glosses could make a good informed joke, but the analysis is useless if it does not reveal the overall meaning of the word.

Examples of the relevance of semantic variation in the analysis of words abound. The root *cast* means both "purify" and "fortify"; without knowing the two meanings we would not recognize that *castrate* and *castle* are cognates. The allomorphs *tag, tang* gloss as both "touch" (concrete) and "perceive, feel" (abstract); this semantic information is the essential link between the fairly concrete notion *contact*, and *tact*, the abstract perception of social propriety and respect for other people's feelings. The root *lev* "rise" appears in the homophonous words *levee*. First, *levee* has the concrete meaning of "embankment," but the second word *levee* "a reception, an assembly" is arrived at indirectly; it comes from the royal habit of receiving visitors after rising from bed, especially an afternoon siesta. It is a rather big jump from the *radish* in one's salad to the mathematical *radical*. Why would *regular* and *regal* mean such different things? What is the relationship between a *regent* and a *region*? No discussion of semantic pitfalls can supply all the answers. All we can do is flag the existence of variant meanings for one root and hope that etymological good sense and a good dictionary in hand will produce the right analysis.

9   Multiple derivatives – multiple meanings

Finally, we turn our attention to yet another pitfall – the shifting of the semantic focus, or the complete change of the semantic content of a root in derived words. This can happen either within the scope of a single root, as in *radish* and *radical*, or in the process of suffixation. This section addresses the possibility that two suffixes with the same grammatical meaning can attach to the same root and produce two different words.

Let us look at the two frequent adjective suffixes *-ic* and *-al*. They can be added to some roots twice, compare *diabolic* vs. *diabolical*, *problematic* vs. *problematical*, *rhythmic* vs. *rhythmical*. In these examples the stacking of suffixes with identical grammatical function does not seem to affect the meaning or usage of the words. In another set, the *-ic/ical* variants have the same meaning, but one of the forms is used more commonly: *academic, angelic, ethnic, iconic, semantic, symbolic*. On the other hand, *radical, conical, critical, logical, vertical* appear only in the form with *-ical*. Adjectives ending in *-ic* are easily converted into nouns: *academic, cynic, logic, tropic*, while the corresponding adjectives ending in *-ical* are mostly used as adjectives: *cynical, epical, logical, tropical*, etc. Finally, there are some word pairs in this set where the *-ic* vs. *-ical* distinction is both formal and semantic: *comic* vs. *comical*, *economic* vs. *economical, historic* vs. *historical*. Here are some more instances of multiple derivatives with different meanings:

-al (adj. /noun) vs. **-tion** (noun):

    → soci**al** vs. associa**tion**

    → propos**al** vs. propos**ition**

-al (adj.) vs. **-ous** (adj.):

    → factu**al** vs. fictiti**ous** (vs. facile)

    → offici**al** vs. offici**ous**

    → sensu**al** vs. sensu**ous** (vs. sensitive, sensible, sensory, sensational)

    → virtu**al** vs. virtu**ous**

-ic (adj.) vs. **-al** (adj.)

    → dialect**ic** vs. dialect**al**

    → gener**ic** vs. gener**al**

    → (geo)centr**ic** vs. centr**al**

    → ton**ic** vs. ton**al**

-ity (noun) vs. **-ness** (noun):

    → commun**ity** vs. common**ness**

    → enorm**ity** vs. enormous**ness**

    → nice**ty** vs. nice**ness**

    → gentil**ity** vs. gentle**ness**

Think further of *animosity–animation–animism, audience–audition, integrity–integration*, and many, many more. These examples illustrate the incredibly rich gamut of possibilities that our language allows on the basis of a finite set of formative elements.

10   Multiple affixes – same meaning

As noted in Chapter 5, the meanings that affixes carry are not specific; affixes are subject to semantic bleaching. The more general the meaning of a morpheme, the more likely it is to overlap the meaning of another morpheme. Thus, *ab-, cata-, apo-, de-*, and *ex-*, are all used with the meaning "away." Affixes from different classical sources may also be (near) synonymous, thus: *multi-, pan-, poly-; mono-, uni-; dys-, mal-, mis-; bi-, di-*. Finally, there are synonymous pairs where one of the items is from Greek, while the other one comes from Latin: *hemi – semi-* (Latin), or *demi-* (Medieval Latin and French), *hypo – sub, hyper – super*.

9 Semantic change and semantic guesswork

1   Terminology

Homophony. The term **homophony** ("sounding the same") is commonly used to cover three types of semantic identity: **homonymy**, **homophony**, and **polysemy**. All of these count as homophones:

corn: on the cob vs. *corn* on toe
ear: of corn vs. *ear* of head
flight: from danger (*flee*), vs. *flight* in an airplane (*fly*), vs. *flight* of stairs
load: of dirt vs. *lode* in a gold mine
meal: ground up vs. *meal* at dinner time
mettle: in the sense of courage vs. *metal* in the sense of iron, copper
pupil: of your eye vs. *pupil* who is a student
score: score the table with a nail, vs. *score* high in game
sea: body of water vs. *see* verb of perception
sole: type of fish vs. *sole* only vs. *sole* the base of a shoe, vs. *soul* in a
    religious sense
trip: journey vs. *trip* to obstruct, cause to fall
waist: of a person vs. *waste* squander

To be **homonymous** ("having the same name"), words that sound alike must have different meanings and different origins: thus *bear* "carry," *bear* "grizzly," and *bare* "nude," *riddle* "puzzle" and *riddle* "pierce with holes," *rock* "stone" and *rock* "sway to and fro," fit this definition. **Homophony** means approximately the same thing but even more broadly: words that sound alike but have different meanings, whether they have different origins or not. Dictionaries have separate entries for homonyms and homophones, thus *fast*(1) "quick, swift," while *fast*(2) is "to abstain from food, or from some kinds of food." Some of the above examples are also **homographs** – spelled alike.

Polysemy refers to a single word with several different meanings. The differentiation from one into several meanings is a consequence of the change from concrete to abstract meaning – i.e., figurative use of language. If you look at almost any root whatever, you will find that it has several different meanings. This is typical of what is meant by the word **polysemy**. At some point, words which start out as one and the same word get differentiated and lose connection with each other. Such pairs are *gentle–genteel, petty–petite, genre–gender, flower–flour, metal–mettle, of–off*. Each of these pairs goes back to one single word, yet no one today would consider them to be the same word. However, the etymologies of these words in any dictionary will indicate that they started out as the same word.

1.1   Diversity of meanings

Check in some dictionary the number of separate meanings it lists under everyday words like *about, beak, chair, devil, eat, fine, go, happy*. It is not always easy to decide at which point two meanings of one polysemic word merit separate entries in the dictionary. Until the fifteenth century English had one word *hull* with two meanings; today *hull* "husk, shell" and *hull* "the hollow portion of a ship" are treated as two words. The semantic divergence between the adjective *continent* and the noun *continent* is about the same as that between the different meanings of *base, piano, volume, sensation, sentence* and *solution*, but the decision on how to list these items in the dictionary is a matter of editorial policy. The Third Edition of *The American Heritage College Dictionary* (1993) lists the different senses of *base, continent* and *piano* separately but *volume, sentence* and *solution* are one entry each.[1] These decisions reflect the editors' judgment on which of the senses is "central" and "most commonly sought" (p.xxv). That sense of the word is recorded first. We are all aware of the multiple meanings of *chair, club, honey* in our language, and more recently, with the computer, *load, mouse, window*, but these words are still single dictionary entries.

1.2   Other -onyms

Traditionally the study of meaning has been understood as the study of how we "name" objects, properties, events, processes, and actions we encounter in the world around us. It is not surprising, then, that a number of terms coined on the basis of the root **onym** "name" are used to cover a variety of semantic relations between words in the language. Some of these terms will be familiar to you. Others are more technical and specialized. All reflect some peculiarity of the "naming" process which is the foundation of semantics.

***antonym*: anti** "opposed" + **onym** "word opposite in meaning" *soft* vs. *hard, love* vs. *hate, early* vs. *late*

---

[1] For comparison, note that the 1991 *Random House Webster's Collegiate Dictionary* has two separate entries for *base* and *piano*, but only one entry for *continent*, noun, and *continent*, adj.

heteronym: **hetero** "other, different" + **onym** – a word spelled like another, but having a different pronunciation and meaning: *bass* "fish" vs. *bass* "male voice," *lead* "metal" vs. *lead* "to conduct," *wind* "to coil" vs. *wind* "air in motion"

metonym: **meta** "changed" + **onym** – a word used for another, with which there is some special association, as in space or time: "I always support the point of view of **Buckingham Palace**."

synonym: **syn** "with, together" + **onym** – a word approximately equivalent in meaning to another word: *quick, fast, rapid*

hyponym: **hypo** "under" + **onym** – a word whose meaning is subsumed under the more general meaning of another word: *oak, beech, poplar* ⊏ *tree*

2   How meanings change ("semantic change")

Semantic change is very difficult to describe and explain. It is unlikely that scholars will ever be able to predict the directions in which particular words will change their meanings. The development of new material and social conditions may cause words to become unnecessary – e.g. *merlon* "the part of a battlement between the crenels," *wimple* "a medieval head-covering," *caboose* "early nineteenth century cast-iron cooking range used in ship galleys." A shift of attitudes may render some words socially unacceptable (*coolie, frog, girlie, Jap, pansy*), while others become highly fashionable or socially relevant (*cool, ecology, infomercial, outsource*). Nonetheless, by looking at a wide range of examples of semantic changes that have happened in the history of the language, one can begin to develop a certain sense of what kinds of change are likely. Information about the original meaning of the morphemes and the intuition developed from observing various patterns of semantic change will help us make better-informed guesses about the meanings of unfamiliar words that contain familiar morphemes.

We shall focus, first, on the **mechanisms** of change – what forces in our society, or what forces in our thinking, typically have brought about semantic change? Then we will turn to a classification of the **results** of semantic change: looked at in a long perspective, how do these changes affect the lexicon?

2.1   External forces

2.1.1   Technology and current relevance

When new technology changes the way we conduct our daily life, the words which refer to it change also. Consider the word *compute* and its derivatives – *computer, computation*. It used to mean "to count, to reckon, to calculate." Indeed the word *count* is a direct descendant (through French) of the Latin verb *computare* "to count." The computer, however, is no longer a "counter": it has given its name to a new branch of science, *computer science*, we talk of *computer addiction*, *computer-aided design*, *computer ethics*, *computer literacy*, *computer viruses*, and even *compusex*. Computers deal with text, graphics, images, symbols, music; the original meaning of "counting" in computer language has been completely supplanted by the new associations of "computing."

As computers became common, many words changed their meanings because they could conveniently be used to refer to aspects of computing. For example, you can *customize* your *commands*, where *customize* refers to setting up specialized *function keys*. Think of the range of meanings that the word *custom* has outside the computer domain: *custom* as in "characteristic behavior of a society," *custom* as in "to collect duty as you pass through customs at the airport," *customer* as in "one who shops at a store." The word *command* in *customizing your commands* is a specialized sense of a word that once meant "an order given to a person of higher rank to a person of lower rank" – now it means "give a signal to the program by pushing a certain key or clicking the mouse on the right icon." In defining *command*, we have introduced two new meanings: *mouse*, and *icon*. Until the computer age, *icon* most commonly referred to pictorial representations of sacred personages in the Eastern Orthodox Church. The lively *mouse* is an input device, it can be *mechanical* or *optical*, it is connected through a *mouseport*, and it can cause *mouse elbow*. The computer revolution has given rise to new meanings for ordinary words. You can open two *windows* on your *screen*, select computing operations from a *menu*, use hyphenation *tools* from your *tools menu*, select a *hyperlink*, *paste* a section from one document into another, look at something called a *clipboard* which is neither "clipped on" nor a board, you find the *bug* in your program, you *surf* the *net*, and so on.

The computer-related examples are numerous and striking, but the process they illustrate is neither new nor isolated. The word *shuttle*, whose original meaning is "a device used in weaving," is more frequently used today in its later, extended figurative meaning of anything that goes back and forth: a *shuttle bus*, a *shuttle flight*, the *space shuttle*, and, in politics, *shuttle diplomacy*. For some less-dramatic examples, think of the nineteenth-century meaning of *station wagon*, "a horse-drawn covered carriage." Going further back, notice the difference between the literal sense of *shepherd* vs. its meaning in a phrase like "The Lord is my *shepherd*, I shall not want." In many religions, *pastor* is the name for the leader or minister. Its original meaning is "shepherd," and of course it is cognate with *pasture*.

Another example comes from the history of the word *hierarchy*. Today it means "a system of ranking," but it started out as a term referring to the three divisions of angels and their ranking, from which it developed the meaning "sacred rule," used by the Church to describe the successive order of pope, cardinals, archbishops, bishops, priests, all arrayed from top to bottom in a branching structure of authority. Since it provided a natural model for the dissemination of authority, it spread to military and governmental structures as a superior model for organization, and from there, in a more abstract way, to the natural sciences. *Disaster* "a bad, unfavorable, star or planet" refers to astrology, in which the future is supposed to be predicted by configurations of stars. Our faith in such predictions was shattered long ago, but the word maintains its meaning in a changed society. *Doctor* meant "teacher," and in that meaning it survives as an occasional title for professors. The medical sense, now the norm, was acquired gradually from the association with higher education that was characteristic of physicians.

2.2   Accidental associations

Elegant means "one who selects out," based on √leg, i.e., someone who picks wisely. An elegant person, for example, is taken to be elegant because he or she selects clothes and accessories wisely. By association with the high price of quality goods, the word comes to mean "exclusivity," as in a phrase like "the elegance of Rodeo Drive."

What is the relation of *logic* to words? Logic has to do with the study of reasoning; and since reasoning is associated with language (√log means "word," originally), the association takes over the meaning and now logic is not thought of as having much to do specifically with words.

Consider *adore*. It means, literally, "to speak to." At some point in history, the kind of speaking came to be the speech of prayer, "speaking to God." Eventually the association went even further: looking heavenward, imploringly, would now be described as "adoration." Wordsworth has a wonderful line in a sonnet about a strikingly beautiful evening: "It is a beauteous evening, calm and free, The holy time is quiet as a Nun, Breathless with adoration." The point is, the root which meant "speak" has come to refer to silent worship, a change brought about by association with prayer.

Scripture just meant "writing," but by association with religious writing, in particular the Bible (which itself just meant "book"), it came to mean "religious writing," and not just any religious writing but that which is found in the holy bible of the Christian tradition. On the other hand, by a quite different association, the verb *prescribe* and its associated noun *prescription* are now limited almost entirely to what a physician writes out to allow one to obtain medication. The association with medicine is what has driven the particular semantic change we find in it.

The connection between *amble* and *ambulance* is an accident of war: *ambulance* comes from a longer phrase, *hospital ambulant*, a "moveable hospital," one which could be present on the battlefield to tend to the wounded. It was merely shortened to the second part of the phrase, giving us *ambulance.*

Metonymy is an association of a particular type, usually accidental association in space or time. The real referent and the transferred referent are associated by virtue of being in the same place, as when we speak of *The White House* and we are in fact referring to the current President of the United States and his staff (association of both place and time, since *The White House* can only refer to the president identified with a particular period of time); *pigskin* "football" is an example of association through material. Metonymy can be extended to cover changes resulting from other associations such as part and whole – *drink the whole bottle, give me a hand, live by the sword.* From the classical vocabulary of English, an example is *exposition*, which meant "putting things out." Now the event at which new cars are displayed, or new computer technologies or whatever, is called an exposition. Another classical example is *commissary*, which in America means a place where food and other supplies are dispensed in the military. Its meaning still, in Britain, and its only meaning earlier in history, was an officer of the law or of the military forces to whom responsibility was assigned for – among other possibilities – the supply storehouse. The association is between the person (to whom the term originally referred) and the place of his work.

2.3   Internal forces

2.3.1   Analogy

The association covered by the notion of metonymy is due to a more general cause: analogy. Analogy involves the perception of similarity between some concrete object or process and some abstract concept or process. The basic meaning of a word is related to another meaning in such a way that by analogy there can be a transfer or extension of meaning from one to the other. For example, if someone is the *head* of a department, the relationship of the head to the body – the **literal** sense – is being used in an **extended** or **figurative** sense, in which there is an analogical ratio set up: *head* is to *body* as *head (=leader)* is to *department*. It can be seen as an equation:

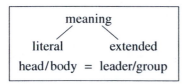

Thus if we say that "The population is mushrooming all over the world," we are comparing the rapid growth of population to the unmanageable fecundity of a mushroom. If we say, "The New Hampshire primary will be the acid test of his candidacy," we are comparing the ability of his campaign to survive the results of close scrutiny in New Hampshire with the well-known test for genuine gold by means of using nitric acid. If we speak of "The strong arm of the law," we are comparing an individual's strong arm and the abstract notion of law enforcement. If we speak of a "traffic bottleneck," we are comparing some narrowing of traffic flow with the neck of a bottle where the contents flow more slowly (think about getting ketchup out of the bottle!).

Virtually any perceived similarity can be the basis of analogical change and the source of a new meaning. Thus √cad means "fall," and the analogy in *recidivism* is between returning to crime and falling backwards – returning to crime is like falling backwards. All analogies can be stated in a similar manner: some abstract relationship reminds one of a concrete relationship. The concrete relationship may be topological (above, below, behind, in front of, inside of, beside), or it may be temporal (before, after), or it may be a matter of sense perception (smell–hear–feel–touch–taste).

The analogy can be quite remote and even unlikely, but if it catches someone's fancy it may easily stick in the language. Here are some examples in which the etymology depends precisely on analogy of the type seen in the phrases above. In each example we try to formulate the basis for the comparison, even though it is sometimes tediously obvious:

companion con "together" + L. panis "bread" → "any partner, comrade, associate"
    (basis: sharing bread, i.e. eating together)
construct "piled up together" (like stones forming a house)
    → construct a sentence (piling up words like stones)
culminate "reach the top of a hill"
    → "to reach a decisive point, after struggling as if climbing"
dependent "hanging from something"
    → "supported by virtue of someone else's money or power"

educate "to lead forth, to bring up"
    → "to make competent, to raise to a higher social or cultural level"
illustrate "to purify, to give physical light to, to throw light on"
    → "to make clear, demonstrate visually or by reasoning"
offend "strike against"
    → "create bad feelings"
precipitate "head in front, falling forward"
    → "to behave in a manner that lacks forethought"
progress "to step forward"
    → "to improve, to move toward a better existence"
provoke "call forth, summon"
    → "to incite with anger or desire, to irritate"
understand "be located beneath"
    → "grasp concept" (like having it fall on one)

The role played by analogy cannot be overestimated. It is fair to say that the mind looks for concrete ways of representing abstract concepts, and the concrete meanings clarify the intended abstract relationships. Analogy is the most frequent and most important source of semantic enrichment of the language.

2.4   Loss of specificity

This process could equally well be called **over-generalization**, but loss of specificity has the slight advantage of reflecting a common human failing. All of us are prone to generalizing, prone to failures of specificity. One of the techniques we study when we are learning to write acceptable prose is how to be more specific, how to provide details and examples, how to find the right word for the meaning we have in mind. Nonetheless, in everyday speech and casual writing we choose the more general meaning because most of us have no particular talent for words. This tendency shows up historically when words acquire broader and more general meanings. A word like *docile*, from the same root as *doctor*, originally meaning "teachable," has developed the sense of non-resistant, pliable, a kind of over-generalization of the notion "teachable." *Guy Fawkes'* infamous first name lost its specificity with the proliferation of November 5th effigies of the criminal; then *guys* began to be used of males of strange appearance, then it was broadened to refer to any males, and now it is generalized (especially in the plural) to any group of people, including groups of females. Let us examine this notion of overgeneralization more deeply.

All the words of a language can be arranged in **hyponymic sets**. What is a hyponym and how does it help us understand the notion of overgeneralization in historical semantic development? A hyponymic relation exists between two words when one can replace the other without changing the reference, but not vice-versa. Thus *scarlet* is more specific than *red*: if one can say, "Her face was scarlet," one can always say "Her face was red." Here is a hyponymic diagram which helps make the notion clear (the symbol [⊃] "contains as a subset" means the term to the right is a hyponym of the term to its left, and the leftmost one is the key word; two terms on the same level, not hyponyms of each other, are separated by a comma)

> *go* ⊃ *walk* ⊃ *amble, shuffle, stride,* . . .

What this says is, "*Go* is the most general and least specific of these words; *walk* is a type of *going* but not all going is walking; *amble, shuffle, stride* are types of walking but not conversely." When, as in this example, there are several equally good hyponyms and none of them is a hyponym of the other (e.g. *shuffle* is not a hyponym of *amble*), we call them **co-hyponyms**. Now, when we say that language tends toward loss of hyponymy and favors the more general category – the one at the head of such a hyponymic diagram – it is somewhat clearer what it means to lose specificity.

Where would one look for examples? Answer: that is what a thesaurus is about. A thesaurus lists vocabulary under a small number of the most general categories, the ones that are most likely to come to mind when one is formulating a concept. Peter Mark Roget, the Frenchman who constructed the first useful thesaurus, in the middle of the nineteenth century (1852), called the most general term the "key word," and he tried to compress the language to just one thousand such key categories, which were in turn grouped into a small number of logical categories: abstract relations, space, matter, intellect, volition, and affections. These days nearly all computer word-processing programs include both a dictionary and a thesaurus. A thesaurus is about the same as a dictionary of synonyms. Both are arranged with a keyword that the editors hope we will think of as the general category for an idea, and we will follow from there to more and more specific words with the special senses that we are looking for. Here are some typical sequences available from the *Merriam-Webster's New Dictionary of Synonyms*:

Expert ⊃ *adept* ⊃ *artist* ⊃ *virtuoso* – note how the items on the right necessarily imply the meanings of the ones to the left, but not conversely. You cannot be a virtuoso without being an expert, but the converse is not true at all.
honor ⊃ *glory* ⊃ *renown, fame* ⊃ *celebrity*
likeness ⊃ *similarity, resemblance, similitude* ⊃ *analogy*
limp ⊃ *floppy* ⊃ *flaccid, flabby* ⊃ *flimsy*
lure ⊃ *entice, inveigle* ⊃ *decoy, tempt* ⊃ *seduce*

mistake (v) ⊃ *confuse* ⊃ *confound*
parsimonious ⊃ *miserly* ⊃ *penurious* ⊃ *niggardly* ⊃ *penny-pinching*
partiality ⊃ *prepossession* ⊃ *prejudice* ⊃ *bias*
enthusiasm ⊃ *fervor, ardor* ⊃ *passion* ⊃ *zeal*
small ⊃ *petty* ⊃ *puny* ⊃ *trivial* ⊃ *trifling, paltry* ⊃ *measly* ⊃ *picayune*

We can now define the notion "loss of specificity" with some precision: the more the words on the right side of these hyponymic rankings approach in meaning the ones on the left, the more general they have become and the more they have lost specificity.

3   The results of semantic change

We turn now from the mechanisms of change to the consequences of change. Traditionally, the results of semantic change are described and classified in terms of two properties: (1) Scope, and (2) Status. Other categories of traditional classification, like relation to culture and technology, have been considered above, because they are part of the **causes** of change.

3.1   Scope

How broad is the range which the meaning of a word covers – how much does it include? A familiar example will illustrate this property: *meat* used to mean "any kind of solid food," as in the familiar expression "meat and drink," and now it means only a particular kind of food, namely the flesh of animals. The scope of the word has been **narrowed**. The scope of a word's meaning can, of course, change in the opposite direction: originally the word *escape* meant "to get out of one's clothing, lose one's cape while fleeing," (ex "out of" + √cap "head [covering], cape"). Today we can escape and keep our cape on, if we wore capes any more. The scope of the word has been widened.

3.2   Status: amelioration and pejoration

Has the reference of the word gone up, or down, in its social status and content? One classic example of a word that has risen in status is *knight*, which used to mean, quite simply, "boy, manservant." Rising in status is called **amelioration** (from Lat. *melior* "better"). A development of the meaning in the opposite direction, which is perhaps more frequent, is called **pejoration** (from Lat. *pejor* "worse"). *Hussy* used to mean "house wife." *Demagogue* in ancient Greece meant "a leader of the people," completely lacking the negative connotations it has today (Hitler and Mussolini were demagogues). The Latin adjective *praeposterus* describes a "before-behind" relationship, a typical "cart-before-the-horse" situation. Such situations are undesirable; such inversion is illogical and contrary to reason. The English word *preposterous* now has a strong pejorative meaning and can be used in much broader negative contexts.

Another type of status change is **semantic bleaching**, where the original meaning of the word has been eroded away and generalized by heavy usage, as in words like *very* (originally "true"), *awful* ("full of awe"), *terrible* ("able to cause terror"). The ultimate examples of bleaching are the words *thing*, *do*, *nice*, and *okay*, and of course the more a word is bleached the further left it moves on a scale of hyponymy. *Thing* originally referred to a sort of parliamentary town-hall meeting, hence *affair*, *act*, any kind of *business*.[2] *Do* meant "to put, lay, cause" – "I did him (to) cry" meant "I caused him to cry." *Nice* (ultimately from Lat. *ne* "no" + *sci* "know," *nescius* "ignorant") was used in English until the thirteenth century only with the meaning "foolish, stupid," then in the fifteenth century it developed the meaning "coy, shy," and from that, in the sixteenth century, it changed into "dainty, fastidious, accurate," "delightful" in the eighteenth century, and a very loose positive adjective today. And *okay*, though there has been debate about it, seems to have started as a sort of joke, an acronym for "Oll Korrect," attributed to President Andrew Jackson. It was probably distributed widely as an abbreviation of "Old Kinderhook," Martin van Buren, who followed Jackson in the presidency and whose supporters formed "OK clubs" to solicit money for his campaign. This very general affirmative word was apparently needed and has been borrowed into virtually every language in the world whose speakers have had any significant amount of international contact.

3.3   Mixed examples

We classified the various types of semantic change above according to various criteria, but in reality most individual instances of semantic change can be seen as examples of two or more of these types simultaneously. The word *vixen* is clearly an instance of figurative use (analogical extension – it used to mean only "female fox" and now means both the animal, and, you might say, "foxy female"); it has also undergone generalization of meaning (i.e. the scope of the word has been widened to include not only foxes but also humans). It has furthermore undergone a change in status, namely pejoration (i.e. its associations have become negative). The word *offend* is an example of

---

[2] The bleaching of this word is so complete that people have come up with variations such as *thingumbob*, *thingamajig*, *thingumabob*, possibly in the desire to restore some of the "lost color" of *thing*.

widening of meaning, analogical extension, and pejoration. Since the late seventies psychologists have been using the word *bonding* in a highly specialized manner (scope change), extended from its original context, and positive with respect to social values (status change); this is especially obvious if you note the cultural associations of the two cognate nouns: *bonding* vs. *bondage*. *Nepotism*, although historically related to the word *nephew*, is favoritism no longer restricted to one particular family member; its scope has been widened and at the same time its status has gone down. It now refers to any hiring or other practice of favoritism in the workplace which gives an advantage to one's relatives or friends. Our simple everyday phrase *good bye* is a contraction of the phrase *God be with you*. The change involves both semantic bleaching and a shift in cultural reference (it no longer refers to God).

3.4   Narrowing/specialization[3]

Narrowing is an unnatural change in that it requires moving to the right on a hyponymic scale – we have already seen that the natural change is to the left, toward greater generality and less specificity. But narrowing takes place quite frequently when common words with non-specialized meanings are borrowed into some scientific field where they are given a highly specialized meaning within the context of one area. The transfer from one area of human experience to another is frequently accompanied by a figurative shift from the more concrete to the more abstract. We have noted recent examples where technology has given specialized meanings to ordinary words: recall terms like *bootstrap, clipboard, desktop, icon, software, style, toggle, tools, vaccine, virus, window* in the analogical and specialized sense we use in reference to our computers. In television, an *anchor* is primarily a "newscaster," and only secondarily a nautical object. In linguistics, a syntactic or prosodic *tree* can have *nodes* and *branches*; in these words the analogical transfer is also accompanied by narrowing. The *crescent* of the moon has a very specific shape, but the adjective from which the word is derived, √cre(s) "grow" + *ent* means simply "waxing, on the increase." The words below are transparent examples of narrowing:

> *acquiesce* "become quiet" (general)
> → "agree without further comment" (narrow, specific)
> *actor* "one who does something" (general)
> → "one who has a role in a dramatic production" (specific)

---

[3] Some of the examples in this section are taken from John Algeo, *Problems in the Origins and Development of the English Language*, Harcourt, Brace, and Jovanovich, 1992.

ammunition "military supplies of all kinds" (general)
    → "bullets, rockets, gunpowder" (military supplies which explode)
biblical "relating to a book"
    → "relating to a particular book"
hound "dog"
    → "type of hunting dog"
liquor "beverage, including water"
    → "alcoholic beverage of certain types, excluding wine"
science "knowledge of any kind"
    → "knowledge acquired through controlled experimentation"

4   Types of status change

Pejoration/degeneration. In one sense, status change is also a scope change. The scope that changes, in both pejoration ("getting worse") and amelioration ("getting better"), is **social** scope. When we focus on status, we ask whether the things these words refer to are higher or lower in the social scale? The examples below give the earlier higher-class or neutral meaning first, and then one or more of the lower-scale meanings the word has acquired in the course of pejoration:

aggravate "add weight to"
    → "annoy"
animosity "high spirits, courage"
    → "strong dislike"
artificial "skillfully constructed"
    → "fake"
brutal "animal, non-human"
    → "extremely cruel, ruthless"
censure "judgment, estimate"
    → "blame, severe criticism"
chaos "chasm, gulf"
    → "total disorder"
obsequious "following along"
    → "groveling"
officious "hard-working in carrying out one's duties"
    → "over-zealous and offensive in carrying out one's duties"
pretend "to stretch forth, to assert"
    → "to feign"

Amelioration. Some roots and words are better "social climbers" than others – from a neutral, or even negative original meaning they have attained an improved "social" status. Instances of this type of semantic shift are not as frequent as instances of pejoration; for some reason words are more likely to lose their status and respectability in the language than to "go up in the world." Note the social unacceptability, or near unacceptability, of *poor, cripple, idiot, stewardess* – we have replaced them with *underprivileged, disabled, mentally challenged, flight attendant.* However, examples of **amelioration** do exist, as the more recent uses of the adjectives *hopping, designer,* and *cool* testify. The words listed below are instances of amelioration:

> *dexterity* "right (handedness)"
> → "skill"
> *knight* "stable boy"
> → "feudal warrior"
> → "lower rank nobility in Britain"
> *mellifluous* (*mel* -"honey" + flu- "flow") "flowing like honey"
> → "smooth and melodious," especially of voice, tune, etc.
> *meticulous* "fearful, timid"
> →"very careful and precise in performance"
> *pastor* "one who tends sheep"
> → "one who ministers to the religious needs of people"
> *pedagogue* "a slave who takes the children to school"
> →"any teacher"
> *sensitive* "capable of using one's senses"
> → "perceptive, keenly observant, responsive"

5   Changing cultural relevance

As our world changes, we change the meanings of the words which refer to it. Consider the *default setting* of some parameter in a computer. *Default* means "failure." It stills refers to bank failures or individual failures to live up to financial obligations ("to default on a loan"). The current computer meaning does not appear even as recently as the first edition of the *American Heritage Dictionary* of 1973, namely "the setting to which the program returns when no special setting is selected." Computers have become widely used and understood subsequent to that date, and that fact has established very recently what is now one of the two principal meanings of the word, the computer sense. Thus, we can say that the cultural relevance of the word has changed.

Changing cultural relevance is inevitable. All languages at all times reflect the needs, perceptions, interests, attitudes of their speakers. As the speakers and their social environment change, so do the words they use, both in form and in meaning. Our language is full of amusing examples of changing cultural relevance, most of which pass by without notice. Living in a *duplex* does not evoke the image of something folded twice. *Trivia* is transparently "three ways" or "three roads," but that etymological sense is so far removed from the present meaning that we have to be told that it comes from the casual chatter occurring at a major three-way intersection where people gathered in ancient Rome. We do not think of the word *suffrage* in a phrase like *women's suffrage* as having anything to do with breaking, but it means literally "broken under," referring to the use of broken tiles for ballots in ancient Greece. During World War II, the word *axis*, a neutral geometric term, was adopted for the alliance of Germany and Italy in 1936, later including Japan and other nations. Subsequent history cast a blight on this word, and now it is a negative word, identifying those who were opposed to the Allies. The Allies, on the other hand, were "the good guys," from an anti-fascist perspective, though the word *ally* is a neutral word meaning "associate, kinsman," related to *alloy* "something bound up." More recently, the adjective *affirmative* in the phrase *affirmative action* has been interpreted to carry either positive or negative meaning depending on the context and the political views of the speaker and the audience. All such changes are of course unpredictable: they depend on changing technology, changing customs, even historical accidents of all kinds.

6   Semantic guesswork

Parsing. The first step in figuring out what an unfamiliar word means is to parse it – that is, divide it into morphemes. We have seen many examples of this and need not go over it again. Given a correct parse, the question is how to go about figuring out the meaning. First we **gloss** it morpheme by morpheme, dividing the surface form into its meaningful components, then showing the basic forms of the morphemes, then the meanings. At this stage of the exercise the result may look dangerously like gibberish. In these examples, the parse is marked by hyphens and the morpheme-by-morpheme gloss is given to the right in single quotes:

> *homeo-stas-is* < *homeo-stat-is* "same"-"stay"-"AN"[4]

To make sense of this, we have to try reading the gloss in both directions to see which makes more sense (usually right to left works better). In this case, a right-to-left reading produces something like "state of staying the same." So our full analysis looks like this:

> *homeo-stas-is* < *homeo-stat-is* = "same"-"stay"-"AN"
>   "state of staying the same"

---

[4] AN stands for "abstract noun."

Another example that works well in the same direction:

necrophobia < *necro-phob-ia* =   "dead body"-"fear"-"condition"
"condition of fear of corpses"

With the word *hieroglyphic*, on the other hand, the easier reading goes from left to right: "sacred" + "carving" + ADJ., that is, "having the properties of sacred carvings," though in this case, too, the last morpheme in the string determines whether we are dealing with a verb, a noun, an adjective, or an adverb. The gloss "having the properties of sacred carvings" is not very helpful: the problem is to figure out what those properties might be. In order to understand what *hieroglyphic* really means, you have to deduce that the carvings are ancient, that they are like letters cut into stone, and that they are hard to read, or at least that it caused a lot of trouble to decipher them. Only in that way can you discover that in addition to referring to the sacred writings on the temples of Egypt, the word can mean simply "hard to read."

Consider a word like *supererogation*.

super-ex-rog-ate-ion = "above"-"out of, beyond"-"ask, payout"-"V"-"AN"

If we leave off the *super*, we get "paying out beyond" or "something which is paid beyond what was asked for" (no way to know which, in this case: the first is active, the second passive, and either is possible). When we add *super* to the first guess, the meaning is sensible enough: "something which is far beyond asking." It could mean, therefore, a really nice favor you might do for someone, something that no one would ask for. That is roughly what it means: "something which is above and beyond what was asked for." It refers to the behavior of people who go that extra mile, but it can also mean "superfluous, unnecessary".

Now consider the word *apheliotropic*:

ap – heli-o-trop-ism < *apo-* = "away"-"sun"-"turn"-"state, condition, process"

To produce a good reading for this word, we have to supply a sensible relationship between "away," "sun," and "turn"; the *-ism* is the easy part. Starting from the end, first we get "the state of turning" and then, left-to-right, "away from the sun." As soon as we see that, the full reading is obvious, "condition or state of turning away from the sun."

One really acquires the ability to make such guesswork come out right only after looking at hundreds of examples, guessing, and not being afraid to be wrong: guess, then check the dictionary, and after a while you get the knack of it.

10 The pronunciation of classical words in English

1   Unassimilated classical words

English contains classical words and phrases of two types:

(1)   Those that have been fully assimilated into English, and have simply become English words (all the early borrowings, also most borrowings during and before the Renaissance); and

(2)   True classical words that are either recognizably recent borrowings, or words and phrases fossilized in legal or scientific language.

The bulk of this book has been concerned with the former group, the words of classical origin that are now fully assimilated into English, and this chapter will be no exception. Before turning to the main topic, however, it may be useful to deal with the **second** group and recount briefly how **un**assimilated classical words and phrases are pronounced in English. The issue with these is: to what extent does one try to reproduce or simulate "authentic" Latin pronunciation? There are five traditional methods of Latin pronunciation found in modern times: (1) the classical Ciceronian, (2) the Italian, (3) the Continental, (4) the British, and (5) the American. The British system, though the one most commonly recorded in dictionaries, including some American dictionaries, is not in fact the one most commonly used in American English. It is, however, strongly favored in Britain. The essence of the British system is that not only the consonants but also the vowels are pronounced completely as they would be in a similar English word. Thus even *a priori*, which is almost universally pronounced [ɑ pri ′o ri] (it rhymes with "see glory") in America, is pronounced [e prai ′o rai] in Britain, rhyming with "say pry OH rye." As we will point out below, neither the British nor the American system is thoroughly consistent. For unassimilated words and phrases in America the most acceptable approach is to follow one fairly easy rule: English consonants, Continental vowels.[1] And

---

[1] In this section we follow closely two articles by H. A. Kelly which from their titles and place of publication ("Pronouncing Latin Words in English," in *Classical World* 80: 33–37 (1986-87) and "Lawyers' Latin: *Loquenda ut Vulgus*?," in *Journal of Legal Education* 38: 195-207 (1988)) might appear to be too formidable for the general reader, but which in fact are accessible and strongly recommended.

before reading further here, it would be well if you were to review the phonetic explanations and special symbols found in Chapter 5.

1.1   The pronunciation of consonants in unassimilated classical words

It is now generally accepted that the consonants of any classical words in English should be pronounced in accord with the standard values associated with those letters in **English** orthography. In most cases, of course, the values of the consonant letters in Latin and in English have remained the same. In other words, treat the Latin consonant letters in the way that they would most commonly be pronounced in English orthography. Take a phrase like *prima facie*. In ancient Rome, it would have been something like [pri ma 'fa ki e]. In modern English, however, it is generally pronounced [prai ma 'feš i i]. Other examples of familiar words: *ex officio* would have been something like [ɛks o 'fi ki o] in ancient Rome, but it is now pronounced [ɛks o 'fiš i o]. *Ceteris paribus* would have been ['ke te ris 'pa ri bus], now ['se te ris 'pa ri bus]. *Sui generis* would have been [su i 'ge ne ris] but is now pronounced [swi 'ǰe ne rəs]. The consonant spelled <v> was pronounced [w] in classical Latin; only classical scholars today are aware of this fact. For this consonant, too, it is best to follow an Anglicized pronunciation, so that an expression such as *volenti* "to a consenting person" which used to be pronounced [**wo len** ti] is now pronounced [vo "**len** ti]. If you want to warn your friends that wine will loosen their tongue, *in vino veritas* is pronounced [in '**vi** no '**ve** ri tas] and not with [w] for [v].

The table summarizes the main differences between the classical and the Anglicized pronunciation of consonants:

Letter	Classical Sound	Anglicized Sound	Example
c	[k] always	[s] before i, e	*pace, et cetera*
g	[g] always	[ǰ] before i, e	*ab origine, genius*
t	[t] always	[š] before iV, e	*ab initio, ratio*
v	[w]	[v]	*verbatim, (modus) vivendi*

1.2   The pronunciation of vowels in unassimilated classical words

While we can treat the consonants in unassimilated words and phrases as if they were just unfamiliar English words, the vowels can be pronounced in accord with two quite different systems:

(1)   as normally pronounced in English in that position in the word, the system used in Britain, or

(2)   roughly, as normally pronounced in other European languages such as Spanish, German, French, the system used in America.

In either case the consequence is that they are not pronounced in the way they would have been in classical times, though the European-American tradition is much closer.

European values. It is indeed easiest to be consistent in the pronunciation of the vowels of classical words if one simply follows the European values of the vowels, given below. The angle brackets < > are used to enclose the letters with which a word is spelled, the square brackets enclose our representation of the pronunciation of the letters.

<a> or <au> as in *father, nausea*, represented as [ɑ] in our pronunciation guides[2]

<e> as in *fiancé*, represented as [e]

<i> or <y> as in *machine*, represented as [i]

<o> as in *hope*, represented as [o]

<u> as in either *boot* or *cute*, represented as [u] or [yu][3]

<oe> like <i> if long, but [ɛ] if short (e.g. *Oedipus*)

The letter <a> is not treated consistently in Anglicized Latin pronunciation, even though the value given above is generally favored. This letter has three main values in English: the vowel of *cash* [æ], the vowel of *father* [ɑ], and the vowel of hate [e]. The first of these does not correspond to any Latin sound spelled with <a>, and should not, speaking from a technical view, be used in pronouncing unassimilated Latin words, though in practice it is the sound you will hear in *caveat, magnum (opus), lapsus*, etc, a spontaneous and natural assimilation of the classical [ɑ] to the English [æ]. The last one, [e], is what we commonly find in *prima facie* because the <a> appears before a single consonant and two bare vowels in the following two syllables. But except for that situation and a few others that cause the same choice to be made, the letter <a> is usually pronounced as indicated above, [ɑ], in the proper circumstances or by people who want to preserve more of the authentic classical flavor of the word or phrase they are using. Thus the expressions *tabula rasa, pater familias*, and *alma mater* are pronounced ['tɑ bu lɑ 'rɑ sa], ['pɑ ter fa 'mi li əs], and ['ɑl mə 'mɑ tər], respectively.

---

[2] About half of all American English speakers – roughly speaking, those who live west of the Missouri River – have this vowel in both *father* and *nausea*. In the northeast and south, the two words will have two somewhat different vowels, but there is little uniformity about **which** two different vowels.

[3] These are not the same; both pronunciations are widely used, even though the latter is actually the English version rather than continental, e.g. *humanum est errare* "to err is human," would have [hu-] in the Continental version, [hyu-] in the English version.

Fossilized pronunciations. One should make the point once again that our recommendations here would be more straightforward were it not for the considerable diversity of pronunciations inherited from the past. We have to take into account the fact that many Latin words and phrases (though not fully integrated into the language) have a well-established and widespread pronunciation that deviates from the general principles formulated above. For instance, our recommendation for the phrase *prima facie* would have to be ['**pri** mə '**fe** ši] if we followed our rules exclusively; but this phrase is so well known in the British pronunciation ['**prai** mə . . .] that we think that that variant is perfectly acceptable. Vacillation may occur even with relatively well-defined patterns. An example of this is the pronunciation of <-i> at the end of borrowed words. It is very likely to be pronounced [-ai], as in *alumni, a priori, loci*, yet while most borrowed Latin nouns whose plurals end in <-i> do indeed follow that model, e.g. *gemini, magi, nuclei*, all with [-ai], the <-i> in phrases such as *advocatus diaboli* "devil's advocate," *anno Domini* "in the year of the Lord," *memento mori* "remember that you will die," *modus vivendi* "a way of living," or *vox populi* "voice of the people" both [-ai] and [-i] are freely used, while in *lapis lazuli* the most common pronunciation is with [-i].[4]

2   The pronunciation of fully assimilated classical words

By definition "fully assimilated" is a qualification which suggests that words in this category are treated exactly like English words. There are some peculiarities of pronunciation, however, which are specific to the classical vocabulary of English. The pronunciation of the consonants spelled <ch>, <g>, <x> varies depending on whether the source of the word is Greek or Latin.

	Latin	Greek
<ch>	[č]	[k]
<g>	[ǰ]	[g]
<x>	[ks]	[z]

Thus the <ch> in a word derived from Latin is what you would expect, namely the sound that <ch> has in words like *channel, chart, chapel, chisel*. If an etymologically Latinate word was borrowed into English not directly from Latin, but via French, the <ch> may represent [š]:

---

[4] Our discussion of this particular pattern is strictly confined to Latin borrowings. Thus the plural of *alumnus* "male student" is alumni, with [-ai], but non-Latin loanwords: *salami* and *tutti frutti* from Italian, *corgi* from Welsh, *yogi* from Sanskrit, *colibri* from Caribbean via Spanish *pastrami* from Yiddish, *hara-kiri, kabuki, tsunami* from Japanese, all have *only* [-i].

chammy < *chamois, chute, cliché, douche, machine, moustache.* Note that in the latter group – words which are etymologically Latinate, but come to English through French, there is a tendency for the replacement of the [š] by [č], as in *avalanche, niche*; clearly the innovative pronunciation with [č] is due to the influence of spelling. Yet a third way of pronouncing <ch> is found in words derived from Greek. These are consistently [k], as in:

ar**ch**angel	A**ch**illes	**ch**i	stoma**ch**
chaos	**ch**ronology	**ch**aracter	e**ch**o
chimera	te**ch**nology	**ch**arisma	

Some familiar roots with this pronunciation are *chem* "alloy," *chir* "hand," *chlor* "green," *chrom* "color," *mechan* "device," *tachy* "speed," *machy* "battle."

When **the letter <g>** is followed by a front vowel, *i, y,* or *e,* it is normally pronounced as the first sound in *gem, gin, gym,* i.e. [ǰ]. This is generally true of both Latin and Greek words, (though, notice, there are exceptions to the rule in the **native** vocabulary: *gear, geek, geezer, geld, get, gill, gimmick, giggle*). One Greek root, *gyn* "woman" has an interesting history: in some derivatives the consonant appears to contradict the rule, so we have *gynecology, gynecocracy, gynecoid, gynogenesis* pronounced with initial [g-], a pronunciation which was probably artificially introduced and is now maintained by the professional community. Notice that both [g] and [ǰ] are allowed by the *American Heritage College Dictionary*. Inside the word, *-gyn-* is always [ǰ]: *androgynous, heterogynous, protogynous.*

The letter <x>, the third letter in the list above, is normally pronounced [ks], as in *cortex, dexterous, expert, sextet.* In some cases the sequence [k]+[s] can even be reconstructed: *flec* "bend" +*s*+*ible* becomes *inflexible, para*+*dog* "teach" +s becomes *paradox, seg* "cut" +*s* becomes *sex* – notice that there is no change of pronunciation in such cases; the only change is in the spelling, a change that has not been fully agreed upon on the two sides of the Atlantic. The accepted British spelling for the phonetic sequences of [k]+[s] is <-x->, while the most widely used spelling in the US is <-ct-> as in *connexion, inflexion* vs. *connection, inflection.* Both traditions have only *complexion* and *crucifixion.* The Yiddish word *laks* "salmon," German *Lachs* has now been re-spelled as *lox,* and Americans are familiar with spellings such as *thanx, (White) Sox,* and the clever attention-getter *truxtop.* One can never tell, just from spelling, which language the word has come from. Even in a word for which one *does* know the origin, as in the Greek name of the letter *xi,* the *OED* records four pronunciations: [s-], [z-], [ks-], [gz-], though only [z-] is common in Modern English. It is safe to assume that if the initial <x> in a word is not capitalized, or hyphenated as in *X-rated*, *x-ray*, the word is Greek and its first consonant is [z].[5] In transcriptions from non-classical alphabets <x> is usually [š] as in the place names *Xian* [šia*n*], *Xin-xiang* [ši*n* šiang], except in the transcription of *Xosa*, also *Xhosa*, the people and the language of the Eastern Cape in South Africa in which X stands for a sound similar to [kh].

These minor complications are predictable in a language which is constantly expanding its vocabulary. Putting the inconsistencies aside, and looking at the vast body of loanwords in English, we can say that the consonants and vowels of the classical words are well on their way to becoming fully assimilated into the corresponding English values: the one-time loanwords are English words now, and both vowels and consonants should be treated in standard English ways.

3   Finding the main stress[6]

There is one respect in which words from classical sources can catch us by surprise: which syllable gets the main stress? This is not always obvious because it depends on some information which does not show up in the spelling, namely whether certain vowels were long or short in Latin. The importance of this question is developed below. But this chapter makes no attempt to deal with the rules of stress placement in general. To deal with the full lexicon, the rules are numerous and complex, with many exceptions to any formulation. The stress placement for words which have been in the language since Anglo-Saxon times presents no serious problems and we hardly need "rules" to describe the situation: it is **the first syllable of the root** that is stressed, e.g. *blóssom*, *bódy*, *hóly*, *néver*, *súmmer*, *unpáck*; these are mostly mono- or disyllabic words anyway. However, once we look into the polysyllabic vocabulary, for the words borrowed into English from Latin and Greek or formed by the addition of foreign suffixes, the rules can become fairly intricate. Knowing them will usually enable us to pronounce correctly a long classical word even if we don't know all the details of its meaning or how to parse it.

---

[5] This convention is so well established that puns can be based on it. In the *Los Angeles Times*, November 30, 1997, a story about Xena, the "Warrior Princess" of TV, was headlined "Princess of the Xeitgeist." The pun is based on the Americanized pronunciation of *Zeitgeist* with an initial [z-], a word borrowed from German meaning "spirit of the time" and pronounced [tsait gaist] in German.

[6] Many of our examples of stress placement are drawn from Eric Fudge, *English Word Stress* (London: Allen and Unwin, 1984). Our rules, however, differ from his in significant ways. A good introduction to the linguistic principles governing word stress in English can be found in Chapter 7 "Word Stress," in *English Phonology. An Introduction* by Heinz Giegerich, Cambridge University Press, 1992.

First, what is meant by "stress?" A syllable is said to be stressed if it is given more prominence than the syllables on at least one side of it, commonly both; if it is the most prominent syllable in the word it is said to carry the **main stress**. If you can figure out where the main stress is, then all the subsidiary stresses will fall into place automatically. Some people have trouble identifying the stressed syllable in a word; one way of training yourself to hear which syllable in a word is the most prominent is by pronouncing the word in a loud, emphatic manner: imagine a fiery speaker addressing a large audience: "I say deMOcracy . . . we want eduCAtion . . . let's give every child the opporTUnity . . ." Try yelling a word across a noisy room – soon you will develop the knack of recognizing stress.

How shall we mark stress? Obviously, stress is not normally orthographically marked on the printed page, though sometimes authors will insist on italicizing a particular syllable or word for special effect. In dictionaries and philological descriptions such as this one, it is common to indicate the prominence of the main-stressed syllable by the use of capitalization, thus: *capitaliZAtion*, *PROminence*, *unaccountaBIlity*, *DICtatorship*, *senSAtional*, *aristoCRAtic*, *arisTOcracy*, *TElegraph*, *teLEgraphy*. There are various other, equivalent, systems of notation found in dictionaries and in textbooks, employing stress diacritics, accent marks before, over, or after the stressed syllable. They are usually explained in the front matter. We find the system which uses capital letters for the most prominent syllables most readily recognized, and we will therefore use it here.

3.1   The role of final syllables

Stress neutrality. The determination of stress position depends on certain facts about the last two syllables on the right-hand edge of the word. However, not all such syllables affect the location of the stressed syllable. Inflectional suffixes, whether they are separate syllables or not, remain invisible to the stress placement rules. Certain final syllables which happen also to be suffixes are **stress neutral** too. You can add them onto the stem to which stress has already been assigned, and that stress does not change. Most of these suffixes are from earliest English times, even though, as one can see below, they combine freely with familiar classical roots. There are also historically non-native suffixes which belong to this set: *-ist* and *-ize*. The following suffixes are stress neutral:

-dom as in *MARtyr – MARtyrdom*
-en as in *forGIVE – forGIven*
-er as in *inTERpret – inTERpreter*
-ess as in *PROphet – PROphetess*
-ful as in *reGRET – reGRETful*

-hood as in *GRANDfather – GRANDfatherhood*
-ish as in *FEver – FEverish*
-ist as in *perFECtion – perFECtionist*
-ize as in *CApital – CApitalize*
-less as in *comPASSion – comPASSionless*
-ly as in *MAtron – MAtronly*
-man as in *FORestry – FORestryman*
-ness as in *inVINcible – inVINcibleness*
-some as in *adVENture – adVENturesome*
-ward(s) as in *HEAVen – HEAVenward(s)*
-wise as in *WEATHer – WEATHerwise*

It should be noted that while the borrowed suffixes *-ist* and *-ize* are normally stress-neutral, they remain so only if the form they attach to is a free-standing form as in *perFECtion–perFECtionist*, *ACtive–ACtivist*, *CApital–CApitalize*, *Union–Unionize*, but when attached to non-free forms, they require stress on the third syllable from the end as in *reCIdivist*, *anTAgonize*, or on the preceding syllable, if there is no third syllable from the end, as in *BAPtist*.

The most common stress-neutral suffix, not listed above, in classical vocabulary is the noun-forming suffix **-y** as in *HEterodox–HEterodoxy*.[7] We list the examples with it separately; unlike most of the other stress-neutral suffixes above, *-y* can affect the phonetic shape of the word but not its stress: it changes [k] to [s], it triggers T-Lenition as described in Chapter 6, and it changes the [g] to [j] in the derived suffixal form *-(o)logy* from the root *log* "speak, write" + *y* as in *morphology*, *musicology*, etc., and in stems ending in *-agog* "teach, induce" as in *demagog–demagogy*, *pedagog–pedagogy*. Also, since *-y* is frequently added to words which contain three or more syllables, nouns formed in this way can have a rather exceptional main stress position – four syllables from the right-hand edge. Except for examples with a stress-neutral suffix, it is impossible to have the main stress appear further than the third syllable back from the right-hand edge of the word:

ACcuracy	efFEminacy	INtricacy
CElibacy	imMEdiacy	leGItimacy
deGEneracy	inDElicacy	LIteracy

Other suffixes are **stress demanding**. When you add them to a stem, they always steal the stress away from the stem and require that it be placed on them. Some standard examples of these appear below:

---

[7] The suffix is generally stress-neutral only when it attaches to free-standing forms, e.g. *ALlomorph – ALlomorphy*; otherwise it pushes the stress leftwards onto the third syllable from the end as in *MAjesty*, *geOmetry*.

-*aire* as in *doctriNAIRE*   -*esce* as in *acquiESCE*
-*ee* as in *absenTEE*   -*ese* as in *CantoNESE*
-*eer* as in *auctioNEER*   -*esque* as in *araBESQUE*
-*elle* as in *villaNELLE*   -*ette* as in *drum majoRETTE*

More **final stress**. Some word-endings, which may or may not be productive suffixes, behave in the same way: they demand main stress. You will recognize the stress-demanding elements in the following words:

cruSADE   *kangaROO*
promeNADE   *shamPOO*
canTEEN   *balLOON*
velveTEEN   *monSOON*

Furthermore, a significant number of words take main stress on the final syllable, like the stress-demanding suffixes, usually because they were borrowed from some other language in which they already had final stress. They simply count as exceptions to the general rules of stress placement, and they include examples like these:

aBYSS   *guiTAR*
baROQUE   *hoTEL*
baZAAR   *inTRIGUE*
caNAL   *masSEUSE*
craVAT   *miNUTE*
cuLOTTES   *mouSTACHE*
doMAIN   *personNEL*
gaLORE   *raVINE*
giRAFFE   *terRAIN*

3.2   Steps in determination of main stress placement

To determine main stress placement, follow these steps:

STEP ONE: **Remove inflectional suffixes and stress neutral suffixes.**

All inflectional suffixes in English are stress-neutral, as discussed above – they never affect the position of stress in the word. By "remove" these suffixes, we simply mean "treat them as invisible in calculating the stress placement."

STEP TWO: **If the word has two syllables, stress the first one.**

There are many exceptions such as the ones listed above, all of which "feel" foreign, because they were borrowed recently into English. There is, however, one completely native and entirely systematic set of exceptions: pairs of words, one of them **a verb** and the other the corresponding **noun**, where only the nouns follow STEP TWO:

Verb	Noun
esCORT	*EScort*
ferMENT	*FERment*
fragMENT	*FRAGment*
perVERT	*PERvert*
segMENT	*SEGment*
surVEY	*SURvey*
torMENT	*TORment*

In some cases the pairings involve an adjective which has the same structure as a verb, but differs from it in the placement of stress. If there is a corresponding noun, adjectives and nouns pair together, while the verbs remain end-stressed:

Verb	Noun	Adjective
absTRACT	*ABstract*	*ABstract*
freQUENT	–	*FREquent*
preSENT	*PREsent*	*PREsent*
perFECT	–	*PERfect*
susPECT	*SUspect*	*SUspect*

There are about 130 pairs in English in which the difference in stress is based entirely on whether they are verbs or nouns. The systematic character of the examples listed above has wider implications: even outside these otherwise homophonous pairs, disyllabic nouns in English have stress on the first syllable, while verbs are more likely to frustrate the expectations of our STEP TWO. This is especially true of those verbs, either of Anglo-Saxon origin, or later fully naturalized loans, which contain a recognizable prefix as their first syllable:

beGRUDGE	*proPEL*
comPEL	*reSIGN*
eJECT	*subTRACT*
exPLODE	*transCEND*
forGET	*unDO*

With these exceptions and the ones noted above, it is generally true that the first syllable of disyllabic words is stressed: *anxious, bias, bonus, carnage, common, current, donkey, ethics, exit, famous, finger, govern, horror, pepper, person, verdict, weather.*

A large number of the words we analyzed in the central chapters of this book, however, are words which contain more than two syllables. The next three steps will help decide where the main stress should be in such polysyllabic words.

STEP THREE: In words of three syllables or more, determine whether the penult is heavy or light.

The **penult** is the next-to-last syllable (*pen* "almost" + *ult* "last"). The important thing to discover about the penult is whether it is **light** or **heavy**. A **heavy** syllable consists either of a long vowel or of any vowel, long or short, plus at least one consonant following it in the same syllable. Consonants which precede the vowel do not count in determining weight. The penults in these words are heavy: *recruitment, entailment, confrontation, detergent, extremely, escapist, abysmal*. A **light** syllable consists of a single short vowel and nothing else following it in the same syllable. The penults in these words are light, because in each instance the consonant after the vowel of the penult belongs to the next (final) syllable: *average, bungalow, edible, regiment, syllable, ultimate, resolute*. A fair number of words have penults that are **spelled** as if they were heavy, and therefore they count as heavy for stress assignment even though we pronounce only a single consonant and they are, strictly speaking, phonetically light: *baccillus, compassion, discussion, dismissive, falsetto, occurrence, rebuttal, spaghetti*.

STEP FOUR: If the penult is heavy, stress it.

It may help you determine whether the penult is heavy or not if you understand somewhat better the notions "long vowel" and "short vowel," especially since the labels "long" and "short" have mostly historical relevance – a genuine quantitative distinction between longer and shorter vowels once existed in English, but now the vowels are not always clearly different with respect to "length" but rather only with respect to quality (i.e., they sound different, but not in terms of actual duration). "Long" and "short" should therefore be thought of mostly as arbitrary labels, like "vowels of class A" and "vowels of class B." A long vowel, which always makes a syllable heavy, is one which corresponds in sound to the "name" of the vowel – A, E, I, O, U. In addition to these five, the diphthongs OU as in *house* and OI as in *noise* count as long. Thus the stressed syllable of each of the following words contains a long vowel, in the order just named:

spAcious
spEcious
spIcy
Ocean
mUtant
profOUnd
rejOIce

On the other hand, the stressed syllable of each of the following words contains a **short** vowel:

fAbulous
respEct
tItillate
harmOnic
profUndity

Here are some more examples which behave in accord with STEP FOUR:

confronTAtion	*eLECtric*
encycloPEdic	*eNORmous*
innuENdo	*proFESsion.*
pronunciAtion	*repliCAtion*
spaGHEtti	*verANda*

STEP FIVE: If the penult is light, stress the antepenult.

"Antepenult" is a word which is etymologically fairly transparent. Here is how it parses:

> *ante* "before" + *pen* "almost" + *ult* "last" – that is, "before the almost last syllable," therefore the third-from-last syllable.

Some examples in which the stress is assigned correctly by STEP FIVE (notice that it does not matter whether the final syllable is light or heavy, only whether the penultimate syllable is light or heavy) are as follows:

ACtivate	*reVItalize*
MULtiply	*UNderline*
syLAbify	*TElephone*
MEnopause	*VACcinate*
COMpliment	*aSPAragus*
eSOphagus	*reCIprocal*
encycloPEdia	*reSIdual*
pharmaCEUtical	*eMEritus*
non SEquitur	*hypoTHEtical*
hyPOthesis	*Adequate*
comPArison	*PLEnary*
reciPROcity	*menDAcity*
phiLOlogy	*ambiGUity*

The difficult examples are those where the spelling system does not reflect whether the penultimate syllable is light or heavy; that is, our spelling system does not indicate whether vowels are long or short (or were in Latin or Greek). Consider examples like these:

caesura – if light, stress *CAEsura*; if heavy, *caeSURa* (it's heavy)
corona – if light, stress *COrona*; if heavy, *corOna* (it's heavy)

decorum – if light, stress *DEcorum*; if heavy, *deCOrum* (it's heavy)[8]
detritus – if light, stress *DEtritus*; if heavy, *deTRItus* (it's heavy)
integer – if light, stress *INteger*; if heavy, *inTEger* (it's light)
quietus – if light, stress *QUIetus*; if heavy, *quiEtus* (it's heavy)
stamina – if light, stress *STAmina*; if heavy, *staMIna* (it's light)

In a significant number of words, English speakers have not been able to make up their minds (or they had some misinformation when the word was first borrowed). Words like these can go both ways:

abdomen – either *ABdomen* or *abDOmen*
acumen – either *Acumen*,[9] or *aCUmen*
Caribbean – either *CaRIBbean* or *CaribBEan*
cerebral – either *CErebral* or *ceREbral*
choleric – either *CHOleric* or *choLERic*
decorous – either *DEcorous* or *deCOrous*
vagary – either *VAgary* or *vaGAry*

And in a small number of words, the rules above make the wrong predictions (figure out why, in each case).

deCREpit	*deLIver*
deVElop	*eLEven*
eNAmel	*soLIcit*
disPArage	*INterval*
iMAgine	*CAlendar*
apPArel	*PArallel*
caDAver	*CYlinder*

You should have concluded that the rules predict STRESSED + unstressed + unstressed for *decrepit, deliver, develop, eleven, enamel, solicit, disparage*. For *calendar, interval*, they predict stress in the middle. It should be easy to figure the reason why the rest of the words: *cadaver, cylinder, apparel, parallel, imagine* are considered "irregular."

4   Stress-changing affixes

Regular exceptions. Exceptions like *decrepit* and *develop*, discussed in the immediately preceding paragraph, are real exceptions not governed by any rule. On the other hand, words which contain

---

[8] It is a curiosity of English stress that *decorous*, unlike *decorum*, allows the stress to appear on either one of the first two syllables. This appears to be a consequence of the common assumption that the penultimate vowel is short, resulting in the widespread but originally mistaken pronunciation *DEcorous*. It may be contaminated by something like *decorate*, which has the initial stress legitimately from STEP THREE above.

[9] In spite of the fact that it is historically wrong, this is now the more common pronunciation.

stress-changing affixes are regular in their own way, though they often appear to violate the general rules. You can think of the effect of the affix as a sort of override effect: no matter where the stress would be fixed by the general rules, the general rules are overridden by the special affix effect.

4.1   Affixes which attract the stress to the syllable on their left

With a small number of exceptions (*arithmetic, heretic, lunatic, politic, rhetoric, arsenic, Catholic, choleric, Arabic*), the suffix **-ic** (also **-ical** and **-ics**) attracts the stress to the penultimate syllable even if it would not normally be entitled to get the stress:

genetic	*encyclopedic*
orthopedic	*demonic*
athletic	*microscopic*
telepathic	*hygienic*
algebraic	*telephonic*
cyrillic	*Pacific*
acoustic	*calisthenics*
mathematics	*robotics*
hysterical	*political*

The suffix **-id** also does this, but it is not so common a suffix: e.g., *carotid. Invalid* and *pyramid* are exceptions. The suffix **-ity** behaves in the same way, whether alone or in combination with other suffixes: it attracts stress to the syllable immediately preceding it: *divinity, masculinity, authority, vulgarity*. In the compound suffixes **-id+ity** as in *frigidity, liquidity, morbidity, stupidity* and **-ic+ity** as in *authenticity, infelicity, periodicity, specificity*, the stress is controlled by the rightmost suffix, while the stress-attracting properties of **-id** and **-ic** remain invisible.

Stress in long words of non-classical origin. It may help to understand the stress rules in classical words if you recognize that the same rules work even for the many words, such as names of places, that we have borrowed from other sources like American Indian languages. Consider these words: *Chattanooga, Winnebago, Minnesota, Oklahoma, Mississippi, Okeefenokee*. All have a heavy penult, and the stress falls there. On the other hand, these all have a light penult, and so the stress falls one syllable earlier: *Potawatomi, Florida, Oregon, Temecula, Canada, Tehachapi*.

Appendix I: an introduction to dictionaries

1   The origins of dictionaries

Dictionaries are a recent invention. Human language, in a form that must have resembled modern languages pretty closely, has existed for at least 50,000 years, and it may have been developing in ways unique to humans for more than a million years. But writing systems of any kind are quite recent, originating in the Near East no more than a few thousand years ago. Obviously writing systems have to exist before there is any need for dictionaries. The earliest alphabetic writing system, the kind that is universally used in western languages, is that of Greek, developed around the Aegean Sea less than a thousand years before the birth of Christ, and from it all the others are descended, either in the eastern version (Cyrillic) or the western (Roman). But inventive as the ancient classical civilizations were, they did not invent dictionaries – they invented grammars, they invented geometry, they invented the Olympic games, but not dictionaries. Dictionaries, curiously, are a quite accidental by-product of ignorance. The monks working in scriptoria (places where books were copied by hand, since printing had not been invented) in the Middle Ages often did not know Latin very well. Most of the texts they were copying were written in Latin; but the monks could not read it easily, and they jogged their memories as any elementary language student might do today. They wrote translations ("glosses") between the lines. Other monks later made lists of the glosses, and these were the earliest Latin-to-English "dictionaries." All this took place about 700 years before someone realized there might be money to be made by publishing lists of hard words with explanations of their meanings. The first such publication appeared within the lifetime of Queen Elizabeth I, who died in 1603. The first moderately complete English dictionary was another 150 years later, the work of Samuel Johnson published in 1755. Modern lexicography is therefore only 250 years old.

2   Types of dictionaries

Dictionaries either give information about equivalences between two languages – so-called bi-lingual dictionaries, which we use in translating a language we do not know well; or they give information about a language we already know and want to know better. These latter books are monolingual dictionaries. Such dictionaries now exist for virtually all national languages and for many local languages. We are concerned here specifically with monolingual English dictionaries.

Monolingual English dictionaries are of two distinct types, depending on the audience to which they are addressed: (1) specialized dictionaries, aimed to clarify the technical jargon of various professional and scholarly areas; and (2) general-purpose dictionaries, aimed to help native speakers understand the precise meanings, pronunciations, spellings, usages, and histories of the words of their language, including some of the technical words. The technical words that are found in a general-purpose dictionary usually constitute only a small fraction of the technical terminology of any specialized field, and the more recent coinages rarely appear. Furthermore they almost never have the kinds of encyclopedic explanations and illustrations that make a special-purpose dictionary useful to specialists. It is impossible to assess the technical dictionaries unless you are already an expert in the relevant field. We will refer briefly to some specialized dictionaries of interest to a general audience (for example, dictionaries of slang, dictionaries of Americanisms). Our main concern, however, is with the general-purpose dictionaries of English that all of us consult with great frequency, simply as part of being or becoming educated users of English.

General-purpose dictionaries are of two types also: (1) so-called unabridged dictionaries, and (2) desk dictionaries, which are shortened forms of the full dictionaries, either for college use or for use at lower educational levels. Desk dictionaries are the ones that we consult most of the time, in part because the unabridged dictionaries are ungainly and over-sized, in part because most of us don't have access to an unabridged dictionary at home or in our offices.

2.1   Unabridged

What does "unabridged" mean? First, it does not mean, as one might think, that an "unabridged dictionary" contains every English word. Nobody knows how many words English has. The blurbs on the jackets of various dictionaries may state that the dictionary contains "more than" 200,000 words, but that is difficult to determine. All one can count is "entries" or "headwords," and even that turns out to be a slippery notion because what is a headword in one dictionary may be subordinated – listed below the main entry – in another. Landau (*Dictionaries: The Art and Craft of Lexicography*, p. 84) characterizes the American system of entry counting thus:

(1)   Every word or phrase that is explicitly or implicitly defined, so long as it is clearly identifiable, usually by appearing in boldface type, is an entry.

(2)   The more entries one has or can claim, the better.

He goes on to point out that in a particular dictionary the entry for *parachute (n.)* counts as five entries because the forms *parachuted, parachuting, parachute (v.)* and *parachutist* all appear down inside the entry. But there is surely a large difference in the "counting value" of some of these "countable" entries. Size alone, measured by number of entries, does not make a dictionary better. In fact entry-counts are good mostly for publicity purposes. "Unabridged" means only this: the dictionary is not a shortened version of some other dictionary. It was compiled from scratch, which is to say, largely from its own files of citations, with all definitions and arrangements of meanings and examples determined by its own editors. However, dictionary producers are notorious plagiarists, and in fact have to be: every dictionary of the last 250 years has depended heavily on its predecessors, simply because the job is too big to be done really from scratch. The extremely high degree of originality of the *Oxford English Dictionary* (discussed below), the only one certainly compiled from its own files of citations, is in part due to necessity: it was the first (and still the only) dictionary ever to try to include every word that had appeared in English since the Norman Conquest, barring only technical terms that had not become common parlance. Probably the best understanding of "unabridged" is therefore something like "too big to serve easily as a desk dictionary, and having considerably more entries than desk dictionaries typically do, normally at least twice as many."

2.2   The *Oxford English Dictionary*

The *OED*, as it is generally called (or simply *The Oxford*), is the only English dictionary compiled totally from its own citation files. Its editors, wisely, also consulted the work of their predecessors, especially Samuel Johnson. Though it excludes most technical words, it nevertheless has to be viewed as the greatest of all unabridged dictionaries – not just in English but in any language. Nothing exactly comparable to it exists for Russian, German, Spanish, French, or Italian. Its size cannot be compared with other modern dictionaries of English because it includes, in principle, all the words that have ever appeared in the English language subsequent to 1150, a date which corresponds roughly to the beginning of the Middle-English period (the period of Geoffrey Chaucer, who died in 1400). The other great modern unabridged dictionaries like the *Merriam-Webster's* have excluded older obsolete and obsolescent words, but they considerably exceed the *OED*'s coverage of technical words from all the major fields of knowledge. Of the 291,627 entries in the *OED*, half or more than half are older words that no longer occur in modern usage. To say that more than half the words are no longer in contemporary use is not a criticism: the *OED* set out to create a record of the history of the English vocabulary and the historical development of the meanings of English words. It is a historical work par excellence.

The fully-up-dated second edition of 1989 is available in three formats: (1) twenty very large heavy printed volumes, which one is likely to find only in libraries; (2) a two-volume "compact edition" in which four regular printed pages of the full-sized version are reduced to one-quarter size and printed together on a single page – and a magnifying glass is provided; and (3) a compact disk, containing the whole dictionary as well as search programs which enable you to bring up onto your computer screen information which would take days to assemble from the printed versions. Unfortunately, the only one of these three versions which might be called "inexpensive" or even "moderately priced" is the compact edition, which has on several occasions been made available at a very reasonable price as a bonus for joining one book club or another. The CD-ROM version is between $200 and $400, depending on which version you choose; the hard-copy version is about three times that much. A third edition, which will certainly be available in electronic form also, is projected for the year 2005.

This great dictionary is so important to all work on the history of the English language that one should know how it came in existence. The first edition of the *OED* was compiled between 1884 and 1928; it contained about 240,000 entries. Recall, however, that this number included all the earlier as well as current words of English, so probably half the headword entries were obsolete. Furthermore, the *OED* explicitly chose not to include technical terminology from the sciences and medicine unless these terms had become common parlance outside the jargon of specialists. The policies of later dictionaries like *Merriam-Webster's* have been somewhat inconsistent on this issue, but they have generally included much more such terminology than the *OED*.

2.2.1   The editors

In spite of its staggering size, the *OED* is to an astonishingly large extent the work of a single individual, Sir James A. H. Murray, the first official editor after the task was taken over by Oxford University Press. Prior to that there were two very important earlier editors, under the loose control of The Philological Association which had initiated the entire project of data collection by hundreds of readers: Herbert Coleridge, a descendant of the poet, who died after two years; and

Frederick Furnivall, who installed a hierarchical structure of sub-editors to organize the citation slips that were sent in by the readers. He was otherwise negligent, and the project nearly died. But he was responsible for bringing into the work both Murray himself, and the backing of the Oxford University Press. Murray edited, starting in 1879, more than half of the first edition, the one which appeared in fascicles over a period of forty-four years, and these were assembled in the first edition of twelve tombstone-sized[1] volumes in 1928. He worked at it continuously for the last thirty-seven years of his life,[2] eighty to ninety hours a week. He collected and organized citations from the hundreds of individual readers who were solicited from all over the English-speaking world though mainly from England and Scotland. While it was Samuel Johnson (1755) who first provided citations to defend and illustrate his definitions, citations usually chosen by Johnson from learned authors and often written down straight out of Johnson's own prodigious memory, it was Murray who made a science of it, insisting that every nuance of every word be justified by citations from published and dated sources. He carefully sorted his citation slips and arranged them in historical order by senses, so that one can see for every word what the date of the earliest occurrence[3] was and what the earliest sense was and how, step by step, the meaning changed or new meanings arose from older ones. The *OED* citation file, at the time that publication of fascicles began in 1884, was already in excess of six million; and it has continued to be enriched to the present day under the later editors. The editor who produced the four-volume supplement of 1986 (incorporating the 1933 supplement) was R. W. Burchfield. The second edition of the *OED*, in 1989, which fully integrates both supplements, contains two-and-a-half million quotations selected from the citation files to support the definitions. The CD-ROM versions appeared in 1992 and 1994. The second edition was produced by J. A. Simpson and E. S. C. Weiner, who were also responsible for directing the work that put the dictionary into its present computer-accessible form on CD-ROM for either Macintosh or PC's.

2.2.2 Reduced versions of the *OED*

The *OED* has twice been the source of highly selective reduced-size versions. The first of these is *The Shorter Oxford English Dictionary* [4]

---

[1] This felicitous phrase is borrowed from Simon Winchester's *The Professor and the Madman*, New York: Harper Collins 1998. His delightful book recounts in detail the twenty-year relationship between Sir James Murray and Dr. William C. Minor, Murray's most prolific supplier of citations.   [2] He died in 1915 at the age of 78.

[3] The *OED*, first edition and supplements, was not always correct about earliest occurrence, and there are many learned articles in the lexicographic literature citing earlier occurrences than those that Murray and his readers found – about 40,000 of them up to this time. All this new information of course has been included in *OED*2, and the scholarly game of finding earlier dates starts all over again.   [4] Edited by William Little.

published in 1933. It has been revised twice, once in 1944[5] and most recently in 1993[6] under the title *The New Shorter Oxford English Dictionary.* This version was released on CD-ROM in 1997. This dictionary, in its various editions and formats, has been very popular and has sold well, though it is somewhat difficult to appreciate how so many purchasers have put it to use. It is too big for a desk dictionary and it is certainly not unabridged. As Onions wrote in his Preface to the second printing of 1936, "The aim of this Dictionary is to present in miniature all the features of the principal work."

The etymological portion of the *OED* – just the etymological portion –was the basis for the second selective version, *The Oxford Dictionary of English Etymology* (1966).[7] This version is wonderful for etymology, and it is the right size for a desk dictionary, but in fact since it has neither extended definitions nor illustrative quotations, it is not useful as a desk dictionary and is useful even for etymological purposes only if you can't get your hands on the *OED2* CD-ROM. In 1986 Oxford published *The Concise Oxford Dictionary of English Etymology,*[8] with a paperback reprint in 1993. The *Concise* version succeeds in reducing the Onions version from 1,024 pages to half that length, with most information preserved in spite of the reduction, to say nothing of the quite affordable price. But it is really difficult to use because it is so compact and abbreviated; and it does not serve at all as a desk dictionary and rather minimally as an etymological dictionary.

2.3   Merriam-Webster

Webster's Third New International Dictionary of the English Language, published by the Merriam-Webster Company in 1961 (*NID*3), is the only other relatively complete unabridged English dictionary of recent times. It differs from the *OED* in that it does contain very large numbers of technical words, going far beyond just those that have moved out into common parlance. It has some 450,000 entries. The fact that it is almost forty years old says something about the incredible expense and time required to update or replace a great unabridged dictionary. It replaced *Webster's New International Dictionary* of 1934 (*NID*2), which remains the largest of all English dictionaries, having over 600,000 entries. *NID*3 was shortened (at the same time that over 100,000 new entries were included, which means that 250,000 entries were dropped from *NID*2) mainly to make it possible to bind it by machine (it would have been prohibitively expensive,

---

[5] Edited by C. T. Onions.   [6] Edited by Leslie Brown.
[7] Completed by Dr. C. T. Onions in 1966 (he died while it was going through final editing; the work was completed by Dr. G. W. S. Friedrichsen and R. W. Burchfield). Onions was himself the sixth and last editor of the original *OED*.
[8] Edited by T. F. Hoad.

in 1961, to bind it by hand-stitching in the way that *NID2* was bound during the Great Depression when labor was cheap).

The name "Webster's," at least in America, is almost synonymous with "dictionary." One should know, however, that the name "Webster's" is in the public domain. The only publishing company whose work is directly descended from that of the nineteenth-century American lexicographical giant, Noah Webster, is the G. and C. Merriam Company of Springfield, Massachusetts. Its founders, after Webster's death in 1843, bought out the rights to the 1841 edition of Webster's *American Dictionary* (first edition 1828). But the Merriam-Webster dictionaries are not the only ones that use the Webster name to add prestige to their product. One of the best desk dictionaries with the Webster name, *Webster's New World Dictionary of the English Language* (first edition 1953) is totally unrelated to the Merriam-Webster company or to the Webster family. Another great desk dictionary (also unrelated to the earlier Webster's), the *Random House Webster's College Dictionary* (1992), simply has the name "Webster's" inserted into its earlier title, which was *The Random House College Dictionary* (1968, 1975).

2.4   Webster's competitors

Although the name "Webster's" has great visibility in the modern marketplace, and though the cachet of the name certainly helps to sell dictionaries in modern America, it is worth pointing out that this is due to a considerable extent to hype and mythology. Noah Webster was not the best lexicographer even of his own time, though he was the most influential one because of his *Speller* – which was the textbook of choice throughout most of the century. In his own time the best American lexicographer was probably Joseph Worcester, whose *Universal and Critical Dictionary of the English Language* appeared as the only American competitor for Webster in 1846, the final revised version in 1860. At both dates it was superior to Webster's in almost every way, but in 1864 a vastly improved version of the Webster's appeared (reworked by two scholars hired by Webster's son-in-law, and consequently known as the *Webster-Mahn* in deference to the German scholar who totally replaced the Webster etymologies). This was really the first "unabridged" Webster's dictionary, and it won the competition against Worcester in the marketplace. Near the end of the century William Dwight Whitney, a Sanskrit scholar at Yale University, produced the great *Century Dictionary*, which, in the words of Sidney Landau "is surely one of the handsomest dictionaries ever made."[9] It was never revised, however, and is now of historical interest only. But

[9] Sidney I. Landau, *Dictionaries: The Art and Craft of Lexicography*, Cambridge: Cambridge University Press, 1989: 72.

Whitney was not the only end-of-century competition for Webster's place in lexicography: There was also the 1893 Funk and Wagnalls unabridged *Standard Dictionary of the English Language*, revised and enlarged in 1913 as the *New Standard Dictionary*, with 450,000 entries, making it a true competitor for the unabridged Webster's. Though it was never later fully revised, and it therefore dropped out of competition, this dictionary made many important changes in dictionary practice which are continued in the various dictionaries connected with the name of Clarence Barnhart and with the dictionaries published by Random House.

2.5   Writing dictionaries

All modern dictionaries draw much of their historical and etymological information from the *OED*. Etymologies and definitions are based on citations. What is a citation? It is an index card (or, these days, a computer file) which lists a word and a quotation containing that word – if possible in a context that clearly implies a specific meaning – and gives the source, author, and date of the citation. As Landau says, "In spite of other sources [such as earlier dictionaries, either your own or your competitors"], a large ongoing citation file is essential for the preparation of any new general dictionary or for the revision of an existing dictionary."[10] We have already mentioned the citation file of the *OED*, and a bit about how it came into existence. In America, the G. and C. Merriam Company is reputed to have the largest continuously updated and current file of citations of the words they enter into their dictionaries. Both Random House and Barnhart have independent citation files. The quality of a dictionary ultimately depends on the quality of the writing and editing.

2.6   Desktop dictionaries

2.6.1   For British users

There is really only one desktop dictionary likely to be satisfactory in Britain – *The Chambers Dictionary*. This great dictionary is available in many editions, with small variations in the title. An edition called *The Chambers 21st Century Dictionary* was ambitiously published in 1997, three years in advance of the millennium bug. Its ultimate ancestor, *The Chambers 20th Century Dictionary*, first edition, came out in 1901. The 1998 edition does away with the centennial puffery and goes simply under the name *The Chambers Dictionary*. The one-page discussion (p. xx) of what American English is like (i.e., how it differs from

---

[10] Landau, *Dictionaries*, p. 152.

British English) is about as useful as a comparable American one-page explanation of British English would be that was supposed to include the southern counties of Britain, the north country, Scotland, and Ireland. However, *Chambers* often records American usage in pronunciation, a favor which is not reciprocated by some American dictionaries. For instance, *schedule* is recorded by *Chambers* with the [sk-] pronunciation marked as "esp. US," but *The American Heritage Dictionary* (see below) does not record the British sh- pronunciation at all, even though it is widely favored in Canada. *Merriam-Webster's* (every modern edition), however, does record the difference.

The most conspicuous feature of *Chambers* is that all derived forms are listed within the entry under a single headword. Thus if you want to find the computer term *descriptor*, you have to look under *describe*. If you want to find *repentance* you look under *repent*. Thus there are many fewer headwords in *Chambers* than in typical American dictionaries, though the total number of words defined in *Chambers* is actually somewhat larger than we find in any American desk dictionary. *Chambers* also has an appendix that lists common phrases and even quotations from the classical languages and modern foreign languages, and another appendix which gives the origins of many first names. *Chambers* does not give the dates when a word entered English, which is a useful feature of several American dictionaries and of the *OED*. In general, etymology is treated with minimal detail in *Chambers*.

2.6.2 For American users

At least four possible choices have to be considered.

(1) *The American Heritage Dictionary*
(2) *Merriam-Webster's Collegiate Dictionary*
(3) *Random House Webster's College Dictionary*
(4) *Webster's New World Dictionary of the American Language*

2.6.2.1 The *American Heritage Dictionary*.[11] This dictionary was innovative in two important ways:

(1) Rather than placing all the etymological information in the entry, in case the word contained a root derived from Proto-Indo-European (the parent language of most European languages, discussed in Chapter 3) the entry provided a reference to an appendix called *Indo-European Roots*, where one can find, for every root, not only the word

[11] Ed. by William Morris. Boston: Houghton Mifflin, 1969, reprinted with minor updating, 1979. (*AHD*1) – Now superseded by the Third Edition of 1992 (*AHD*3), ed. by Anne H. Soukhanov. In between *AHD*1 and *AHD*3 appeared a "College Edition" (*AHD*2, 1982) which is so drastically shortened, especially in the word histories (etymologies), that it is of much less value than the other versions of the *AHD*, for any purpose whatever.

in question but often dozens of other words which are related by virtue of being derived from the same point of origin. Although fine for our purposes in this book, most readers found the appendix of little value because they did not know how to use it. It is unlikely ever to be valued highly by the general public.

(2) Since there had been much negative publicity about the usage labels in *Merriam-Webster's Third New International Dictionary*, the *American Heritage Dictionary* took advantage of the bad publicity to step into the breach and created a "Usage Panel" who made judgments, reported in the dictionary, about their preferences in several hundred instances of disputed usage (e.g., as between "He laid down on the bed" and "He lay down on the bed"). The panel's recommendations were sometimes too sensitive to "establishment" usage; they were often keen to protect the language from decay and corruption, metaphorically speaking. But the *Heritage* received lots of good publicity from this ploy: as a merchandising technique it was successful. As a record of actual usage, which is what dictionaries are obligated to report, it is dubious, at best, and cannot be viewed as especially authoritative.

2.6.2.2 The *Merriam-Webster's Collegiate* Dictionaries.
Produced by The G. and C. Merriam Co. of Springfield, Mass. The latest edition is the 10th (1993). The 9th (1983) and the 8th (1973) are also excellent dictionaries, but the 7th (1963) is too old to use today. These dictionaries, depending on when they were printed, go by slightly different names, such as *Webster's New Collegiate Dictionary*, *Webster's Ninth New Collegiate Dictionary*, *Webster's Seventh New Collegiate Dictionary*. New printings with minor revisions come out almost every year, but as the dates above indicate (1963, 1973, 1983, 1993), major re-editing to produce a really new *Collegiate* takes about ten years. Several editors have been responsible for these superb dictionaries over the years, beginning with Philip Babcock Gove.[12] The important thing to realize about all the *Collegiate* dictionaries that the G. and C. Merriam Company has produced is that they are based squarely on the citation files of the two greatest unabridged American dictionaries of this century, namely Second (1934) and Third (1961)*Webster's New International Dictionaries*, and of course all of them draw on the *OED* for etymological information and much else.

2.6.2.3 *Random House Webster's Collegiate Dictionary.*[13] Based
on *The Random House Dictionary of the English Language*,[14] 1966 and 1973. The latter is claimed to be an unabridged dictionary, and is the

---

[12] Gove edited the unabridged *3rd International* and the *Seventh Collegiate*); Henry Bosley Woolf and Frederick C. Mish, respectively, edited the *Eighth* and *Ninth Collegiate* dictionaries.

[13] Ed. by Robert Costello, New York: Random House, 1991.   [14] Ed. by Jesse Stein.

basis of the 1993 *Random House Unabridged Dictionary*. But this excellent dictionary is just too large to serve as a desk dictionary, and one is probably better served by the 1991 College version. Both for etymology and for general use, the College version is hard to improve upon.

2.6.2.4 *Webster's New World Dictionary of the American Language*.[15] The third edition is available in both full and college versions, like the *Heritage*. In spite of the gimmicky title (it has no special connection with Webster, and there is nothing specific to the New World or to American English about it except for the fact that it gives etymologies for American place names, a feature which is not found in other general-purpose dictionaries), this is a good desk dictionary, one of the very best when it first appeared in 1953, and it remains highly competitive in quality after its 1988 revision.

2.6.3   Important differences between dictionaries

Most words have several different, though related, meanings. These are called senses. Dictionaries divide up their definitions into categories, one for each discernible sense. Thus the *OED*, for the noun *work*, divides the senses into 23 main categories, with up to seven or eight subcategories under each of the main ones. *Chambers* has 20, though unlike most dictionaries they are not labeled a, b, . . . x, but are only set apart by semicolons. The *Heritage* has 15 categories. *Merriam-Webster's Collegiate* has 11. Such distinctions are a necessary part of providing comprehensive definitions, and it is to be expected that all dictionaries will have similar if not identical categories of sense. But the order in which the senses are presented is radically different, and has been known to lead to serious misunderstandings on the part of dictionary users.

2.6.3.1 Historical order vs. logical order. The *OED* and all the Merriam-Webster dictionaries arrange their senses according to the dates when each sense first came into English. Quoting from Frederick C. Mish, the editor-in-chief of the *Ninth Collegiate*,

> The order of senses within an entry is historical: the sense known to have been first used in English is entered first . . . When a numbered sense is further subdivided into lettered sub senses, the inclusion of particular sub senses within a sense is based upon their semantic relationship to one another, but their order is likewise historical. Divisions of sub senses . . . are also in historical order with respect to one another (*Merriam-Webster's Ninth Collegiate*, p.19)

Since the word *fatal* is used in the example quoted just below by the *Heritage*, let us see how the *Ninth Collegiate* defines it:

---

[15] First edition by David Guralnik and Joseph Friend. New York: Simon and Schuster, 1953, rev. 1970, 1976, 3rd edn. 1988.

1 obs: fated 2: fateful <a ~ hour> 3 a: of or relating to fate b: resembling
fate in proceeding according to a fixed sequence c: determining one's fate
4 a: causing death b: bringing ruin.

This is terribly misleading unless you know that the first three definitions are ancient history, as it were, and only the fourth one applies to
current usage. And this fact is not even made apparent in the definition
itself (e.g., by saying "current meaning," or marking the ancient meanings with an asterisk (except for the first one, marked obsolete). One
understands why the Merriam Company uses historical order: using
historical order is determinate. We know the history, because the
history has been thoroughly investigated and reported in the *OED*. But
it has a very big disadvantage for the ordinary user, as is pointed out by
the editorial staff of the *Heritage*:

> Entries containing more than one sense are arranged for the convenience
> of contemporary dictionary users with the central and often most com-
> monly sought meanings first. Senses and sub senses are grouped to show
> their relationships with each other. For example, in the entry for *fatal* . . .
> the commonly sought meaning "Causing or capable of causing death"
> appears first and the now obsolete sense "Having been destined; fated"
> comes last in the series of five.   (*Heritage 3rd edn.*, xxxix)

This is called logical order or frequency-determined order, the idea
being that the meanings which are most frequent or most central come
before those that are less common or more peripheral. The problem is
that unlike historical ordering this ordering is not determinate. Most
frequent in what kinds of texts? at what style level? in what context of
use? Does the "logical" order somehow reflect a fundamental fact
about the mental storage system of the typical speaker of English,
thereby having claim to genuine psychological reality? Are there
enough frequency studies to base these preference judgments on? The
answer is, there are some, but not enough yet to provide consistent
answers. This means that the ordering really depends on the shrewd
guesses of the editors. They will differ.

To see how editors can differ on this crucial judgment, consider the
definitions of the adjective *appreciable* found in the *Collegiate*, the
Heritage, the *Random House*, and *Chambers*. In the *Collegiate*, the definition is correctly historical: "capable of being perceived or measured."
In the *Heritage*, the definition does not differ, surprisingly: "possible to
estimate, measure, or perceive." In *Random House* the definition differs
in a crucial way, namely it does not include the notion "measure." It
says "enough to be felt or estimated, noticeable, perceptible." *Webster's
New World* agrees with *Random House* from its very first edition in
1953. *Chambers* supports the latter two but includes the traditional
sense "measurable."

It is clear from actual usage of the word *appreciable* in sentences like
"There was no *appreciable* amount of moisture on the grass this

morning" that, of these four, only *New World* and *Random House* are correct, while *Chambers* has split the difference. The modern sense of the word is clearly vague and does not include literal measurement, since with instrumentation any amount of anything can be measured, and that is not what *appreciable* means. Therefore the *Collegiate* definition is historically correct but misleading about modern usage. One would not expect this lead to be followed by *Heritage*, which agrees with *Chambers* and *Random House* as to theory of presentation and the logic on which definitions should be based. The reason they differ is that it is often difficult to know what the "most commonly sought meaning" is, or what the logical "core" meaning is, and when they are uncertain, it appears that they fall back on history. History is, nevertheless, not only the easy way to go, but clearly the less desirable, except in an explicitly specialized historical dictionary like the *OED*.

2.6.3.2 The position of etymologies in dictionary entries. This correlates with the arrangement of sense ordering. In all dictionaries produced by the Merriam Company, where the earliest sense is first, the etymology is also first (right after pronunciation). This is also true of *Webster's New World*, which arranges senses according to their historical semantic development, except that technical meanings are at the very end. The other two desk dictionaries – *Chambers* and *Random House* – place the etymology at the end of the entry, just after the oldest senses. *Heritage* has a uniquely different manner of presenting etymologies, as we noted in our discussion of it above (the *Indo-European Roots* appendix), but when they place an etymology in the text rather than in the appendix, it is placed at the end, in agreement with *Chambers* and *Random House*.

2.6.3.3 Dating of earliest examples. The tenth *Collegiate*, like its competitor the *Random House* (both College version and the unabridged version), gives the date of the earliest example of the first sense of each word (the earlier *Collegiates* do not, nor do *Chambers* or the *Heritage*). This procedure is standard in the specialized historical dictionaries but not usual in contemporary general-purpose dictionaries, though it is an extremely useful piece of information for etymology.

2.6.3.4 Specialized dictionaries. The number of specialized dictionaries is vast, and, as we remarked earlier, one cannot even judge whether a specialized dictionary is good or not unless one is a specialist in the field. There is virtually no end to specialized dictionaries – dictionaries of Old English, of Middle English, pronouncing dictionaries, reverse dictionaries, chronological dictionaries, frequency dictionaries, rhyming dictionaries, dictionaries of proverbs, dictionaries of loanwords, bibliographical dictionaries, legal terms, medical terms, music, astronomy, geography, computer terms. Because this book is primarily about etymology, especially the classical origins of vast numbers of English words, it is appropriate to discuss specialized etymological dictionaries here, at least briefly, because they are the places where one would go – beyond our desk dictionaries – to learn more about the history of words and phrases.

But first, why should one study etymology? In view of the fact that etymology often concerns itself with aspects of language that are sometimes fossilized and no longer relevant to our ordinary synchronic understanding of what words mean or how they are used, one may legitimately ask why one should bother. It generally turns out to be true that the study of the etymology of words enlightens us both as to interesting accidents in their history and, from a practical point of view, it gives us insights into their present meanings and into the meanings of other words which are related to the same sources, thereby expanding our vocabularies substantially and sharpening our awareness of the meanings of complex words. It also often enables us to guess correctly at the meaning of a new word we have never encountered before, which happens to contain some of the parts of words we have learned to analyze by the means discussed in this book. But the most important reason is to know our language history, just as we want to know the history of our social institutions, our technology, our ancestry, our government, and so on.

How study etymology? Happily, in this area of specialization we are well served indeed. The finest historical dictionary of any language, the basis for the historical information in all subsequent general purpose English dictionaries, is the *OED*, which was discussed at some length above. However, no dictionary can meet all imaginable etymological needs. In particular, the *OED* is incomplete with respect to American English. For more information in that area, four important resources exist:

(1) *A Dictionary of American English on Historical Principles*, ed. by William A. Craigie and James R. Hulbert, Chicago: University of Chicago Press 1938–44 (*DAE*), the main source of information about words that originated in the United States and words that are "representative." Dr. Craigie was one of the editors of the *OED*, and in fact received his training with Sir James Murray himself, having started to work for Murray in 1897. He moved to Chicago specifically to create an American version of the *OED*.

(2) *A Dictionary of Americanisms on Historical Principles*, ed. by Mitford M. Mathews, Chicago: University of Chicago Press, 1951 (*DA*), specifically dealing with words or expressions that originated in the United States.

(3) *The Dictionary of American Regional English*, ed. by Frederick G. Cassidy (*DARE*) (as of this writing, three volumes of a projected five had been published, covering the alphabet through the letter O). *DARE* is expected to provide definitive information about the regional distribution of vocabulary items, based on almost 3,000 interviews with individuals living in over 1,000 communities all over the United States.

(4) *Historical Dictionary of American Slang*, ed. by J. E. Lighter et al., vol. I (A–G) and II (H–O), of three projected volumes, published by Random House in 1994 and 1997. Fun to peruse, but one does not find in it a sharp differentiation between slang and ordinary usage: Lighter's dictionary has many words and phrases that under a stricter definition would have to be excluded.

2.6.3.5 Thesaurus. There is one type of dictionary which categorizes words only according to their semantic similarities, without regard for shared form or ancestry: this is called a thesaurus. The most famous such listing is *Roget's Thesaurus of English Words and Phrases*, first published in 1852 and in many editions subsequently. For expanding one's vocabulary, a thesaurus is likely to be even more useful than a standard dictionary, because it is arranged according to a universal set of concepts (e.g. *space, matter, intellect, abstract relations*) and then each of these is divided further and further until finally all the words can be grouped together which refer to closely similar meanings. Definitions are not given, or at least not normally very detailed definitions, just synonyms; and much of the book is an elaborate index to help you find the head entry under which all the semantically similar words of a particular category are listed.

2.6.3.6 Dictionaries of synonyms. Besides *Roget*, there are dictionaries of synonyms in which the headword is more or less arbitrarily chosen, and of course alphabetically listed: i.e., the editor's choice of headwords is not part of an elaborate universal classificatory system, and in the entry all the semantically similar words are listed with explanations of the distinctions among them. *Webster's New Dictionary of Synonyms* is an excellent such dictionary, as also is the Funk and Wagnall's *Modern Guide to Synonyms*. These are basically tools for writers, to help them avoid repeating the same word in different contexts (since English style has always placed a premium on variation and non-repetition).

2.7   Dictionary shelf-life

Several really excellent dictionaries like the *Century* and the *Funk and Wagnalls* have disappeared from the scene because they have not been updated. The language is constantly changing, constantly in flux, and dictionaries must stay current – i.e., not more than ten to fifteen years out of date. The turnover rate is fairly shocking. For example, in 1977 the *Chambers Twentieth Century* put out a supplement to its 1972 edition which included these **new** entries:

> *alternative*, adj. – as in *alternative technology, alternative life-style*
> *amniocentesis* – the testing for foetal abnormalities
> *bananas* – adj. mad, crazy, wild
> *-bashing* as in *union-bashing, boss-bashing*

Going further down the list we find: *catch 22, database, day care, digital clock, floating currency, gang-bang, greenhouse effect, hype, liquid crystal display, modem, Ms., pixel, safari park, sitcom, skateboard, skin-flick, tunnel vision, up-market, voice-over, yucky, zap, zero in on, zilch, zip code, zonked.* These words are so much part of British as well as American vocabulary today that it is difficult to imagine that the parents of the current college student generation would not have been familiar with them. Yet they became dictionary-worthy in the UK only between 1972 and 1977!

The G. and C. Merriam Company has dealt with this problem by releasing new versions of the *Collegiate* at intervals of approximately ten years, though the *Third International* is over forty years old. Other companies like Barnhart, whose most recently released full dictionary is twenty-five years old, have tried to deal with the updating issue by periodically releasing new material from their constantly updated citation files, such as *The Barnhart Dictionary of New English Since 1963* (1973) and at five-year intervals subsequently. This is an enormous service to the lexicographers, though it is not as obviously a valuable tool for the ordinary dictionary user. It is a terrible nuisance to look from one volume to another hoping to find the word in question. It now appears likely anyway that the updating of the future will be done on computer disks and/or CD-ROMs. This is relatively easy and relatively cheap. As we all move into cyberspace, the conventional printed dictionary may become one of the casualties, and we'll simply check in at a Web site (or, unfortunately, more likely a dozen Web sites) for the latest lexicographical information.[16]

---

[16] For over fifty years, the journal *American Speech* has been recording the appearance of new words and the development of new meanings for old words in American English. *The Barnhart New-Words Concordance* by David Barnhart (Cold Spring, NY: Lexik House, 1944) provides an index to ten sources listing new words. The current web site for the American Dialect Society, which also has a discussion group on new words and other issues of American English, is:
http://www.et.byu.edu/~lilliek/ads/index.htm

Appendix II: morpheme list

This list includes all the morphemes[1] cited in the root exercises of the *Workbook* (part b in each chapter), plus the affixes cited in chapter 5 of the main text. The numbers in parentheses correspond to the chapter of the Workbook in which the morpheme is introduced for study or memorization. In the SOURCE column, asterisks mark Proto-Indo-European forms.

This appendix does NOT include the many other morphemes introduced as examples in the textbook.

MORPHEME	MEANING	EXAMPLES	SOURCE
1. **a-, au-, an-**	"lacking" (5)	asymmetric, amoral, atonal	G a/an-
2. **ab-, a-, abs-**	"from, away" (5)	abnormal, abstinence, abjure	L ab-
3. **-able**	"fit for" (5)	agreeable, comfortable, incalculable	L-abil(is)
4. **ac, acer, acerb**	"sharp, tip" (10)	acumen, acrid, acerbic, acme, exacerbate	G ak(os)
5. **-acy, -asy**	"state or quality" (5)	advocacy, intricacy, accuracy, ecstasy	L-cia
6. **ad-**	"toward" (5)	admit, advance, admonish	L ad-
7. **-ade**	"an action done" (5)	fusillade, tirade, masquerade, arcade	Fr -ade
8. **ag, act**	"act, drive" (9)	agent, act, agile, ambiguous, litigate, navigate	*ag
9. **-age**	"condition, state" (5)	anchorage, postage, coinage	L-atic(um)
10. **agog**	"teach, induce" (2)	pedagogue, demagogue, synagogue	*ag
11. **agon**	"struggle" (11)	antagonize, protagonist	*agon
12. **agr**	"field" (11)	agriculture, agrarian	*agr
13. **-al**	"act of" (5)	renewal, revival, trial	L-al(is)
14. **-al (-ial,-ical,-ual)**	"having the property of" (5)	conjectural, fraternal, dialectal, sensual	L-al(is)
15. **al(i), ol(t)**	"grow, nourish" (11)	adolescent, adult, alimentary (canal), coalesce	*al
16. **al, all(o)**	"other" (5)	alibi, allegory, allomorph, alien	*al
17. **alg**	"pain" (11)	analgesic, analgesia, algolagnia	G alg
18. **alt**	"high" (5)	altitude, altimeter, alto	L alt
19. **ambi, amphi**	"both," "around" (5)	ambidextrous, ambivalent, preamble, amphiarthrosis	*ambhi
20. **ambl**	"walk" (5)	ambulance, perambulate	L ambul
21. **ampl**	"large" (10)	amplify, amplitude	L ampl
22. **-an, -ian**	"belonging to, resembling" (5)	reptilian, Augustan, plebeian, patrician	L -anus
23. **ana-**	"back" (5)	anatomy, analogy	G ana-
24. **-ance, -ence**	"state, act, or fact of" (5)	repentance, perseverance, emergence	L -antia
25. **ander**	"male" (6)	android, androgynous, androgen	*andr
26. **ang**	"constrict" (7)	angst, anxious, anxiety, anguish, angina	*angh

[1] We have chosen base morphemes which are, with a few exceptions, near the top of the text-frequency and list-frequency counts found in Thorndike, E. L and I. Lorge (1959), *The Teacher's Wordbook of 30000 Words* (3rd edn.). [New York: Columbia University]. They are also high on the *American Heritage Frequency List*.

MORPHEME	MEANING	EXAMPLES	SOURCE
27. anim	"mind" (3)	animate, animosity, animadversion, animal	L anim(us)
28. ann	"year" (2)	annals, annual, superannuated, annuity	L annu
29. -ant, -ent	"one who" (5)	agent, defendant, participant	L -antem
30. ante-	"before, old" (5)	antenuptial, ante	L ante
31. ante-	"preceding" (5)	antechamber, ante-Norman	L ante-
32. anth	"flower, collection" (11)	anthology, anthophore,	G anth(os)
33. anthrop	"man, human being" (6)	anthropology, anthropoid, anthrolatry	G anthrop(os)
34. anti-	"opposed, instead" (5)	antidote, antisemitic, antacid, anti-Chistian	G anti-
35. apt	"fit, capable" (3)	aptitude, ineptitude, inept	L apt
36. arch(aeo)	"rule, begin, foremost" (2)	archaeology, archaic, archaism	G archae-
37. arch-	"chief, principal, high" (2)	archbishop, archduke	G arch
38. -arian	"member of a sect" (5)	utilitarian, egalitarian, euthoritarian	L -arian(us)
39. art	"skill"	artful, inertia	OFr art
40. -ary	"having a tendency" (5)	secondary, discretionary, rudimentary, tributary	L -ari(us)
41. aster	"star" (2)	asteroid, astronomy	G aster
42. -ate	"cause X to happen" (5)	create, contaminate, frustrate, terminate	L -at(us)
43. -ate	"full of" (5)	passionate, affectionate, extortionate	L -at(us)
44. -ation	"state of being X-ed" (5)	purification, organization, contemplation	L -ation
45. aud	"hear" (4)	audit, auditory, auditorium, audience	L aud(ire)
46. aug	"increase" (7)	auction, augment, augur, august, August	L aug
47. auto-	"self, same" (5)	automaton, autobiography, automobile	G auto(s)
48. av(i)	"bird, fly" (11)	aviary, aviation, aviator	L avi(s)
49. barbar	"uncivilized" (12)	barbarian, barbarous	L barbar(us)
50. bell	"war" (8)	bellicose, belligerent, antebellum	L bell(um)
51. bene, bon	"good, well" (8)	benefit, beneficent, beneficiary, bonanza	L ben
52. bi-	"twice, double" (5)	bifocal, biennial, bipolar, bisulphate	L bi-
53. bio	"life" (6)	biology, biogenic, biography, biogenetic	G bio(s)
54. bol, bl	"throw" (10)	symbol, hyperbole, metabolism, parabola, parable	G ball(ein)
55. brev	"short" (2)	abbreviate, breve, breviloquent	L brev(is)
56. burs	"pouch, money" (9)	bursar, bursa, bursitis, disburse, reimburse	L burs(a)
57. cad, cas	"fall" (5)	cadaver, cadence, decadence, case, casual, occasion	L cad(ere)
58. camp	"field" (11)	camp, campaign, campus, decamp, encamp	L camp(us)
59. can, cyn	"dog" (11)	canaille, canary, canine, cynic	L can(is)
60. cant	"sing" (4)	incantation, incentive, enchant	L cant(are)
61. cap(it)	"head" (3)	cape, capital, capitol, capitulate, recapitulate, captain	L cap(ut)
62. cap, cup, ceiv	"to take, contain" (9)	capable, capsule, captive, accept, anticipate	L cap(ere)
63. car(n)	"flesh" (3)	carnal, carnage, carnivore, carnival, carrion, incarnate	L carnal(is)
64. card, cord	"heart, agree" (3)	cardiac, cardiology, accord, accordion, concord, record	G kard
65. cast	"purify, fortify" (3)	caste, castigate, castle, castrate, chateau, chaste	L cast(us)
66. cata-	"down, away, back" (5)	catapult, catastrophe	G kata-
67. ced, ceed	"go, let go" (7)	concede, precede, proceed, access, accessory, ancestor	L ced(ere)

	MORPHEME	MEANING	EXAMPLES	SOURCE
68.	ceive	"take" (9)	conceit, conception, deceit, deception	L cip(ere)
69.	cele(b)r	"swift, frequent" (2)	celerity, accelerate, celebrate, celebrity	L celebr
70.	cer(t), cr	"separate, judge, settle" (9)	certain, certify, critic, crime, excrement, secret	L cert(us)
71.	cere, cre	"come forth, grow" (7)	accrue, create, decrease, recruit	L cre(are)
72.	chrom(at)	"color, embellishment" (10)	chromatic, chromatophilic, chromosome	G khrom(a)
73.	chron	"time" (12)	chronology, chronic, chronicle, anachronism	G khron(os)
74.	cid, cis	"cut, kill" (11)	decide, fratricide, genocide, concise, incisor, precise	L incid(ere)
75.	circum-	"around" (5)	circumnavigate, circumspect, circumcise	L circum
76.	cit	"arouse, summon" (9)	cite, excite, recite, solicit, resuscitate	L cit(are)
77.	civ, cit	"city, refined" (8)	civic, civil, civilian, civilization, citadelle, city	L civil(is)
78.	clam	"call out" ( )	exclaim, declaim, exclamatory, proclamation	L clam(are)
79.	clar	"clear" (12)	clarity, declare, clarify	L clar(us)
80.	class	"group" (7)	classic, classical, classicism, classify, déclassé	L class(is)
81.	cli, cliv, clin	"lean, lie, bed" (5)	client, climate, climax, clinic, decline, incline	G cli(ma)
82.	clud, claus, clos	"close" (2)	conclude, exclude, include, preclude, closet, disclose	G claus(us)
83.	co-, con-	"together, jointly" (5)	coexistence, cooperate, concur	L com-
84.	col, cult	"live, inhabit, grow" (11)	bucolic, colonial, cultivate, culture, horticulture	L cult(is)
85.	com	"comic, comedy" (12)	comic, comedy, comedian	G com(os)
86.	contra-	"against, opposite" (5)	contradiction, contrary	L contra-
87.	cor, curv	"round, around" (10)	corona, coroner, coronary, corolla, corollary	L curv(us)
88.	corp	"body, flesh" (3)	corporal, corporate, incorporate, corporeal, corpse	L corp(us)
89.	cosm	"universe, world, order" (12)	cosmic, cosmology, cosmos, cosmetic, microcosm	G kosm(os)
90.	counter-	"against, opposite" (5)	counterfeit, counterbalance	L contra
91.	crat	"rule" (8)	autocrat, aristocracy, bureaucracy, democracy	G krat(os)
92.	cre	"grow" (12)	creature, creation, excrescence	L cre(are)
93.	cre, cred	"believe, trust" (8)	credence, credential, credible, credit, credo, creed	L cred(ere)
94.	crit	"discern" (12)	critic, criticize, critical, criticism	G kritik(os)
95.	crypto-	"secret, hidden" (5)	cryptography, cryptoanalytic	G krupt(os)
96.	cub, cumb	"lie, hollow" (5)	concubine, cube, cubicle, incumbent, succumb	G kub(os)
97.	cur, car, cor, cour	"run" (9)	current, cursive, incur, recur, car, career, carry	L curr(ere)
98.	de-	"away from, down" (5)	decay, debase, deny, depend	L de-
99.	dei, div	"god, augury" (2)	deify, deism, deity, divine, divinity	L de(us)
100.	del	"erase, wipe out" (11)	delete, indelible, deleterious	L del(ere)
101.	dem	"people" (8)	demagogue, democracy, endemic, epidemic	G dem(os)
102.	den, odon	"tooth" (3)	dent, dental, indent, indenture, dandelion, mastodon	L den(s)
103.	dexter	"right hand, adroit" (3)	dexterity, dextrorotatory, dextrose, dextrous	L dexter

	MORPHEME	MEANING	EXAMPLES	SOURCE
104.	di-	"two" (5)	dioxide, ditransitive, dichloride	G di-
105.	dia-	"across, through" (5)	diameter, diachronic	G dia-
106.	dic(t)	"speak, give" (4)	dictate, edict, verdict, benediction, contradict, addict	L dic(ere)
107.	dis-	"apart, reversal, lacking" (5)	displease, disallow, distaste	L dis-
108.	dis-	intensifier (5)	disturb, disgruntle, disannul	L dis-
109.	doc, dog	"teach, praise" (4)	doctrine, indoctrinate, doctor, document, dogma	L doc(ere)
110.	dol, dolor	"suffer" (11)	condolence, doleful, indolent, dolorous	L dolor(e)
111.	dom, domin	"control, lord, master" (8)	domestic, domicile, domain, dominate, domineer	L domin(us)
112.	don, dat, dot, dor, dos, dow	"give" (7)	donate, data, addition, editor, antidote, dose, endow	L don(are)
113.	du-	"two, double" (5)	duple, duplicate, duplicity	L du(o)
114.	dubi	"doubt" (12)	dubious, dubiety, indubitably	L. dubi(um)
115.	duc(t)	"lead, pull" (8)	abduct, aqueduct, conduct, deduce, educate, induce	L duc(ere)
116.	dur	"hard, lasting" (11)	durable, duration, duress, endurance, endure, obdurate	L dur(are)
117.	dys-	"bad, badly" (5)	dyslogistic, dyspeptic	G dus-
118.	eco	"environment" (12)	ecosystems, ecology	G oik(os)
119.	-eer	"one who deals in X" (5)	engineer, balladeer, mountaineer, profiteer	Fr. -ier
120.	ego	"self" (3)	ego, egocentric, egoism, egoist, egomania, egotism	L ego
121.	electr-	"electric" (12)	electricity, electrode, electron (Gk. root = "amber")	G elektron
122.	-en	"to become" (5)	darken, chasten, cheapen, deafen	OE -en
123.	en-	"in, into" (a form of in-) (5)	encapsulate, enclose	G en-
124.	epi-	"on, over" (5)	epiglottis, epidermis, epicycle	G epi
125.	equi	"even, level" (10)	equanimity, equator, equilateral, equinox, equity	L aequ(us)
126.	-er	"agent" (5)	baker, thriller, worker, sweeper, retriever	L -arius
127.	erg, urg, org	"work" (9)	energy, erg, synergism, metallurgy	G organ(on)
128.	ero	"physical love" (6)	erotic, erogenous	G ero(s)
129.	err	"wander, go wrong" (12)	aberrant, err, errant, erratic, erratum, erroneous, error	L err(are)
130.	-ery, -ry	"collectivity" (5)	masonry, carpentry, slavery, savagery	L -ari(a)
131.	-esc	"become" (5)	tumescent, coalesce	L -esc
132.	-ese	"belonging to a place" (5)	Japanese, New Yorkese, journalese	L -ens(is)
133.	-esque	"having the style of X" (5)	romanesque, lawyeresque, statuesque	Fr -esque
134.	esth	"feel" (11)	esthetic, phonaesthetic	G aesth
135.	-ess	"feminine of X" (5)	tigress, laundress, stewardess	Fr -ess
136.	etym	"true, source" (12)	etymology, etymon	G etum(on)
137.	eu	"good, well" (8)	eucalyptus, eugenics, eulogy, eupeptic, euphony	G eu
138.	ex-, ec-	"out from, away" (5)	exconsul, exwife; eccentric; educate, eradicate, emit	G ex-
139.	extra-	"outside the scope of" (5)	extraordinary, extramarital	L extra-
140.	fa, pho, fe, phe	"speak, spoken about" (4)	fable, affable, fame, famous, infant, preface, aphasia	G phe, L fa
141.	fac	"do, make" (7)	fact, affect, infect, office, suffice	L fac(ere)
142.	fem	"effeminate, female" (12)	feminine, female, effeminate,	Fr fem(elle)
143.	fend	"strike, ward off" (8)	defend, defence, fence, fend, fender, offense	L defend(ere)

MORPHEME	MEANING	EXAMPLES	SOURCE
144. **fer, pher, phor**	"bear, send, bring" (5)	circumference, conifer, defer, differ, fertile, infer	L fer(re)
145. **fess**	"admit, acknowledge" (12)	confess, confession, profess(or), profession(al)	LL fess(us)
146. **fid, feder**	"trust, faith" (8)	affidavit, *bona fide*, confide, federation, infidel	L fid(es)
147. **fig, fing**	"form" (10)	figure, figurative	L figur(a)a
148. **fin-**	"end" (12)	final, finish, define, definite	L fin(ire)
149. **firm**	"strong" (12)	affirm, affirmative, affirmation, infirm	L firm(us)
150. **flec**	"bend, turn" (2)	flexible, reflect, reflex, deflect, circumflex	L flect(ere)
151. **flict**	"strike" (3)	inflict, conflict, afflict	L flict(us)
152. **flu, fluc, fluv**	"flow, river" (5)	fluent, fluid, influence, affluent, effluent, fluvial	L flu(ere)
153. **fore-**	"before" (5)	(in time or space) forecast, forefinger, foreskin	OE fore
154. **form**	"shape" (12)	conform, uniform, formation, formal	L form(a)
155. **fort**	"strong" (12)	comfort, effort, fortification	L fort
156. **frag, frang**	"break, deflect" (7)	fragment, fraction, fracture, refraction, frangible	L frang(ere)
157. **fug**	"flee, flight" (12)	refuge, fugitive, fugue	L. fug(ere)
158. **-ful**	"full of X" (5)	peaceful, powerful, skillful	OE full
159. **fuse, fund**	"pour, melt, blend" (12)	fuse, confuse, diffuse, effusive, infuse, profuse	L fund(ere)
160. **gam**	"marriage, sexual union" (6)	bigamy, gamete, monogamy, polygamy	G gam(os)
161. **gen(er), gn, gon, germ(in)**	"birth, origin" (5)	general, generate, gender, genesis, genius, germ	L gen(us)
162. **geo**	"earth" (11)	geodesic, geology, geometry, apogee, George	G geo
163. **ges(t), ger**	"carry, bring, offer" (5)	gesture, gestation, digest, congest, ingest, suggest	L ger(ere)
164. **glos, glot**	"tongue, speech" (4)	gloss, glossary, glottis, epiglottis, polyglot	G glossa
165. **gn, gnos, gnor**	"to know" (4)	cognition, incognito, recognize, agnostic, ignore	G gnos
166. **grad, gress**	"step, go" (5)	grade, gradation, gradual, graduate, degrade, aggressive	L grad(us)
167. **graph, gram**	"make lines, write, record" (4)	agraphia, autograph, telegraph, biography, grammar	G graph(e)
168. **grat**	"thankful, pleased, kind" (8)	grateful, gratify, gratis, gratitude, congratulate, grace	L grat(us)
169. **grav**	"heavy, serious" (10)	aggravate, gravity	L grav(em)
170. **greg**	"flock, gather" (8)	aggregate, congregate, congregation, egregious	L greg
171. **gyn, gynec**	"woman, female" (11)	androgynous, gynarchy, gynocracy, misogynist	G gun(e)
172. **hab, hib**	"to have, hold" (11)	inhibit, exhibit, habitable	L hab(ere)
173. **heli**	"sun" (7)	heliotrope, parahelion, helioscope	G heli(os)
174. **hem, em**	"blood" (3)	hemoglobin, hemophilia, hemoptysis, anemia	G haim(a)
175. **hend**	"seize" (7)	apprehend, comprehend, prehensile	L (pre)hend-
176. **her, heir**	"heir" (10)	inherit, inheritance, hereditary	L her(es)
177. **hes, her**	"stick, hold back" (2)	adhere, coherent, incoherent, inherent, cohesive	L haer(ere)
178. **hetero-**	"other" (7)	heterosexual, heteronym, heteromorphic	G hetero

MORPHEME	MEANING	EXAMPLES	SOURCE
179. **hom(o), homeo**	"same" (6)	homogeneous, homomorphic, homonym	G hom(os)
180. **hon**	"worthy" (10)	honor, honorable, dishonor, honesty	L honor
181. **-hood**	"state of, condition of" (5)	childhood, womanhood, priesthood	OE hood
182. **hor**	"shudder"(7)	abhor, horrible, horror	L hor(er)
183. **hum**	"damp, wet" (7)	humid, humidity	L hum(ere)
184. **hyd(r)**	"water" (11)	dehydrate, hydrant, hydrate, hydraulic, hydrogen	G hudr(o)
185. **hyper-**	"over, to excess" (5)	hyperactive, hypersensitive	G hyper-
186. **hypo-**	"under, slightly" (5)	hypotactic, hypoglossal, hypotoxic	G hypo-
187. **-ia**	"condition" (5)	amnesia, paranoia	G L-ia
188. **iatr**	"treat (medically)" (3)	iatrogenic, geriatric, psychiatry, pediatric, podiatry	G iatr(os)
189. **-ic**	"having the property X" (5)	alcoholic, atheistic, naturalistic, romantic	L ic(us)
190. **-ician**	"skilled in art/science" (5)	physician, musician, magician	L ic + ian
191. **-icity**	"abstract noun from -ic" (5)	historic/historicity, electric/electricity	Fr -icité
192. **idio**	"particular" (7)	idiom, idiolect, idiot, idiosyncratic	G idios
193. **-ify, fy**	"to cause to (be) X" (5)	purify, denazify, sanctify, verify, amplify	L fac(ere)
194. **in-**	"in, into, within" (5)	inaugurate, inchoate	L in-
195. **in-**	"negative" (5)	indiscreet, ineffectual, incredible, illegible	*n-
196. **infra-**	"below, underneath" (5)	infra-red, infrastructure	L infra-
197. **inter-**	"between, among" (5)	interchange, interpose, intersect, interloper	L inter-
198. **intra-**	"inside" (5)	intracity, intramural, intracellular	L intra
199. **is-, iso-**	"equal" (5)	isochrony, isosceles, isotope	G iso-
200. **-ish**	"to become like X" (5)	churlish, boyish, peckish, stylish	Gmc -ish
201. **-ism**	"doctrinal system of principles" (5)	communism, realism, romanticism	G -isma
202. **isol, insul**	"island" (11)	isolate, insular, insulate, peninsula	L insul(a)
203. **-ist**	"one connected with" (5)	socialist, perfectionist, dentist, pugilist	G -ist(es)
204. **-ity**	"state, quality" (5)	agility, diversity, actuality	Fr -ité
205. **-ive**	"characterized by" (5)	abusive, contradictive, retrospective	L -iv(us)
206. **-ize**	"to cause to be X" (5)	popularize, legalize, plagiarize, miniaturize	Fr -ise
207. **jac(t)**	"throw, lay, lie" (2)	ejaculate, adjacent, reject, inject, eject, project	L eic(ere)
208. **journ**	"day" (9)	journal, sojourn, journey	L diorn
209. **jug, jung**	"join" (2)	jugate, conjugal, conjugate, jugular, juncture	L iung(ere)
210. **kine, cine**	"move" (5)	kinetic, kinesics, kinesiology, telekinesis, cinema	G kine
211. **lab**	"take, seize" (5)	epilepsy, narcolepsy, prolepsis, syllable, astrolabe	L lep, lab
212. **lat**	"carry" (6)	correlate, elated, legislate, relate, translate	L lat(us)
213. **lat**	"hidden" (10)	latent	L lat(ere)
214. **later, lat**	"wide, broad, side" (10)	lateralization, latitude	L lat(us)
215. **leg, lect**	"choose, gather" (4)	legion, elegance, sacrilege, elect, select, neglect	L leg(ere)
216. **leg**	"law, charge" (4)	legal, legislate, allege, delegate, legitimate, privilege	L leg
217. **leg, log**	"speak, write, read, reason" (4)	logo, logic, apology, biology, eulogy, prolog	G log(os)
218. **-less**	"without, free from" (5)	forms adjective from noun, as in faultless, keyless	OE less

	MORPHEME	MEANING	EXAMPLES	SOURCE
219.	-let	"diminutive" (5)	leaflet, driblet	Fr -(l)ette
220.	lev	"light, rise" (2)	levity, levitate, lever, elevate, alleviate, leavening	L lev(is)
221.	liber	"free" (9)	liberty, liberate, deliberate	L liber
222.	lig	"bind" (2)	ligature, ligament, oblige, religion	L lig(are)
223.	liqu	"fluid" (9)	liquidate, liquid, liquor	L liqu
224.	liter	"letter" (9)	illiterate, literature	L liter(a)
225.	lith	"stone" (11)	lithograph, lithosphere, monolith	G lith(os)
226.	loc	"place" (2)	locus, local, locative, locomotion, allocate	L loc(us)
227.	loqu, locu	"speak" (4)	locution, circumlocution, loquacious, colloquial	L loqu(i)
228.	lud	"play" (9)	allude, delude, elude, interlude, prelude, ludicrous	L lud(us)
229.	lumin	"light" (12)	illuminate, lumen, luminous	L lumen
230.	-ly	"appropriate, befitting" (5)	friendly, timely, shapely, fatherly	OE -lice
231.	macro-	"large, broad scale" (5)	macroeconomics, macroclimatology	G makr(os)
232.	mag(n), maj	"great, large" (10)	magnanimous, magnify, maximum, major, majority	L maior
233.	mal-	"ill, evil, wrong" (5)	malfeasance, malodorous, malpractice	L male
234.	mal, male	"bad" (8)	dismal, malady, malaise, malapropism, malaria	L male
235.	mand	"order" (9)	mandatory, command, reprimand	L mand(are)
236.	mani	"intense desire" (6)	bibliomania, mania, maniac, megalomania	G mania
237.	mar	"sea" (9)	marine, submarine, mariner	L marin(us)
238.	mater, metr	"mother, womb, surrounding substance" (6)	material, maternal, matrix	L mater
239.	medi	"middle" (10)	mediocre, media, medieval, Mediterranean	L medi(us)
240.	memor	"recall" (9)	memorize, memorial, memorable, memory	L memor
241.	men, min, mon, mn	"think, remind, warn" (3)	mental, mentor, dementia, monitor, mnemonic	L mem(or)
242.	-ment	"condition of being X" (5)	advancement, treatment, abandonment	L -ment(um)
243.	merc	"pay, trade, sell" (7)	mercantile, mercenary, mercy, commercial	L merc
244.	merg, mers	"dip, plunge" (9)	emerge, merge, merger, submerge, immerse	L merg(ere)
245.	meta-	"transcending, changed" (5)	metaphysics, metamorphosis	G meta-
246.	meter	"measure" (10)	metric, metrics, metronome, perimeter, symmetrical	G metr(on)
247.	micro-	"tiny, small scale" (5)	microorganism, microscope	G mikr(os)
248.	mid-	"middle" (5)	midwinter, midlands, midnight	OE midd
249.	migr	"wander" (6)	emigrate, immigrate, migrate, transmigration	L migr(are)
250.	min	"little, least" (10)	diminish, diminutive, minor, minority, minuscular	L min(or)
251.	mis-	"badly, wrongly" (5)	misspent, miscalculate, mislead	OE mis-
252.	misc	"mix" (9)	promiscuous, miscellaneous, mixture	L misc(ere)
253.	miso	"hate" (6)	misanthrope, misogamy, misogyny	G mis(ein)
254.	mit, mis	"send, go" (5)	emit, omit, transmit, admission, promise, missive	L mitt(ere)
255.	mob, mot	"move" (5)	motion, motor, promote, remote, emotion, mob	L mov(ere)
256.	mod	"moderate, measure" (8)	mode, model, accommodate, commode, modal	L mod(us)

MORPHEME	MEANING	EXAMPLES	SOURCE
257. mon	"advise, warn" (9)	monitor, monster, admonish	L mon(ere)
258. mono	"one" (7)	monochrome, monogamy, monograph, monologue	G mon(os)
259. morph	"form" (10)	amorphous, morphology, morphogenesis	G morph(e)
260. mor(t)	"death" (11)	immortal, mortal, mortgage, moritfy, mortuary	L mort(us)
261. multi-	"many" (5)	multifaceted, multivalent, multiform	L multi-
262. mun	"common, public, gift" (8)	communion, communism, community, immune	L mun(us)
263. mus	"one of the muses" (9)	music, muse, museum	G mousa
264. mut	"change" (9)	mutate, immutable, mutant	L mut(are)
265. nat	"be born" (9)	natural, native, innate	L nat
266. nav(t)	"sail, swim, boat" (9)	naval, navy, aeronaut, aquanaut, nautical	L nav(is)
267. nec(ro), noc(s)	"death, harmful" (11)	nectar, nectarine, internecine, pernicious, necrophilia	G nekr(os)
268. neg	"not, no" (7)	negate, neglect, renegade, renege	L neg
269. neo-	"new, recent" (5)	neonatal, neolithic, neotype	G neos
270. -ness	"state, condition" (5)	bitterness, fairness, idleness	OE -ness
271. nom	"law, system" (8)	autonomous, anomie, economy, antinomy	G nom(os)
272. nom, onom, onym	"name" (4)	anonymous, antonym, homonym, ignominy	G onum(a)
273. non-	"not" (5)	nonsense, non-resident, non-intervention	L non-
274. nunc	"speak" (8)	annunciate, enunciate, pronunciation, renunciation	L nunti(us)
275. -ob-	"inverse" (5)	(in the opposite direction) object, obverse	L ob-
276. -oid	"having the shape of, resembling" (5)	humanoid	G oeid(es)
277. oligo-	"few" (5)	oligarchy, oligotrophic	G olig(o)
278. omni-	"all" (5)	omnipotent, omniscient, omnidirectional	L omni(s)
279. op(t,s)	"eye, sight, look at" (3)	presbyopia, amblyopia, myopia, optical, optometry	G opt(os)
280. oper	"work, creation" (7)	opera, operate, operand, opus	L oper
281. ordin	"order" (7)	ordinal, ordain	L ordin
282. ortho	"straight" (10)	orthography, orthodontist, orthopedics	G orth(os)
283. -ory	"connected with" (5)	obligatory, inflammatory, dormitory	L -ori(us)
284. os, or	"mouth, speak" (4)	adore, oral, oratory, peroration, osculate	L os, or
285. -ose	"full of, abounding in" (5)	verbose, morose, jocose	L -os(us)
286. -ous	"of the nature of X" (5)	virtuous, torturous, glorious, grievous	L -us
287. pac	"bind, agreement, peace" (8)	pact, compact, impact, *pace*, pacific, pacifism	L pax
288. palp	"touch, feel" (3)	palpate, palpitate, palpable	L palp(are)
289. pan, panta	"all, all embracing" (7)	panacea, pandemonium, panorama, panoply	G pan
290. par	"beget, produce" (6)	parent, viviparous, repertory	L par(ere)
291. par	"show" (7)	parade, apparition, appear, transparent	L par(ere)
292. par, por	"part, share, equality" (6)	compare, disparate, parity, parse, part, depart, impart	L pars
293. para-	"beside, along with" (5)	paramedic, parallel	G para
294. pass	"spread out, go" (6)	pass, compass, encompass, passport, surpass	L pass(us)
295. pass	"suffer" (7)	passion, impassionate, impassive	L pass(ionem)
296. past, pan	"food, dough, bread" (9)	companion, pannier, pantry, pasta, repast	L pan(is)
297. pater	"father, sponsor" (6)	paternal, patriarch, patrimony	L pater

MORPHEME	MEANING	EXAMPLES	SOURCE
298. **path(et)**	"feel, suffer, illness" (3)	apathy, allopathy, electropathy, hydropathy, empathy	G path(os)
299. **pati**	"suffer, endure" (7)	patience, patient, impatient	L patient
300. **ped, paed**	"child, training, education" (6)	pediatric, encyclopedia, orthopedics, pedagogy	G paed
301. **ped, pod, pus**	"foot" (3)	biped, centipede, millipede, expedite, impede	L ped
302. **pel**	"push" (9)	compel, dispel, expel, propel, repel, compulsory	L pell(ere)
303. **pen(i)(t), pun**	"punishment" (8)	penal, penalty, penitent, penitentiary, repent, punish	L penten(s)
304. **pend, pond**	"weigh, hang, consider, pay" (8)	append, depend, expend, pendulum, suspend	L pend(ere)
305. **per-**	"through, thoroughly" (5)	perspire, pernicious, pervade	L per
306. **peri-**	"around, nearby" (5)	perimeter, peristomatic	G peri
307. **pet**	"go, seek" (6)	appetite, compete, competent, impetuous, impetus	L pet(ere)
308. **phag**	"eat" (9)	anthropophagous, dysphagia, necrophagous	G phag(os)
309. **phan, phen, fan**	"show, appear" (2)	phantom, sycophant, phenomenon, fancy, fantasy	G phan(ein)
310. **phil**	"love" (6)	Anglophile, bibliophile, philanthropy, philology	G phil(os)
311. **phob,**	"fear" (11)	phobia, arachnophobia, hydrophobia	G phob(os)
312. **phon**	"speech, sound" (5)	phonetic, microphone, telephone	G phon(e)
313. **phot, phos**	"light" (7)	photography, photosynthesis, phototropism	G phos, phot
314. **phys**	"natural" (11)	metaphysics, physic, physical, physician, physicist	G phus(is)
315. **ple(c), ply**	"fold, tangle" (10)	complex, accomplice, complicate, complicity	L plec
316. **plen, pleo, pleth**	"abundance" (3)	plenty, pleonasm, plethora, complete	*pl
317. **pol(is)(it)**	"city, state" (8)	acropolis, cosmopolitan, police, policy, political	G pol(is)
318. **poly-**	"many" (5)	polychromatic, polyangular, polygamy	G poly-
319. **pon, pos**	"place, put" (5)	composite, deposit, expose, impose, oppose	L pon(ere)
320. **popul**	"people" (3)	depopulate, people, population, popular	L popul(us)
321. **port**	"carry" (6)	deport, export, import, portly, purport, rapport	L port(are)
322. **post, poster**	"after, behind" (10)	post-mortem, post-pone, post-script, posterior	L post
323. **pot, poss**	"be able, powerful" (9)	potent, omnipotent, potential, possible, possess	L pot, posse
324. **prag**	"do" (9)	practical, pragmatic, pragmatics	G prag(m)
325. **pre-, pro-**	"before, in front of" (5)	preconceive, preposition, progress, professor	L prae-, pro-
326. **prec**	"entreat, pray" (8)	deprecate, precarious, imprecate, imprecation	L prec(ari)
327. **prec**	"worth, value" (9)	appreciate, depreciate, precious, preciosity	L preti(um)
328. **prim**	"first, foremost" (10)	primal, primary, primate, prime, primer, primeval	L primus
329. **princ**	"ruler" (5)	"prince, principle, principal ["take first"]	L prim + cip
330. **priv**	"secret, not public" (5)	private, deprive, privy	L priv-
331. **pro-**	"on behalf of" (5)	pro-British, pro-education	G pro

MORPHEME	MEANING	EXAMPLES	SOURCE
332. **prob, prov**	"test, find good" (9)	probable, probe, probation, prove, approve, probity	L prob(are)
333. **prol**	"offspring" (6)	proletariat, prolific, proliferate	L proles
334. **proto-**	"first, chief" (5)	proto-organism, protoplasm, prototype	G proto
335. **pseudo-**	"false, deceptive resemblance" (5)	pseudonym, pseudo-prophet, pseudo-archaic	G pseud(es)
336. **psych**	"spirit, soul, mind" (3)	psyche, Psyche, psychedelic, psychiatry, psychic	G psukhe
337. **publ**	"people" (5)	republican, publicity, publish	L public(us)
338. **pud**	"feel shame, cast off" (6)	impudent, pudendum, repudiate	L puden(s)
339. **pung(t)**	"point, prick" (11)	expunge, punctuation, puncture	L pung(ere)
340. **put**	"cut, reckon, consider" (7)	amputate, deputy, dispute, repute, reputation	L put(are)
341. **pyr**	"fire, fever" (3)	antipyretic, pyre, pyretic, pyrite, pyromania	G pur
342. **ques, quer**	"ask, seek" (4)	question, request, exquisite, query, conquer, acquire	L quaer(ere)
343. **rat**	"reckon, reason" (8)	rational, ration, ratio, ratify	L ratio
344. **re-**	"anew, again, back" (5)	regenerate, rehearse, restore, reward	L re-
345. **re**	"thing" (5)	real, reality, realize	L re(s)
346. **reg(t), roy**	"straight, lead, rule, king" (8)	regal, regent, regicide, regimen, region, regular, royal	L reg(ere)
347. **retro-**	"backwards, back" (5)	retrogression, retrospection	L retro
348. **rig**	"stiff," rigor, rigid" (5)	rigid, rigor	L rigid(us)
349. **riv**	"river, shore, stream" (6)	derive, arrive, rival, river, rivulet	L ripa
350. **rog**	"ask, take away" (6)	abrogate, arrogant, derogatory, interrogate, prerogative	L rog(are)
351. **rrh, rh**	"flow, steam, measured motion" (5)	catarrh, diarrhea, gonorrhea, hemorrhage	G rhein
352. **rupt**	"burst, become unsound" (7)	abrupt, bankrupt, corrupt, disrupt, erupt, interrupt	L rump(ere)
353. **salv**	"safe, healthy" (9)	salvation, salvage, salute, salutation	L salv(us)
354. **sat, satis**	"satisfy" (9)	insatiable, sate, saturate, satisfy	L sat(is)
355. **sci**	"know, discern" (8)	science, conscience, conscious, prescience	L sciens
356. **scrib**	"write" (4)	scribe, proscribe, prescribe, describe, ascribe	L scrib(ere)
357. **se-, sed-**	"apart" (5)	separate, select, sedition, seduce	L se(d)
358. **sec, seg**	"cut, split" (6)	segment, dissect, insect, sect, section, secant, sex	L sec(are)
359. **sed**	"sit, stay" (5)	sedate, sedentary, sediment, supersede, assiduous	L sed(are)
360. **sel(t), sal, saul(t)**	"jump" (9)	salient, assail, assault, somersault, exult, insult	L salt(are)
361. **sembl**	"similar" (5)	resemble, semblance, dissemble	L simil
362. **semi-**	"half, partly" (5)	semicolon, semifinal, semi-annual	L semi-
363. **sen(t,s)**	"feel, agree, think" (3)	assent, consent, dissent, presentiment, resent	L sent(ire)
364. **sequ, secut**	"follow" (5)	sequel, sequence, sequester, subsequent, consequence	L sequi
365. **ser(t)**	"put, arrange, write, speak" (4)	series, serial, assert, desert, dissertation, exert	L ser(ere)
366. **-ship**	"state, condition" (5)	dictatorship, trusteeship, workmanship	OE scipe

	MORPHEME	MEANING	EXAMPLES	SOURCE
367.	sim, simil, sem	"same, one" (10)	simple, simplex, assimilate, facsimile, simile	L simil(is)
368.	soci	"companion" (5)	social, society, socialism, sociable, associate	L soci(us)
369.	sol	"alone, single" (7)	desolate, sole, soliloquy, solipsism, solitary, solitude	L sol(us)
370.	sol	"sun" (11)	parasol, solar, solarium, solstice	L sol
371.	sol, hol	"whole" (7)	solid, consolidate, solder, catholic, holistic, holocaust	L solid(us)
372.	solv	"loosen, unbind" (7)	solve, solvent, insolvent, absolve, dissolve, resolve	L solv(ere)
373.	some	"like, characterized by, apt to" (5)	cumbersome, awesome, bothersome	OE sum
374.	son	"sound" (8)	sonorous, consonant, dissonant, sonata, sonnet	L son(us)
375.	soph	"wise" (8)	philosophy, sophist, sophisticated	G soph(os)
376.	spec, skep, scop, speci	"look, see" (3)	specious, species, speculum, spectator, aspect	L spec(ere)
377.	sper, spor	"scatter, seed" (6)	aspersion, disperse, intersperse, sperm, sporadic	G spor(a)
378.	spir	"breathe, animate" (3)	aspiration, conspire, expire, inspire, perspire	L spir(are)
379.	spond	"pledge" (5)	sponsor, correspond, respond, despondent	L spond(ere)
380.	stat, stit st,	"stay, stand, make firm" (2)	state, statue, apostasy, armistice, substitute	G stat(os)
381.	struct, stru	"build" (9)	construct, obstruct, instruct, superstructure	L stru(ere)
382.	sub-	"under, below" (5)	subdivision, subtraction, subtitle	L sub-
383.	super-	"over, above" (5)	supernatural, supererogatory, superman	L super-
384.	sur-	"over, above, beyond" (5)	surtax, surrealistic	L super-
385.	syn-	"with, together" (5)	synthetic, synchronic	G syn-
386.	tac(s,t)	"order, arrange" (7)	tactics, syntax, syntactic, taxidermy, taxonomy	G takt(os)
387.	tag(t), tang	"touch, feel" (3)	contagious, contiguous, contact, intact	L tang(ere)
388.	tec(hn)	"build, skill" (7)	polytechnic, technical, technique, technology	G tekhne
389.	temp	"measure" (5)	temper, temperature, tempered	L temper-
390.	ten, tain	"hold, maintain" (7)	tenant, tenement, tenet, tenure, sustenance, tenable	L ten(ire)
391.	ten(d)	"stretch, thin" (2)	attend, tend, extend, intend, intense, ostensible	L tend(ere)
392.	ter	"frighten" (4)	deter, determine, terror	L terr(ere)
393.	termin	"limit" (4)	terminate, indeterminate, terminus, terminal	L termin(us)
394.	thanat	"death" (11)	euthanasia	G thanat(os)
395.	the	"place, put" (2)	theme, thesis, anathema, apothecary, hypothesis	G the
396.	theo	"god" (2)	theism, atheism, pantheism, theology, theocracy	G theo
397.	therm	"heat" (9)	thermal	G therme
398.	tom, tm	"cut" (7)	anatomy, atom, dichotomy, entomology, epitome	G tom(os)
399.	top	"place" (4)	topic, topology, topography, toponomy, isotope	G top(os)

	MORPHEME	MEANING	EXAMPLES	SOURCE
400.	tor(t)	"twist" (10)	contortion, distort, extortion, retort, torturous, torture	L tort(us)
401.	tract	"drag, pull" (6)	tractable, traction, tractor, attract, abstract, contract	L trac(ere)
402.	trib	"give, pay" (4)	tribute, contribute, tributary, distribute, attribute	L tribu(ere)
403.	trop	"turn" (10)	tropic, trope, entropy	G trop(os)
404.	tu(i)t	"watch, instruct" (4)	tutor, tutelage, intuition, tuition	L tueri
405.	tum	"swollen" (10)	contumely, detumescence, intumescence, tumor	L tum(ere)
406.	trans-	"across, surpassing" (5)	transalpine, transoceanic, transhuman	L trans-
407.	tri-	"three" (5)	triangle, tridimensional	G tri
408.	ultra-	"beyond, extreme" (5)	ultraliberal, ultramodest, ultraviolet	*ulter
409.	un-	"not" (5)	unclean, uneven, unmindful, unbearable, uncouth	G an-
410.	un-	"opposite" (5)	untie, unlock, uncoil	G ent-
411.	uni-	"in place of, instead" (5)	vice-consul, vice-president	L un(us)
412.	uter hyster	"womb, hysteria" (6)	hysterectomy, hysteria, hysterogenic, uterus	G hustra
413.	vac, van	"empty" (10)	vacate, vacancy, vacation, evacuate, vacuous, vacuum	L vac(ere)
414.	val	"strong, useful" (9)	valid, valor, value, equivalent, convalescence	L val(ere)
415.	ven	"come, bring, happen" (5)	adventure, circumvent, convent, convention, event	L ven(ire)
416.	ver	"true" (8)	veracity, verdict, verify, verisimilitude, veritable	L ver(us)
417.	ver, vers, vor	"turn, roll" (10)	adverse, adversary, controversy, converse, conversion	L vers(are)
418.	via, voy	"way, road" (5)	deviate, devious, impervious, obviate, obvious, trivial	L via
419.	vic(t), vinc	"conquer" (9)	evict, victory, convince, invincible	L vinc(ere)
420.	vid, vis, id, eid	"see" (3)	evident, provide, video, *vide*, advise, television, visit	L vid(ere)
421.	vir	"male, man" (6)	triumvirate, virago, virile, virtue, virtually	L viril(us)
422.	viv	"alive" (4)	vivisection, vivacious, vivid, revive	L viv(ere)
423.	voc, vok	"speak, call" (4)	vocal, vocabulary, advocate, vociferous, vocation	L vox
424.	volv	"turn, roll" (7)	evolve, devolve, involve, revolve, revolt, voluble	L volv(ere)
425.	-y	"full of, characterized by" (5)	mighty, moody, healthy	OE -ig
426.	xen	"foreign, strange" (8)	xenophile, xenophobe, xenon	G xen(os)
427.	zo	"animal" (10)	protozoan, spermatozoa, zoo, zoology	G zo(on)

Index